Practical Guidelines for NOVICE TEACHERS

Practical Guidelines for
NOVICE TEACHERS

Rinelle Evans
Piera Biccard
(editors)

Practical Guidelines for Novice Teachers

First edition 2019

Juta and Company (Pty) Ltd
PO Box 14373, Lansdowne, 7779, Cape Town, South Africa
www.juta.co.za

© 2019 Juta and Company (Pty) Ltd

ISBN 978 1 48512 509 9

All rights reserved. No part of this publication may be reproduced or transmitted in any form or by any means, electronic or mechanical, including photocopying, recording, or any information storage or retrieval system, without prior permission in writing from the publisher. Subject to any applicable licensing terms and conditions in the case of electronically supplied publications, a person may engage in fair dealing with a copy of this publication for his or her personal or private use, or his or her research or private study. See section 12(1)*(a)* of the Copyright Act 98 of 1978.

Project manager: Mmakasa Ramoshaba
Editor: Kathleen Sutton
Proofreader: Simone Chiara van der Merwe
Cover designer: Genevieve Simpson
Typesetter: Wouter Reinders

Credits
Permission was granted to reproduce a table on positive and negative behaviour from Joubert, R. (2008), *Learner Discipline in Schools*, Pretoria: Centre for Education Law and Education Policy (CELP).

Typeset in 11 on 14 pt Rotis Serif

The authors and the publisher believe on the strength of due diligence exercised that this work does not contain any material that is the subject of copyright held by another person. In the alternative, they believe that any protected pre-existing material that may be comprised in it has been used with appropriate authority or has been used in circumstances that make such use permissible under the law.

Contents

About the authors vii
About the cover xiii
Introduction xv

Section A: Teaching as a career 1
1 Teaching in South Africa 3
2 Teaching in rural South Africa 10
3 Making the most of your teaching practice 14
4 Finding the right school 19
5 Understanding the school as an organisation 22

Section B: You as the new professional 29
6 Becoming a professional 31
7 Establishing your teacher identity 35
8 Determining your personality traits 38
9 Acting *in loco parentis* 46
10 Taking care of yourself 50
11 Counting your words 54

Section C: You and your learners 61
12 Equipping learners with 21st-century skills 63
13 Identifying your learners' temperaments 68
14 Identifying your learners' learning styles 74
15 Readying the learner for learning 79
16 Managing aggressive behaviour 83
17 Working with linguistic diversity 88

Section D: In the classroom 93
18 Creating a meaningful, safe and optimal learning environment 95
19 Surviving the first day 103
20 Planning, preparing and starting your lessons 106

21	Managing large classes	111
22	Giving homework	116
23	Keeping up with the marking load	121
24	Making your own inexpensive resources	127
25	Using digital tools to enhance your teaching and learning environment	132
26	Eliciting positive behaviour	140
27	Talking like a teacher	148
28	Teaching PE when you are not a PE teacher	156
29	Teaching Mathematics when you are not a 'numbers person'	160
30	Dealing with sensitive topics	164
31	Revealing the hidden curriculum	170

Section E: Beyond the classroom 173

32	The teacher as coach	175
33	Planning a school function	178
34	Continuing your professional development	185
35	The teacher as reflective practitioner	188
36	The teacher as researcher	191
37	Spending, saving and investing	194
38	Tips from top teachers	200

Concluding comments	207
Sources consulted	208
Appendix A: Outline of a CV for a graduate	215
Appendix B: Code of conduct: South African Council for Educators	217
Appendix C: Determining your personality style	221
Appendix D: Digital resources for teachers	222
Appendix E: Useful expressions to use during lessons	224
Appendix F: Example of a project planning schedule	229

About the authors

Rinelle Evans holds a PhD in Curriculum and Instructional Design with special reference to instructional communication via television technology. She also obtained a Master's degree (cum laude) in teaching English to speakers of other languages from the University of Birmingham, England. She is currently involved with teacher education and facilitates modules related to literacies, communication skills and language teaching methodology in the Faculty of Education, University of Pretoria. Her academic interests relate to English language teaching, instructional design and communication, and language-in-education matters. She is a National Research Foundation-rated researcher and has published articles in refereed journals as well as several academic textbooks and support material for English language learners.

Piera Biccard holds a PhD in Curriculum Studies, where she worked on mathematics teacher professional development. In her Master's degree she looked at mathematical modelling competencies of Grade 7 learners. She is a senior lecturer at the University of South Africa (Unisa) and is currently involved in initial teacher education as the module co-ordinator for a teaching practice module. She is also involved in the BEd (Hons) degree at Unisa. Her interests are mathematics teaching and learning and professional development of mathematics teachers. She has published articles in journals and contributed chapters to books.

Michael Biccard has over 25 years' teaching experience and is a retired deputy principal. He has been a member of the School Management Team (SMT) and School Governing Body (SGB) for many years. He played a role in developing a school code of conduct and disciplinary system based on assertive discipline.

Sarina de Jager holds a PhD in Educational Psychology with special reference to model development and proactive aggressive behaviour. She obtained a Master's degree in Educational Psychology from the University of Johannesburg and is a registered educational psychologist. She co-ordinates the Postgraduate Certificate in Education at the University of Pretoria and teaches Life Orientation to undergraduate and honours students. Her academic interests relate to wellness in education, aggression, growth mindset and mindfulness.

Ronél de Villiers holds a PhD in Music Education with special reference to transformation in multicultural curricula. She has won numerous teacher teaching music theory accolades from Unisa as well as the Faculty of Education Dean's Award for Excellence in Music Education. She currently teaches modules related to music theory, music education and music methodologies. She co-ordinates and presents various music concert productions. She is also involved in a community outreach programme to enhance music theory and practical skills with learners in an inner-city school. She has received a post-doctoral fellowship to launch her research career in collaboration with the Innsbruck University in Austria during 2019.

Chantelle de Wet currently resides in Abu Dhabi, United Arab Emirates, where she teaches Mathematics as Head of Department (HoD) in a British International school. She recently completed her MEd degree (cum laude) at the University of Pretoria, with research on contextual adaptation of teaching and learning resources for ESL learners.

Annelize du Plessis holds a PhD in Educational Psychology with special reference to simultaneous multisensory instruction. She developed a special multisensory reading programme, which was translated into five languages and was successfully implemented in several communities in South Africa. She has vast experience in higher education and specialises in student learning and development, especially the mentoring of student teachers. At present she is actively involved in a funded research project in which she focuses on the development of a mentoring intervention for mentor lecturers, student teachers and mentor teachers in the Faculty of Education at the University of Pretoria. She has published articles in refereed journals as well as in academic and scholarly textbooks.

Hannelie du Preez is a lecturer in Early Childhood Education at the University of Pretoria. Hannelie holds a PhD in Learner Support and two Master's degrees (Research Psychology and Learning Support, Guidance and Counselling). Her research interests pertain to environment psychology and STE(A)M education in the early years. Her international collaboration includes serving as a member on an editorial board, featuring as a guest editor and being invited as a keynote speaker. She is a registered psychometrist (Health Professions Council of South Africa [HPCSA]) and a member of the South African Academy for Science and Art (SAASA) and the South African Research Association for Early Childhood Education (SARAECE).

Eric Eberlein is currently the Head of Teaching Practice for the SANTS group, a private higher education provider specialising in teacher qualifications. This follows on eight years as a lecturer in the Department of Educational Management and Policy Studies, Faculty of Education at the University of Pretoria. He holds a PhD in Education Law Management and Policy, and has 18 years' worth of teaching experience, 10 of these years having been spent at various levels of school management (HoD and deputy principal) in both the public and private education sector. Dr Eberlein's research interests include school leadership and management, the protection and promotion of human rights in education, teacher identity development and the development and maintenance of positive school culture.

Alta Engelbrecht is a senior lecturer in the Faculty of Education at the University of Pretoria and she holds a PhD in Curriculum Studies. She is currently the co-ordinator of the Master's programme in the Department of Humanities Education. Her research areas are cultural stereotyping and textbooks. She is also responsible for the training of second-, third- and fourth-year BEd students in the subject area of Afrikaans methodology. She has authored 11 academic articles, 20 school textbooks and four chapters in scholarly books.

Heather Erasmus is currently engaged in postgraduate studies related to instructional communication and teacher talk. She has vast experience as a teacher, both in South Africa and abroad. Her versatility is demonstrated by the fact that she has taught all grades from preschool to post-matric as well as special-needs learners. She has also been the principal of two leading independent schools. Her further studies in curriculum design, quality assurance and assessment enabled her to work for Umalusi, the SA Council for Quality Assurance of schools. She has an enduring interest and passion for improving teacher effectiveness in the classroom and has taught communication strategies to aspiring teachers at the University of Pretoria for several years.

Mishack Thiza Gumbo is a full Professor and acting coordinator of the postgraduate programme in the College of Education at Unisa. He has extensive experience in conducting postgraduate student research support workshops and supervision, which earned him a certificate of appreciation for his excellent work. He leads and participates in numerous research projects and mentors developing academics and post-doctoral fellows. His research interest areas include indigenous knowledge systems, technology teachers' pedagogical content knowledge, and distance education and e-learning. He writes and presents papers at conferences, heads research and community engagement projects and supervises postgraduate students.

Franklin Lewis is a lecturer in Professional Studies and Practices in the Faculty of Education, University of Pretoria. He is currently awaiting the results of his PhD study. As a music specialist he is also responsible for Methodologies of Music Education for postgraduates. He has extensive experience in music education, curriculum development and assessment practices at primary and secondary school level. He was subject adviser for music as well as senior curriculum planner for the Western Cape Education Department (WCED), South Africa. He was part of the writing team for the National Curriculum Statement (Music) for the Further Education and Training (FET) phase for South African schools.

Candice Livingston is a senior lecturer and the research co-ordinator at the Faculty of Education at the Cape Peninsula University of Technology (CPUT), where she is involved with numerous community engagement projects. She is a member of the faculty research and ethics committees. Her research interests include teaching with technology, cultural competency and the study of fairy tales. Dr Livingston has been part of CPUT's 'Teaching with Technology' programme, where she has presented workshops and mentors other lecturers in the use of technology to improve their teaching.

Mncedisi C. Maphalala is a Professor and dean in the Faculty of Education at the University of Zululand. He has previously worked for the KwaZulu-Natal Department of Education, University of the Witwatersrand (Wits) and Unisa. Between June and August 2015 he was a visiting scholar at the University of North Dakota (USA). His research interests are curriculum studies and assessment in education.

Philip Mirkin has spent the 31 years of his working life in education as a teacher, principal, chair of a school Board of Trustees and university lecturer. He is currently engaged in a doctoral study, after being awarded the prize for best Master's presentation. He has worked in government and in Waldorf/Steiner and Montessori schools in South Africa and New Zealand and is currently lecturing in education at the University of Pretoria. Holism and its application in science poetry, writing and education is his current specialisation. He is currently enrolled for a PhD at the University of Pretoria.

Nhlanhla Mpofu is a senior lecturer at Sol Plaatje University. She holds a PhD in Humanities Education from the University of Pretoria and an MEd (English) and BA (English with Education) from Solusi University. She is a Y-rated researcher. She teaches and researches in the fields of language education, curriculum studies and higher education studies. She also has an understanding of transformative pedagogical strategies in higher education using the blended learning and the flipped classroom approaches, both in conventional and distance education delivery systems.

Elmarie van Wyk holds a Master's degree in Recreation and Sport Management with specific reference to sport management in secondary schools (University of Pretoria). She has been involved in the training and professional development of student teachers in the field of human movement studies and sport management over the last 25 years in the Faculty of Education at the University of Pretoria. Her research interest is situated within the fields of physical education, sport management and recreation. She is a co-published author of several academic articles. She was also a secondary school teacher for nine years prior to the start of her university career.

Johan Wassermann is a Professor at the University of Pretoria and head of the Department of Humanities Education in the Faculty of Education. He teaches on the BEd and Bachelor of History Education Honours qualifications. He also supervises history education students at both Master's and doctoral level. Research-wise he has published widely in both history and history education. His current research interests include history textbooks in Africa, youth and history, and the life histories of teachers.

Yolandi Woest was a secondary school language teacher for 11 years, during which time she completed her Master's degree in linguistics at the University of Stellenbosch. She joined the University of Pretoria in 2012 and completed her doctoral degree, specialising in the development of novice teacher identity. Her area of specialisation in teaching pertains to transformative practices in teaching large classes and teacher assistant/tutor development. Her research niche includes novice teacher identity, novice teacher experiences and emotions, and gender and LGBT+ matters. She has supervised to completion several honours and Master's students.

About the cover

Hands symbolise our connection to each other; we help, create, build, nurture and learn. The open, receptive palm and outstretched fingers express not only the giving and receiving needed in healthy education, but also hard work and creative playfulness. Each unique palm and fingerprint suggests the richness and versatility of the teachers and learners in South African classrooms. The vibrant upward-spiralling pattern points to growth and development as we strive to reach our full potential.

Introduction

Rinelle Evans

'I touch the future, I teach' is a quote made famous by Christa McAuliffe on the eve of her trip into space as the first American not trained as an astronaut. This science teacher was going to conduct some experiments and teach two lessons from outer space while in the spacecraft *Challenger*. On 28 January 1986, the world watched in horror as the shuttle broke apart, 73 seconds after being launched. She was one of the seven crew members who died.

You might share this teacher's sentiments and for that reason have decided to become a teacher. Right now, regardless of your motivation for choosing teaching as a profession, you are possibly scurrying for a placement at a school for your teaching practice. You are also probably thinking about where you would like to eventually take up a post. You may have started preparing a CV, or be hoping for an interview.

Very soon you will be handed the key to your own classroom kingdom. You will be fortunate if you have 40 desks and chairs and a functional chalkboard; very lucky if there is an electronic whiteboard. Any clean surface on which to project images via an overhead projector should please you. You might have a cupboard or bookcase, and enough space to put up visual material. You might want to place your personal stamp on this classroom with a fresh lick of paint, a cut-off carpet, a small pot plant and a bright tablecloth.

That class will soon be filled for the rest of the school year with 40 bustling and often not-so-eager children. You will have the responsibility of facilitating the mastery of subject content, looking after their pastoral wellbeing and coaching them in a variety of extramural activities. You will also have to manage the many organisational and administrative demands of a school's daily routine. Teachers need to be problem solvers and think on their feet as they make minute-by-minute decisions each day.

You might be feeling apprehensive, even overwhelmed now as you approach the start of your career. Perhaps you do not feel adequately prepared. As an author team we trust that this book will provide you with practical ideas that you can use to supplement your book knowledge and practical experience from your university days. We hope that the book provides a platform for reflection so that you will read and reread sections as you start a demanding but very rewarding phase of your career. We have drawn on our many years of classroom experience and have consulted with both academics and seasoned teachers to bring you a book that we believe will be one of a kind and hold a special place on your bookshelf. As you read through it, you may become aware that teaching is not only about transferring knowledge, so we leave you with the African proverb that says: 'True teaching is not the accumulation of knowledge; it is the awakening of consciousness.'

Section A
Teaching as a career

In this first section, we will try to orientate you towards what teaching as a career is all about. We shall go beyond what you may have learnt at university about what it means to be a teacher. Firstly, we spend some time discussing being a teacher in South Africa. Although there are similarities in teaching all over the world, you should not forget that our South African context is unique and complex. We also try to provide you with a starting point for understanding African teaching philosophies and approaches. We advise you to follow this up with your own reading about African philosophy.

South Africa is a country of extremes and we feel that it is important to present to you some orientation to teaching in a rural school. There are unique circumstances and challenges (and benefits) that exist at rural schools. It is important to prepare for these challenges by being aware of some of the issues. Hopefully you can reflect on these issues and succeed at any school where you may find yourself.

We provide a short section on making the most of your teaching practice, for those of you still finishing your qualification. Teaching practice is a time to learn how to manage a classroom and experiment with and consolidate what you have learnt in your various courses.

Since South Africa is such a diverse country and being a teacher is part of your personality and identity, you will need to find the 'right' school, so we look at some of the things you should consider for your first appointment.

Not all schools are the same and they may have different cultures or a different 'feel'. However, there are some basic structures that you will find in most schools. We therefore deal with the school as an organisation to help you fully understand your role and position in the school structure.

Teaching is the one profession that creates all other professions.
Unknown

1

Teaching in South Africa

Mishack Thiza Gumbo

What did last night's news bulletin have to report about education? Was it encouraging or have you started doubting your choice of career? You need only turn to the media to be made unsettlingly aware of the current crises in education at all levels: the high rate of teenage pregnancy, teacher absenteeism, the regular changes to the curriculum, language issues, admissions complications, teacher–learner abuses or disrespect and racial clashes at certain schools still prevail. An unfortunate lack of a teaching and learning culture, parental apathy, demotivated learners, inadequately trained staff, budgetary constraints and internal politics in management make up the rest of the bad news syndrome.

You may be feeling apprehensive right now. Do not lose heart! Few of the problems are insurmountable and with an understanding of why many of these issues exist, you ought to feel less overwhelmed as you prepare to enter what is, in fact, a very satisfying career.

Let's take a closer look at the reasons for some of the dissonance in our current education system. As the legacy of a separatist policy is slowly dismantled at all levels, the restructuring of education is, in turn, directed at initiating fundamental change in the character and content of South African society. The South African education system still shows visible evidence of an inequitable apartheid order and has not transformed adequately or fast enough. A radical reconstruction of its essence is required in order to meet the new and challenging demands of the 21st century. Some very powerful constraints still militate against change:

- There is a shortage of skilled teachers and many need to improve their qualifications.
- Funding is limited, placing strain on all types of resources.
- Productivity and commitment on the part of teachers need to be improved.
- A culture of learning and teaching needs to be established.
- Workloads are heavy and teacher morale is often low.
- Insufficient new schools have been built.

Many schools are overcrowded, while others are trying to cope with increased annual enrolments. The resultant increase in class sizes imposes further pressure on teachers and the prospect of a heavier teaching load has become a reality.

Primarily, teachers have had to face the inevitable changes taking place in their classrooms owing to the merging of historically diverse systems into a unified democracy. Various transformations started taking place even before the euphoria of the first democratic elections had worn off. One year after the first fully democratic elections introduced a national government that was representative of South Africa's population, 19 racially segregated departments of education were legally integrated. This change ushered in a single national department of education with nine provincial departments. The year 1995 also marked the beginning of a phased process, which envisaged access to compulsory schooling for all children up to Grade 9. Since then, high on the list of priorities for educationists have been projects to restore a culture of teaching and learning, the implementation of new curriculum frameworks and the re-organisation of governance/consultative infrastructures. Furthermore, many schools introduced English as an additional means of instruction. This move certainly increased the school's accessibility to learners from several ethnic groups, but it also resulted in new social and organisational challenges that needed to be addressed.

Education as a social issue is a prime concern in most societies. In South Africa it has been highly politicised and emotionally charged for years and is still in a state of flux as representatives from the various groups negotiate a national system of education designed to serve the needs and interests of all South Africans.

Being a teacher in South Africa, particularly now in the democratic era and the 21st century, means you need to start by asking yourself key questions. These questions (see Table 1.1) relate to your identity and culture and are a very much part of you as a teacher.

Table 1.1 Asking yourself key questions

Questions about self	Questions about learners
Who am I?	Who are my learners?
Where do I come from?	Where do they come from?
What is my culture?	What are their cultures?
How does who I am affect my knowledge and teaching?	How does who they are affect their knowledge and learning?

The importance of these questions will assist us to evolve from an 'old' South Africa towards the new South Africa that we aspire to. Building the new South Africa means that teachers ought to be guided by principles entrenched in our national constitution and the values espoused by Ubuntu. The current national curriculum acknowledges these constitutional principles and values that every teacher ought to observe and enact when teaching. These principles are discussed in the following sections.

Social transformation

You have the task to ensure that the educational imbalances of the past are redressed, and that equal educational opportunities are provided for all learners. For instance, you should encourage all learners to be proud of their heritage and languages and to be confident about who they are. Consider using co-operative, team-based learning as a way to build a united South Africa. Research these strategies so that you can use them effectively. Often learners fight in class, and yell slurs at each other. Some of this behaviour is as a result of the social ills that learners are exposed to outside of class, such as dysfunctional families, gangsterism, physical and emotional abuse or neglect in various forms. You will need to teach your learners values (often through example) and about the principles of respect, tolerance, unity and co-operation.

Active and critical thinking

You have the responsibility to encourage an active and critical approach to learning. This may run against the culture of a school that considers rote and uncritical learning of given truths as acceptable. Some communities still consider the teacher as the sole source and dispenser of knowledge, and learners as mere desk warmers. Your teaching should become learner-focused in order to neutralise teacher dominance. Learners should not be treated only as receivers of knowledge but as active participants in the co-creation of knowledge. Their own ideas are important, but they need to learn to critically analyse their own thoughts as well as the thoughts of others.

Knowledge and skills

In line with policy documents, you will determine the minimum standards of performance that your learners ought to achieve in each grade and for the various subjects. In order for our country's learners to have global opportunities, you need to stretch them intellectually as well as extend their skills. Plan learning tasks that challenge them without disheartening them. Many teachers complain of learners not performing well. Indeed, the failure rate in many schools is overwhelming. But have teachers stopped a moment to interrogate their own teaching and content knowledge? Do they really know their learners? What are they doing about their learners' circumstances? Do they know how to involve learners in developing knowledge and skills?

Human rights, inclusivity and environmental and social justice

Teaching in South Africa means being an agent of change and a society builder. Teaching mindfully is a way to help South Africa heal from the atrocities of the past and forge ahead by unifying society and helping to solve our own problems. You should infuse into your teaching the principles and practices of social and environmental justice and human rights as defined in the Constitution of the Republic of South Africa. This implies being sensitive to diversity issues such as poverty, inequality, race, gender, language, age, disability and other factors.

In the spirit of Ubuntu, you will need to act as an 'academic elder' to care for and include each learner irrespective of his or her background, culture or personal problems. You will need to monitor your attitudes and reactions in order to ensure that learning is not hindered by your prejudices. The adage 'No learner cares about how much the teacher knows until he or she knows how much the teacher cares about him or her' rings true. You will consciously need to practise traditional values of inclusion, kindness and respect. As a teacher you will also need to think of ways to address societal and environmental problems through your teaching. For example, Technology teachers could plan tasks based on scenarios that require learners to design technological devices that can help curb certain types of crime or avoid littering and smoke pollution.

Valuing indigenous knowledge systems

You must know, understand, respect and nurture the rich history and heritage of all persons living in South Africa. You will also need to consider other forms of knowledge and ways of knowing as alternatives to the universalised Western forms and colonial systems that currently dominate our education system. For too long, a one-dimensional knowledge set has been enforced. Its related teaching methods and strategies do a disservice and injustice to the richness embedded in the fibre of a multicultural South Africa. As a novice teacher, you can open up the space to allow local forms of knowledge and ways of doing things to thrive. There is so much that you can garner from South African indigenous contexts that could help diversify your subject content and teaching strategies. Learners know much and bring even more to class from their own worlds. The wisdom they have received from elders passed down through many generations should be valued and links should be drawn between indigenous knowledge and that taught in science, technology and mathematics today. African inventors, designers, artists, writers and philosophers should be acknowledged and celebrated. South African learners should know about these voices and not be distanced from what they are learning because of Western hegemony.

Credibility, quality and efficiency

Over the past two decades, the low performance of South African learners in international benchmarking tests has been disheartening. There are several reasons for this, some of which are being addressed at governmental level. You are part of a post-apartheid generation of teachers who can address inequities. You should be committed to providing an education that is comparable in quality, breadth and depth to those of other countries.

Our schooling system unfortunately tends to push learners who are not adequately prepared to a next grade. Matric results, too, are often adjusted to please politicians rather than reflecting accurately how prepared learners are for the next level of education. You will teach learners who are faced with very complex situations, but considering what and how you teach could be a step in the right direction. Reflecting on your practice will help you consciously work towards developing, in line with the national curriculum requirements, learners who are able to:

- identify and solve problems and make decisions using critical and creative thinking
- work effectively as individuals and with others as members of a team
- organise and manage themselves and their activities responsibly and effectively
- collect, analyse, organise and critically evaluate information
- communicate effectively using visual, symbolic and/or language skills in various modes
- use science and technology effectively and critically, showing responsibility towards the environment and the health of others
- demonstrate an understanding of the world as a set of related systems by recognising that problem-solving contexts do not exist in isolation.

Reclaiming an African perspective

In precolonial Africa, education was not separated from life itself – children learnt everywhere and all the time, and they did not have to go to specific places (schools) at specific times to learn. It also meant that all adults were teachers, which helps us understand the phrase 'It takes a village to raise a child'. Learning also took place more by doing and talking rather than by writing – in other words, through 'participatory education', which was mostly informal. Traditional African education (Reagan, 2005: 61) sought to:
- develop a child's physical and intellectual skills
- build a child's character
- inculcate respect for elders and those in position of authority
- help a child to acquire specific vocational training and a healthy attitude toward honest labour
- develop a deep sense of belonging and to enable a child to participate actively in family and community affairs
- understand, appreciate and promote the cultural heritage of the community at large.

These educational goals seem applicable to all groups in our country and truly worth striving for. In the context of African education, the concepts of Ubuntu or Botho are also important. These words broadly mean that human needs are the most important and really determine all other aspects of life. Letseka (2000: 182) translates the expressions *umuntu ngumuntu ngabantu* or *motho ke motho ka batho* as 'a person depends on others just as much as others depend on him/her'.

Unfortunately, the toll of colonialism, industrial revolutions, apartheid, urbanisation, modernisation and a host of other factors have resulted in communities being fragmented (Ntseane, 2007: 118). As a teacher you have the opportunity daily to show learners that we are persons because of other people and to instil values that recognise the importance of each other and the broader communities from which our learners come.

The changing face of the classroom has brought about many uncertainties and challenges. If you are a novice teacher, you are entering a very exciting phase in the history of South African education. Perhaps you actually have an advantage over your seniors, as you will not have to adapt your ways but merely venture into the unknown, which is often more exciting than daunting!

Let's rise to the challenge of Professor SME Bengu, the first minister of education in the democratic dispensation, who urged all citizens to

> *Create a system which cultivates and liberates the talents of all our people without exception ... such a system must be founded on equity and non-discrimination, it must respect diversity, it must honour learning and strive for excellence, it must be owned and cared for by the communities and stakeholders it serves, and it must use all the resources available to it in the most effective manner possible.* (DoE, 1995: 2–3)

2

Teaching in rural South Africa

Rinelle Evans

Teaching in remote areas places particular demands on teachers, but can be just as rewarding. Recent figures (StatsSA, 2015) indicate that South Africa has approximately 25 000 schools. Nearly half of these schools (11 252) are classed as rural schools. Providing education in outlying areas is becoming increasingly difficult. Many farm schools have been closed down as the population ages or moves to urban areas in search of a better life. Most rural schools are situated in KwaZulu-Natal, the Eastern Cape and Limpopo.

You may have grown up in a pastoral, rural area and want to return to your home community. In that case, you would understand what working in such classrooms requires. On the other hand, you may never have left the bustling city lights and would just like a change after spending many years living with your parents. Perhaps you were granted a bursary; you would then not necessarily have a choice in which province you would like to teach. Whatever the reason for taking up a post in rural South Africa, we offer a traditional description of rural life and outline some of the challenges and advantages of teaching in such areas.

In most contexts the concept of rurality is defined in terms of low population density and remote geographic location – that is, isolation from modern infrastructure, facilities, services and technological connectivity due to distance. Often these small settlements also subsist under harsh climatic conditions. Rural regions are also defined in terms of socio-economic growth and sustainability. They tend to be among the poorest in a country, since those living there are often unemployed with no feasible job opportunities. They can thus not rely on a steady income. In the South African context, such areas are primarily inhabited by the elderly, women and young children. These children often suffer from malnutrition or diseases such as malaria or bilharzia. Many could be living with HIV. These are all physically debilitating factors that affect learning.

Rural communities, possibly because they are so isolated from mainstream culture, generally display a strong group cohesion and unique culture. Their close relationships with each other are more than neighbourliness.

Everyone knows each other personally, to the degree of familiarity. They all share responsibilities, and work together for the mutual good of the community. Many parents work in the cities, having left their children in the care of relatives. There are even child-headed households.

These settlements are particularly vulnerable, as traditional leaders seem to control most aspects of life and supposedly represent their communities' interests. Despite the apparent collective decision making and reaching of consensus in rural communities, caregivers are often marginalised, as their own schooling usually does not extend beyond primary level. They are thus inclined to accept the opinions of their community leaders and not question the elders. Many of the adults would be subsistence farmers or traders of firewood, hand crafts or fruit; some may have employment on farms or factories. Electricity or limited solar power might be available, yet most families would generally prefer to prepare food using an open fire.

Teaching in rural contexts has its own challenges. Many schools still depend on boreholes and pit toilets for sanitation. Most learners travel long distances on foot or by donkey cart to get to school, as transportation is non-existent, infrequent or expensive. This also implies many hours in which they are unable to study or do homework, and sometimes they are very tired after walking in the hot sun. They often become sick during winter or when it rains. In addition, they perform domestic chores after school, for example collecting firewood, taking care of the herds until sunset, cutting grass for thatching a mud hut, or fetching water in huge drums transported on a wheelbarrow from some distance away. These routines are performed regardless of the weather and with little regard for the age of the child.

As a teacher, you may also need your own transport or spend a large portion of your salary on travel costs. The great distance from the nearest town may also mean that you and the learners would have infrequent contact with urban areas. Your weekends will not be spent at a movie, mall or club. You may not even have a television or radio to listen to, as there may be no electricity. You may not even be able to WhatsApp friends, as the network coverage is often unreliable. You could, however, spend your leisure time preparing a vegetable garden or reading books. Starting a community or entrepreneurial project with the learners could also be a most satisfying experience. Enrolling for further studies is a sensible option too.

Rural schools, although generally smaller in terms of learner size and with a relatively homogeneous learner profile, are often obliged to combine classes, serving learners across age groups. Teaching multi-grade classes requires dedication. You will need to think of ways to teach different content to the various grades while all the learners are seated in the same classroom, maybe even outside under a tree. Sometimes such classes can be really big, with 60–80 learners needing to be taught. Many teachers complain that the current curriculum does not match the life world of their learners and includes much that is foreign to them. You will have to provide as much context as possible and also take care when setting tests and essay topics that you use material to which learners can respond with confidence. For example, you cannot expect a rural learner to write a letter of complaint about a pizza that was not delivered on time, nor can you give the learner homework that requires him or her to access information. Rural schools are generally under-resourced and seem to have been forgotten by those who determine policy and budgets.

Another challenge you may face is that learners are expected to be taught using English as a language of learning. South Africans living in deep rural areas are generally monolingual, as their isolation also implies that they do not need to use even other regional languages, let alone English. Interaction with authentic speakers of English is very rare and there are very few opportunities to practise communicating in English. Usually, for rural learners, the only chance of hearing and using English happens at school. You are likely to be the only model that rural learners will hear in their everyday lives.

Some single, female teachers complain about their safety and say that senior learners often intimidate them. Some young teachers feel isolated and miss their friends. Currently there are no incentives or extra pay for teaching in rural districts, but there are definitely certain advantages, as a teacher who started her career in a small town explained: 'I experienced that parents and colleagues were more accepting of mistakes I made. The school also gave me more responsibility sooner. The community was very involved with the school and it was never difficult to source a tin of paint or an off-cut carpet to brighten a class.' Other advantages include the following:

- The daily pace is less hectic and the stress of navigating city traffic non-existent. Life is simpler and probably healthier.
- Apart from transport, it is less expensive living in a rural area. Some schools have boarding facilities and you ought to be paid a stipend for staying in the hostel and helping the learners after hours and over weekends. It certainly cuts down on living expenses, as your meals are generally included.

You may temporarily have to sacrifice the convenience of city life, but you may also find the status of being a rural teacher appealing. You will most likely be the only link the learners have to a bigger world. Parents will pin their hopes for their children to escape the cycle of poverty on you. Think of the vast opportunities you have for inspiring those learners and helping them to finally achieve their dreams by getting an education good enough to take them to the cities of promise.

3

Making the most of your teaching practice

Rinelle Evans

Work-integrated learning forms a compulsory part of your pre-service preparation as a teacher. It is also called school placement or teaching practice. Its purpose is that you should gain real-life teaching experience in an authentic school context. Much of the success of this period at schools depends on you. Hopefully you will be placed with an experienced teacher who is willing to offer guidance and allow you to experiment in the class. If you have been able to negotiate a placement with a teacher who is willing to act as a mentor to you, this is ideal. Positive mentorship will enable you to learn in a relaxed, supportive environment. However, you may have been placed at a school where teachers resent the presence of students for a variety of reasons, for example parking under their tree, sitting in their staff room, and generally just being there. To be fair, you do infringe on a teacher's time, progress and privacy. Teachers with senior classes are especially frustrated, as they work against a stringent deadline to finish prescribed work before exams. Many in-service teachers worry that they will have to re-teach the sections allocated to you.

In-service teachers are supposed to be partners in your academic and professional development. Generally, you are placed with competent and experienced staff who consider it their duty to make you feel welcome and who will guide and encourage you as prospective colleagues. Many really go the extra mile to assist you in your professional development.

The purpose of work-integrated learning sessions includes:
- gaining practical experience of how a school functions
- practising your pedagogical skills (including lesson preparation, classroom management, discipline, etc)
- testing in what way theory is implemented in practice
- reflecting on your career choice
- providing an opportunity for personal growth

3 – Making the most of your teaching practice

- learning about all the 'other' activities and duties of teachers (filling in forms, collecting money or doing playground duty). Many experienced teachers complain about these 'other' things more than anything else!

So what would make your presence at a school an asset rather than a burden to the staff? Most teachers consider the ideal student to be someone who:
- has a positive and supportive attitude towards the school and its learners
- is polite, respectful and punctual
- is willing to learn and become involved in the daily operations of a school
- prepares for lessons and offers the teachers assistance.

Before you arrive

- Find out about the school. Many schools have a website that offers information about its vision and mission, the community it serves, after-school activities or services, and any achievements the school is proud of. This information will give you an indication of how to prepare before your arrival and, to a degree, what the school will expect from you.
- Make sure you know exactly where the school is. Plan to arrive well on time and know where or to whom you should report.
- Enquire about the dress code. Most schools have a dress code policy for staff. You do not want to be embarrassed by wearing jeans, only to discover such attire is not permitted. Men may be required to wear a tie and a jacket.
- Some universities will require that the principal signs a document granting you permission to do your teaching practice at that school. Make an appointment to do this.

While at school

- Remember that you are at the school as a guest and should behave accordingly. You are not only showcasing yourself; you are an ambassador of the institution at which you are studying. Make sure your behaviour and speech create a positive impression.
- Wait to be assigned a seat in the staffroom. Students may not even be allowed into this hallowed space! Also do not assume that you have free access to administrative offices or even the obvious cloakroom, let alone parking spots. Ask permission before doing anything. If possible, ask to meet your mentor teacher the day before you start to ask these questions. It will make your first day less nerve-racking.

- Offer to contribute towards the tea fund, if one exists. You may be expected to bring your own flask and mug.
- Use an appropriate and polite register when speaking to staff. Refrain from using first names, even if you happen to know them.
- Respect the privacy of all staff; you may consider leaving the staffroom when teachers enter. If you are invited to stay, keep noise levels to the minimum and do not sit around aimlessly. Never read documents lying around in the class and never check what is placed in pigeon holes.
- Do not smoke in public (where learners or parents can see you) or display body piercings or tattoos, unless these are culturally accepted. Teaching is a career that carries the responsibility of shaping young persons' attitudes towards a healthy lifestyle and responsible citizenship, and modelling appropriate social norms. Most schools tend to be conservative and endorse the values of the particular community they serve. You may need to adjust your own views accordingly for a while.
- Adhere to all school rules. This includes being punctual and not using a cell phone or leaving the grounds without permission. Never use the school phone or photocopier without permission and without offering to pay for the service.
- Remember to sign the daily register.
- Use the opportunity to learn as much as you can about administrative matters such as completing a register, procedures for duplicating learning material, handling school fees or the demerit system.
- Get involved with extramural activities. Offer to do library duty, or help with after-school care of young learners. Every opportunity helps you gain valuable experience of being a teacher.
- Maintain a professional distance with learners; doing so will make your classroom management easier. It will also help you to discourage inappropriate advances from senior learners.
- Be a sponge in the classroom. Use every opportunity to learn as much as you can about everything. Be enthusiastic and offer to help wherever you can willingly. Never just sit around aimlessly. Take notes. Prepare and present your best lessons. Receive feedback graciously. You are at school to learn and grow.
- Return all teaching material or resources borrowed from your teacher or school library.
- You are developing your teaching philosophy, so test your thinking with more experienced teachers and make notes of what you observe and experience. Revise your initial philosophy based on what you learn.

What to do if you have a lousy mentor
As difficult as it is to work with a disinterested mentor, remain positive and enthusiastic. Ensure that your mentor knows that your institution expects you to do certain things (such as teaching a certain number of lessons, or having the mentor teacher evaluate a certain number of lessons). Give your mentor teacher as much notice as possible regarding this. Perhaps even draw up a summary of the things you are expected to complete while in his or her class and give it to him or her in writing.

Re-affirm that you are looking forward to learning from him or her. Many mentors are defensive because they think you are going to know the 'new' methods of teaching and show them up.

Before you leave

- Prepare a neat curriculum vitae (CV) and leave it with the principal. Even if it is not the school you would ideally like to teach at, you may be invited for an interview (which would be good experience) and it may eventually be the only school to offer you a post.
- A much-appreciated gesture is to give the staff some cake, soup or fruit salad upon leaving, if your group is large enough to contribute a few rands each to cover costs. Thank them all for accommodating and helping you. Do not forget the administrative staff in the front office or the persons who clean and make the tea. Consider a thank-you note and a red pen or energy sweets for your mentor teacher.
- Even if you are not sentimental, consider making a scrapbook of your teaching experience for future reference. Ask permission to take photographs of the school facilities or any learners. Collect documents such as the code of conduct or newsletter – anything that may make your career start easier. Ask to make copies of some learners' work or learning material you could use later. Write up your feelings after each week and use these reflections to identify growth points and strengths you have. On occasion, learners will write you a goodbye note. You may be able to put some of these items into your own teaching portfolio once you are appointed.

In conclusion, on very rare occasions after their work-integrated learning experience, some students feel they are not suited to teaching. Before you make radical decisions, consider changing the age group you work with – you may find working with older or younger learners easier. Analyse the school you were at. Each school is very different in nature. Consider a rural school or move to a public school for a very different teaching experience. Private schools often appear more desirable, but offer their own, singular challenges. Spend time in serious conversation with yourself and an experienced teacher to determine why you feel uncertain about teaching as a career. Often factors unrelated to the career have caused these desperate feelings. In most cases, students find teaching practice a life-changing experience filled with many good memories and a confirmation of what they would like to do after graduating. May yours be an enriching experience.

4

Finding the right school

Rinelle Evans

It is important to find a school that is right for you, and not just any school. By this we mean a place where you will feel comfortable and be permitted to grow in your teaching career. Those fortunate learners who were awarded bursaries or scholarships will most likely have positions that are reserved for them. Others will have to scour newspapers and notice boards or trudge from school to school delivering their CVs. Some posts are advertised in the local newspaper, on agency websites, by word of mouth or in a *Government Gazette*, but this does not happen frequently. Apart from these possibilities, keep your eyes open for open days at schools. Attend these to get a sense of what schools offer and how they market their 'brand'. Listen to how the school staff speak to the learners, parents, members of the public and each other. You could even stand outside the school gate when the school day ends and observe the learners coming out. How do they behave? What do they look and sound like? Once you have identified some schools that interest you, you should consult the website for further information. You might even be able to speak to someone teaching there.

It is also important to decide where you want to teach. Consider the affordability and availability of accommodation and transport costs. It is more expensive living in a large city than in rural areas. On the other hand, the city offers more opportunities for excursions and access to resources.

Prepare a neat CV, condensing as much information into as few pages as possible. Tabulating information saves space and looks professional. Make yourself as marketable as possible by gaining experience by volunteering to do afternoon duties, coaching, taking extra modules or enrolling for sport certificates. Register with the professional body the South African Council for Educators (SACE) as well as a teachers' union. Add a covering letter in which you tell the reader more about your capabilities, your teaching philosophy and why you would like to teach at that particular school. Be honest, but showcase your personality and suggest how you could contribute to the particular school. Give a draft copy of your CV and a covering letter to a teacher or lecturer and ask whether he or she would appoint you based on it.

At the start of the fourth term it is generally advisable to have prepared a neat CV (see Appendix A) that you can start taking to schools where you think you might want to work. Even if there are no posts, ask if you may leave the CV with a senior staff member. If at all possible, speak to this person yourself so that he or she has a sense of who you are. You will have to sell yourself.

Should you be invited for an interview, you'll have a further opportunity to find out more about the school and ask about the expectations the governing body has of new teachers. It is most likely that you will have a face-to-face interview, but it could be telephonic or via Skype. Whatever the format, this interview is one of the most important you'll ever experience. Interviews of any form are stressful. Here are some tips for making a good impression:

- Find out exactly where the school is and which routes to take to get there in time.
- Ensure that you arrive punctually. We suggest at least 20 minutes prior to your scheduled time.
- Look professional. Take along a small folder with paper and a copy of your CV. You might even consider taking a portfolio of work you compiled to show lesson plans or certificates.

In face-to-face interviews, the first impression is very important, so remember to make good eye contact and give a strong handshake. Wait until you have been invited to sit down. Make sure that your posture is good and that you sit up confidently, facing each member of the panel. They will ask you questions such as the following:

- Why would you like to teach at this school?
- Why should they appoint you and not someone else?
- How do you deal with conflict?
- What would you do if ...?
- What was the best/worst experience you have had in a classroom?

Take time to think through your answers. Make sure you understand the question. Ask them to repeat it if you don't. You may wish to write down the question so that you can answer all aspects that were asked. You should respond with more than just a yes or a no. Elaborate and provide examples where possible. The panel is trying to get a sense of who you are as you speak. You must also prepare two or three questions to ask at the end of your interview. For example, what opportunities are there for professional development? What extramural duties will you be expected to undertake? How long is the contract for? Is there a probation period?

After the interview, remember to send a short note via email to thank the members of the panel for the opportunity and their time. Indicate that they are welcome to contact you if they need any further information.

Most of the guidelines mentioned above also to apply a telephonic/Skype interview, but here are some very specific ones:

- Be ready for the call at least 15 minutes prior to the scheduled time.
- Choose a quiet place, where you can talk without being disturbed.
- If it is an electronic interview with video, make sure that the background behind you is neat and uncluttered. You may have to ensure that people do not walk across the screen while you are being interviewed.
- Consider wearing the same attire you would have chosen to wear for a face-to-face interview. Conservative and business-like is a good choice. Looking professional even when the panel cannot see you will give you confidence and help you keep to the context of an important interview. If on screen, choose what you wear carefully: shades of blue and green are good colours that complement all skin tones. Avoid wearing all white or black, or very bright or patterned clothing, because electronic media tend to distort colours and patterns. Women should avoid any jewellery such as large earrings or too many bangles that could make an irritating noise that would be amplified via an electronic medium.
- Once the call is connected, have a pen and paper ready so that you can copy down the names of the panel members as they are introduced. Also, ask the chair to describe the room and how the panel is seated. This will help you imagine the setting.

If a school offers you a post, do not accept it immediately. Ask for a few days in which you can consider the offer. State that you wish to discuss the matter with your parents/mentor/partner.

If you decide to accept the offer, immediately ask to meet with the Head of Department (HoD) so that you can be given the prescribed books, lesson plans and any school policies that exist. You may not get class lists for the new year yet, but this year's group might be roughly the same as the group you have been assigned, or an annual yearbook might allow you to see photos of the learners you will work with and memorise some names.

Even if you do not get an offer, learn from the experience of having had an interview. Make a list of the questions you were asked. Formulate answers to those you couldn't respond to well. Ask someone how he or she might have responded. Do not be too despondent if you have still not had an offer by December. Some schools only start their planning once exams are over.

5

Understanding the school as an organisation

Eric Eberlein

If we consider that the word 'organisation' is derived from the Greek word *organon*, which means 'organ', then describing a school as an organisation makes sense. Think of your body. It consists of many vital organs that all have a particular function and need to work properly in order for you to live a healthy life. So too every school, no matter how small or how big, is made up of many different 'organs' all functioning in different ways but focused on providing education. In the school context, these organs or parts are referred to by many different names. So, for example, all the academic year groups that make up the school (seven in primary school and five in high school) are an integral part of the school, and in South Africa these year groups are generally referred to as grades. Another example is the group of mathematics teachers who form a department: the Department of Mathematics. Most of these organs or parts fulfil a specific function – in the example above, all the members of the Mathematics Department teach Mathematics, and it is because they perform this function that they are grouped together in the same department. However, schools are not staffed by teachers alone – every school has support staff such as receptionists, administrative and/or finance clerks, support staff and cleaners who work at the school in support of the core function: education.

Understanding how a school functions as an organisation is vital to your successful adjustment as a novice teacher. Understanding where you fit into that organisation could contribute significantly both to your effectiveness and the way in which you experience the first few months of your new career.

Types of schools in South Africa

Although there are several types of schools – primary schools, secondary schools, faith-based schools, agricultural schools, or schools for learners with special educational needs – the first distinction that needs to be made is whether a school is a public school that belongs to and is funded by the government, or an independent or so-called 'private' school that belongs to a private owner, company or education group. Regardless of a school's public or private status, it functions as an organisation. We focus primarily on public schools because they far outnumber private schools, and also because the vast majority of teachers in South Africa are employed in the public education sector.

Funding models

Within the public education sector, the greatest distinction between schools lies in how they are funded. In South Africa, two major funding models for public schools exist: schools are either fee-paying schools or non-fee-paying schools. Fee-paying schools are legally allowed to charge parents school fees, and can, within the bounds of the law on such matters, enforce the payment of such fees. Please note that a school's legal right to charge school fees comes from the parents of that school, under the leadership of the School Governing Body (SGB). The majority of the parent body of the school must vote in favour of charging school fees before this may happen. Remember, too, that the money collected from parents in this manner then belongs to the SGB, and not to the government. Non-fee-paying schools, on the other hand, may not charge school fees, and this too is determined by a vote by the majority of parents.

The government, because it has to uphold every citizen's right to basic education as stipulated in Section 29 of the Constitution of the Republic of South Africa, remains responsible for the funding of education. It thus has an obligation to both fee-paying and non-fee-paying schools. However, because fee-paying schools are generally situated in more affluent areas, the government, for the purposes of equity (giving everyone what they need rather than giving everyone the same), provides greater funding to non-fee-paying schools than to fee-paying schools, because such communities require a greater share of the government's funding in order to get quality education.

So why this discussion of the funding of education? Well, basically the funding model has consequences not only for the quality of education, but also for the structure of schools as organisations, and who the employer or employers at a school are. In non-fee-paying schools (and in some less affluent fee-paying schools), the government is the only employer. All the employees of the school – teaching as well as support staff – are employed by and paid by the government. However, in a fee-paying school, the SGB can, because it has its own funds collected from the parents, appoint teachers and support staff in addition to those provided by the government. This means that although at most schools the government is the only employer, at some fee-paying schools there are two employers – the government and the SGB. This fact directly affects how a school functions and how the organisation is 'put together'.

Many fee-paying schools are able to appoint additional teaching and support staff, which has not only a number of advantages for the school, but also certain repercussions for the structure of the school as an organisation. The number of teachers appointed and paid for by the government at a public school depends on the number of learners enrolled in that school. If the official ratio of learners to teachers is 30:1, then this means that for every 30 learners, a school qualifies for one teacher. If a school has 900 learners, the government will pay for 30 teachers. However, as a fee-paying school, the parents may, depending on the amount of money available, decide to reduce the learners-to-teacher ratio by employing additional teachers to reduce the size of classes in each grade. These schools may also decide to offer additional subjects or extramural activities, for which they then appoint additional staff. All of this has an impact on the structure of the school as an organisation by expanding the structure, increasing the functions and responsibilities of staff members and complicating the channels of authority and communication.

How are schools structured?

One of the easiest ways to understand the school as an organisation is by looking at a diagram illustrating the different parts of the school and how they fit together – this diagram is referred to as an organogram, which, you will notice, is a clever combination of 'organ' and 'diagram'.

Most schools have a hierarchical organogram. This means that the different levels of the school structure are illustrated in order of responsibility. Figure 5.1 is a good example of a hierarchical organogram.

The School Management Team

The principal and the deputy principal(s) and heads of departments form what is known as the School Management Team (SMT). This team, under the leadership of the principal, manages the day-to-day educational activities at the school. As employees of either the government or the SGB, all teachers and support staff fall under the authority and jurisdiction of the principal and his or her SMT, who take responsibility for effectively managing all the educational activities at the school.

The organogram in Figure 5.1, although not complete, gives a good idea of how a hierarchical school structure works. There are many more functions in a school than just Mathematics, Social Sciences, cricket and a speech festival.

5 – Understanding the school as an organisation

Some smaller schools have no deputy principals, while some large schools may have four or five deputies. At the top of the structure is the principal. He or she is legally responsible and accountable for everything that happens at his or her school. But, as you may well imagine, the principal can't possibly teach every grade and every subject on his or her own, so he or she is supported by teachers qualified to teach different subjects in support of the goal of the school. Furthermore, because education is the core function of the school, and because this core function involves more than just teaching, other functions such as coaching sport or leading cultural, music or art activities have to be included as a function of the school, which means someone needs to support the principal by performing these functions.

Multiple functions in the school imply multiple roles for every teacher

A casual glance at the organogram in Figure 5.1 may suggest that, for example, the teachers in the Mathematics Department perform only one specific function (teaching Mathematics), but as you no doubt already know or will find out within the first few days of your teaching career, all teachers perform many different roles and functions within the school. So, for example, Teacher 1 in the Mathematics Department may also be Coach 1 for cricket and Teacher 2 may very well be Teacher 1 responsible for the speech festival. It is

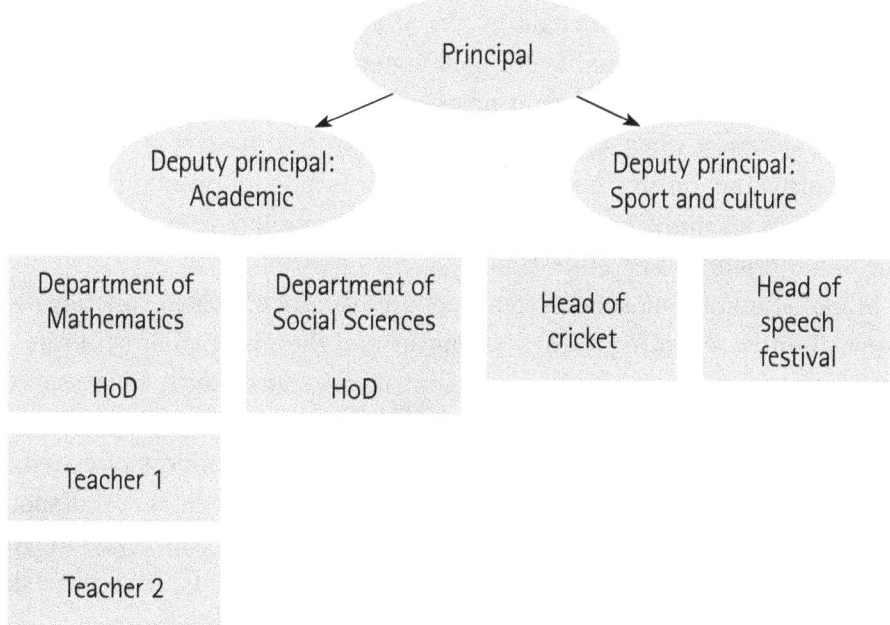

Figure 5.1 School organogram

therefore true to say that every teacher at a school is responsible for and fulfils multiple and often diverse functions, and the success of the school depends to a large extent on the manner in which each individual teacher performs his or her functions.

Another look at the organogram shows that every teacher falls under the authority of a number of line managers – so, for example, Teacher 1 in the Mathematics Department falls under the direct authority of the HoD of Mathematics when it comes to matters related to teaching the subject Mathematics, but he or she also falls directly under the authority of the head of cricket during the cricket season. There are not only clear lines of authority, but also specific channels of communication, both downwards (from the managers to their subordinates) and upwards (from the subordinates to the managers). Find out as soon as you can once you start teaching who are the appropriate persons to approach about the roles and responsibilities you will be assigned.

When it comes to labour matters such as salary payment and increases, benefits additional to the salary, leave privileges (vacation, study and maternity leave) and so on, it makes a big difference who your actual employer is (the government or the SGB) when you need to identify who to speak to when you have a problem. So, for example, a strike by government-paid teachers for a better salary has no impact on the salaries and/or working conditions of those teachers paid by the SGB, and teachers employed by the SGB do not necessarily qualify for paid maternity leave or a 13th cheque, as their counterparts in government posts do. All these matters must be taken into consideration when applying for or accepting a post at a school. They have a profound impact on how the school as an organisation functions, where you as an individual novice teacher fit in and how you experience the school and teaching as a profession.

In high-functioning schools, teachers are usually allocated functions and responsibilities according to their strengths and their particular skill sets – a careful match of person and function contributes significantly to the success of the entire organisation. It would make no sense to place a person who excels at coaching cricket in charge of the school choir, unless of course he or she just happens also to be very good at conducting choirs. You should therefore know what your strengths and interests are. Try to negotiate your involvement in different functions and activities so that your specific skill set and passions are used to the best advantage of the organisation.

Points to remember

In summary, the following points related to the school as an organisation could make the difference to your experience of your first year of teaching:
- Although there are both private and public schools in South Africa, both types have a fairly universal and standard organisational structure.
- Find out when you apply for a post at a South African school whether that post is a government/departmental post or an SGB post.
- As a novice teacher, it is important to know where you fit into the school's/organisational structure, and who you report to for each of your different functions and responsibilities.
- Try to negotiate (as far as is possible) your functions and responsibilities around your strengths to ensure that you are assigned functions that you can do well.

Understanding the structure of the school as an organisation and finding your perfect fit within that organisation will ensure a smooth acclimatisation at your new school. Another common feature regarding the management of school administration is the computer application called SA-SAMS (South African School Administration and Management System), which all schools are required to use. This allows the Department of Basic Education (DBE) to collect data on a national basis, so that systemic evaluation and decisions can be made. SA-SAMS allows for school administration such as class list creation, timetabling and generating reports and schedules. You may find that members of the SMT will require you to either provide information for the SA-SAMS database or input information directly into the SA-SAMS database. It is a good idea to keep your records (absentees or marks) up to date and on school class lists.

Section B
You as the new professional

Not only is teaching part of your identity, but as a teacher, you will be expected to conduct yourself in ways that are acceptable to society and the profession. In this section, we look more closely at the term 'professional' and try to give you some practical examples of what it means to be professional. We look at your new role as a teacher and your responsibility for learning and learners. In many ways, you will become a 'new you'. In doing so, it will be necessary to look closely at who you really are. We provide you with an outline of some of the basic personality traits. This will not only help you to understand yourself better, but also assist you with conflict management and understanding your learners through understanding diversity from a personality perspective. We remind you not to label learners but to try to understand them. In this section we also present the legal term *in loco parentis* and some of the underlying legal responsibilities you have as a professional teacher. The information is by no means complete, but you should be aware of the legal implications of your position and actions (or inactions) as a teacher. We certainly recommended that you understand the South African Schools' Act, the South African Children's Act and the SACE Code of Conduct for Teachers. As a teacher, you are always communicating, whether it be with learners, parents, colleagues or friends. We provide you with some advice regarding communication in your role as a teacher. We conclude this section by acknowledging that a career as a teacher is demanding and stressful (but very rewarding) and we suggest some ways in which you can look after yourself – because your family, your learners, your school and this country needs you to be well and happy!

The future of the world is in my classroom today.
Ivan Welton Fitzwater

6

Becoming a professional

Piera Biccard and Rinelle Evans

You would know that a professional sportsperson earns plenty of money for excelling in a particular sport. The idea of excellence and knowing what you're doing is a key element of being a professional. You will not be considered a professional merely because you have completed your degree.

Dictionary definitions of professionalism refer to someone being paid to engage competently in a skilled occupation, or 'having great skills or experience in a particular field'. Some definitions also refer to being courteous, conscientious and business-like in the workplace.

As a teacher, you will be scrutinised for professional behaviour by the learners, the parent body, your colleagues and the community. So just what is professionalism? Does it mean something different when you refer to a lawyer, doctor, salesperson or teacher? Although we may not find a universal definition for teacher professionalism, we do acknowledge that it relates to prized characteristics unique to teaching and that it is a multifaceted concept.

Perhaps a better term when talking about teachers would be 'integrity'. To quote C.S. Lewis:

Integrity is doing the right things ... even when no one is watching.

Professionals have integrity. This means behaving in the correct or appropriate manner even when you don't feel like it. It also means believing in certain universal principles and consistently living by them. It is easy to be rude to a parent after a long day in the classroom and perhaps an afternoon on the sports field. It is easy to be dismissive of a child who is reporting a bullying incident when your term marks are due. The added burden you have as a teacher when it comes to behaving professionally is that the rights of the child are generally supreme. In a recent video that went viral on social media, a learner can be seen chasing a teacher with a broom. It is clear that the teacher does not retaliate, but walks away. That teacher garnered sympathy from all quarters, not because he was not brave enough to fight back, but because he behaved correctly under those circumstances.

As a teacher you are a role model, whether you choose to be one or not.

Children and teenagers watch adults closely and admire or dislike certain personal qualities. They often strive to be like their teachers and so your behaviour and speech needs to be exemplary.

In the following sections we suggest a few areas in which your professional disposition will be judged.

Being pedagogically prepared

As a professional, you will be expected to have specific knowledge of your content area. You ought to know far more than what is in the textbook. You should also have a broad general knowledge as well as know what is happening in the world around you and have opinions on current affairs. Learners are very perceptive and can easily see through your lack of knowledge. Not only will your anxiety and lack of confidence be evident, but the learners will lose interest in your lessons if they are not challenged to achieve a higher level. You need to prepare thoroughly before teaching a lesson.

Showing who's boss

Even as a novice teacher you will be expected to exercise control over a class for between 35 and 45 minutes at a time. You will need basic managerial and organisational skills to do so. Imagine you are driving a bus full of passengers and you display incompetence in your driving. This incompetence will soon be noticed by your passengers, because you have their safety in your hands. They will become restless and rowdy and will either make their dissatisfaction known to you or report you to your employer or the authorities. A professional teacher is good at what s/he does and constantly seeks to improve.

Personal conduct

Apart from dressing neatly and appropriately for your daily tasks and showing care for your appearance, the way you act and speak adds to the professional image people will have of you. Can your colleagues rely on you? Do you keep your word and honour commitments? Do you speak the truth? How honest are you about being absent or failing to meet a deadline?

People who are positive are generally viewed as being professional. Others appreciate it when we try to solve problems rather than complain. Taking time to help other teachers, for example by stapling exam papers, will be remembered for many years. Listening actively to others when they let off steam or try to explain their point of view is a mature and responsible way of dealing with conflict. Avoid spending time on personal matters at school. Your private life should not intrude on your teaching responsibilities.

Professional behaviour

As a teacher you will be judged more harshly by your words and actions than other people are. How do you display a professional demeanour? The following basics will always apply:

- Be on time for meetings, coaching and especially for your classes. If you are not five minutes early, you're late!
- Be prepared for each and every lesson. Learners pick up very quickly if you are not prepared, and the lesson degenerates into chaos. It is also essential to be prepared for meetings.
- Even if your classroom is poorly resourced or the furniture is old and insufficient, you can keep it clean and tidy. This is your professional space and anyone walking in will make inferences about your professionalism based on their impression of your classroom.
- Listen carefully before responding – especially when you are dealing with an angry parent.
- Keep your promises, and only make promises you can keep. If you have been given a task to complete, do so! The school system can only function effectively when everyone is reliable and keeps to processes and deadlines.
- Do not make excuses – apologise and keep it brief.
- Keep your temper under control. If you are angry with a learner, it should be an 'anger' that you 'put on' and control. It is very difficult to maintain your professionalism when you have lost control of your emotions.
- Never shout in class. Shouting should be kept for emergencies only.
- Stand up straight. You'll be amazed how much better you feel.
- Dress appropriately. (You cannot coach sport in stilettos.)
- Treat all persons with respect. Do not keep parents, colleagues or service providers waiting. Say 'please' and 'thank you' to *everyone* – this includes a naughty learner you are reprimanding (Sam! Sit down! ... please).
- Be very, very, very careful of staffroom gossip.
- Be very, very, very careful of what you say to another staff member in earshot of the learners.
- Do not speak poorly of your school, principal, HoD, colleagues or *anyone* at a social function. It says more about you than it does about them and you never know who knows whom.
- Be careful of what you share on social media – it is permanent and can be easily shared.
- Never use anyone else's ideas without giving him or her credit.

Before you can accept a post, you will have to provide a police clearance certificate to affirm that you are a suitable candidate to work with minors. You will also have to register with the South African Council of Educators (SACE). This is your professional body. The purpose of this council is to uphold excellence in education and ensure that teachers act 'in a proper and becoming way'. They will also investigate any breach of conduct by an offending teacher. By signing the code of conduct, you are committing yourself to behaving in ethical ways towards your learners, their parents, the community and your colleagues. You confirm that you will not act in a manner that brings the teaching profession into disrepute and that you will uphold and promote human rights.

We recommend that you join a teacher union of your choice. If you elect not to, the union contribution is deducted off your salary anyway and divided amongst all the unions, so you might as well join one. Unions play an important role in providing information (for example on salary increases and changes to the curriculum). They can also assist with disputes that may arise while you are employed or if you need legal advice or representation. Check their web page regularly for updates on news, meetings and professional development.

Ask questions about what is expected and permissible at the school. Forming close working relationships with colleagues will enable you to learn the boundaries of acceptable and accountable professional behaviour. Be open to learning, and respond positively to the accepted norms and values of the school that you are in even if they differ from your personal views. Your personality and gifts will be valued if they are displayed appropriately in your new context. Being professional distinguishes you from being just average, makes you marketable and gives you self-worth. If you want to be taken seriously, and have colleagues and parents consider you as an asset to the team, it is essential to do things in a professional manner.

> **Teachers' rights: Discrimination, victimisation and harassment**
> Teachers are protected from direct or indirect discrimination, victimisation and harassment by colleagues, parents and learners. It is unacceptable for teachers to be bullied and harassed by other teachers and/or staff in management positions. Teachers who feel harassed, bullied or discriminated against can raise grievances and bring complaints to employment tribunals about unlawful actions or words. You have the right to teach! You have the right to dignity! Learners, parents and colleagues do not have the right to frustrate teaching and learning in your classroom and nor do they have the right to undermine your dignity as a teacher.

7

Establishing your teacher identity

Yolandi Woest

An identity relates to those unique characteristics you wish to be associated with or recognised by. Identity markers include gender, religion, world view, dress code, interests, citizenship and your physical characteristics or accent. Furthermore, the causes you support, the traditions you uphold and the values and beliefs you subscribe to all constitute your identity. Your identity also has a strong emotional link – a person usually takes pride in his or her identity.

The key to understanding and respecting other people is to know and appreciate who you are. As much as we like to label and put others into categories, you too would be able to give yourself 'labels'. The difference is you *choose* how you wish to categorise yourself, even though this may not be the same way you are viewed by the world (others). Your identity is generally created by how you perceive yourself, but you may accept or reject aspects of who you are considered to be as assigned by others such as friends, parents or colleagues.

One of the biggest challenges for a novice teacher is to get to know, understand and, most importantly, accept the 'new you'. You are not who you were before the annual summer holidays. In a matter of a month, you will move from being a student or au pair or world traveller to a professional with the special title of teacher. In fact, you are the same person about to probably undergo the biggest identity change of your life. You may not feel it as suddenly, but you will immediately be perceived differently by others. Overnight, you will become famous (or infamous) in a way, recognised almost everywhere you go.

Consider these numbers: In a school of 800 learners, you will engage daily with roughly 100 learners in various groups. This means that you are familiar to 100 learners times (approximately) two parents plus at least one grandparent (and their friends) plus one close family friend and their friends. The result of this multiplication is that many people in the community (stretching much further than you think) know who you are and are familiar with your name, probably your face and, significantly, the perceptions their children have of you. You might sneak out in your pyjamas to buy milk or a late-night snack and be greeted unexpectedly by a young teen shouting 'Hi Ma'am!' from across the parking lot. You might be served in a restaurant by the 16-year-old you have scolded during the previous week. You might meet the fresh-faced 14-year-old girl in your class in the pharmacy, accompanied by a much older male, asking for condoms. You might meet the nine-year-old buying liquor together with his clearly drunk dad. You will find that learners react differently towards you when meeting you in public. Do not fret – they are usually more bewildered than you are by the coincidence. That is all part of navigating the new you.

We all have perceptions of the people we observe around us. In a way, we are regularly somewhat judgemental and critical of other people. How often do we not hear statements such as 'I know I am not the tidiest person on earth, but have you seen that person's house?' or 'I know I can be lazy sometimes, but at least I do more than Shabangu.' The educational arena that has now become your professional 'home' consists of various educational stakeholders – all with different perceptions of each other and, often, fixed ideas of what a teacher is and how a teacher should behave. You need to be mindful of the fact that perceptions differ, and that the perceptions other people have of you are not entirely under your control. Managing perceptions is like walking on a tightrope: it is a delicate balance to find, especially during your first years of teaching. Teachers are often expected to be role models, good citizens or flawless individuals. It is not unusual to hear statements such as, 'He is a teacher and he did that!' The truth is that teachers are still human and, more importantly, should be true to themselves.

Other people's social perceptions of you as a novice teacher, together with your many new duties and expectations, can place enormous pressure on you. You may experience feelings of anxiety, frustration, hopelessness or worthlessness because you base your self-worth on what others think of you. This is often an aspect that novice teachers are not very well prepared to handle. Dealing with perceptions requires serious mental efforts: you must teach yourself to self-reflect critically, building empathy toward others and being honest with yourself. Here are a few guidelines to assist you in dealing with others' perceptions of you:

- Know yourself. This 'rule' is the key not only to being a good teacher, but to living a happy and fulfilled life. Getting to know yourself might be the most difficult and continuous venture on which you will embark throughout your career. You get to know yourself better by looking for patterns in your behaviour: you will most probably react fairly consistently

in different situations. The constant in these situations is *you*. You might be a person who tends to avoid conflict at all costs, or the one who immediately blames others. The key is to be very honest with yourself when examining your own behaviour.
- Find 'critical friends'. Invest in someone who works with you but who is not a close friend. Close friends tend to take your side and are mostly subjective. You definitely need them too, but not for getting to know yourself. A 'critical' person in your professional life is extremely valuable. These are the people who are usually honest with you. You can ask someone you trust to play this role in your professional life; an older or more experienced teacher in your environment might be a good choice. However, you also need to be mindful of this person's background, values (which might differ from yours) and social identification. Inexperienced teachers often find a critical friend whose views they accept without questioning them. The tightrope walk is to find your own teacher identity in the midst of what other people think you should be. Another good practice is to ask two very different people to be your critical friends and then synthesise their perceptions of your behaviour and measure it against your own perceptions.

You have, no doubt, heard the maxim that you 'write your own CV'. This is true, but CVs are dynamic and thus change. You do write your own CV, every day. Keep in mind that people are by nature critical towards others – this is a very human characteristic. People tend to feel better about themselves if there are others who make mistakes. The harsh reality is that you might be late for two meetings for very legitimate reasons and thereafter be 'branded' a late-comer or someone who 'always has excuses'. You might be late for every single meeting throughout a school year and be labelled in the same way. The truth is that you are quickly labelled by others as something, whatever that something might be: shy, timid, aggressive or assertive. The key is to know that, accept it and work on it without expecting validation from others.

8

Determining your personality traits

Alta Engelbrecht and Chantelle de Wet

You may have heard about the nature/nurture debate in psychology:
- Are we the mere sum of the genetic DNA inherited from our parents?
- Or are we a product of the social and cultural circle that we grew up in?

This debate does not seem to offer a clear answer, so perhaps a better question to ask is: 'What can we do with what we've got?' You were born with certain characteristics inherited from your parents and we refer to these as your temperament. By being exposed to varied experiences and persons through your upbringing, you have also learnt or acquired several behavioural traits that make up your character. Together your temperament (nature) and your character (nurture) form your personality – your unique way of thinking, feeling, behaving and reacting to the world.

Centuries ago Greek doctors developed a theory that our moods, emotions and behaviours were caused by an excess or lack of body fluids: blood, yellow bile, black bile and phlegm. There had to be a balance of these fluids for a person to have an ideal personality. This categorisation eventually led to someone being labelled as 'sanguine', 'choleric', 'melancholic' and 'phlegmatic'. Here are some characteristics of these personality types:
- A **sanguine** individual is generally light-hearted, fun-loving and a people-person. This person loves to entertain, is spontaneous, has leadership abilities, and is confident. However, he or she can also be arrogant and self-indulgent. This person may day-dream and be off-task often to the point of not accomplishing anything. He or she can be impulsive, possibly acting unpredictably.
- A **choleric** person is a do-er. This person has a lot of ambition, energy and passion, and tries to instil it in others. Cholerics may dominate others, especially phlegmatics. Many great charismatic military and political figures were cholerics. On the negative side, they are easily angered or bad-tempered.

- A **melancholic** is a deep thinker, often very kind and considerate, as well as highly creative in areas such as poetry and art. Such a person may become overly preoccupied with the tragedy and cruelty in the world, thus becoming easily depressed. Melanchodics are often perfectionists, being very particular about what they want and how they want it. This often results in dissatisfaction with their own work, and they tend to always point out to themselves what could be improved.
- A **phlegmatic** person is calm and unemotional. Phlegmatics are very consistent, relaxed, rational, curious and observant, making them good administrators and diplomats. Like the sanguine personality, the phlegmatic has many friends. but the phlegmatic is more reliable and compassionate. These characteristics typically make the phlegmatic more dependable. While phlegmatics are generally self-content and kind, their shy personalities may inhibit others' enthusiasm. They may also be considered lazy and resistant to change.

Even though people cannot be put into boxes, understanding that you as well as your colleagues, the learners and their parents all have a temperament type may help you in your daily interactions in the classroom or staff room. So who are you? Refer to Appendix C for a quick quiz that may help you determine your personality type.

Table 8.1 offers further insight into temperaments, by using birds as metaphors. Which bird are you? Highlight each sentence in the table that truly describes you.

Table 8.1   The four basic temperaments

Peacock (sanguine)	Eagle (choleric)
I love people.	I easily tell people what to do.
I often feel happy and sad on the same day.	I enjoy competing – and winning.
I easily get bored with tasks.	I enjoy it if things are done my way.
I talk too much.	I easily become impatient with other people.
I use my hands when talking.	I want tasks to be completed as soon as possible.
I often act very impulsively.	I easily challenge others.
I am spontaneous.	Normally I have ample self-confidence.
I like to be the centre of attention.	

Owl (melancholic)	Swan (phlegmatic)
I occupy myself for long periods with my own things. I get angry easily. Things must be done perfectly. Normally I'm quiet. People often say I'm too serious. It takes me a while to get to a decision. I am very loyal.	I don't like conflict. I am calm and relaxed. I don't mind doing what others want to do. I don't get angry easily. People say I am a good listener. I'm very reliable. I want to please other people.

In the next sections, we describe some general characteristics of each bird as a teacher as well as how such a temperament manages conflict.

Peacock – sanguine

Peacocks tend to live with the motto '*Carpe diem*' (seize the day), meaning they jump at each opportunity and live life! As teachers, peacocks are very enthusiastic. They are energised teachers who love entertaining others. Learners love their classes, as there is never a dull moment. These teachers thrive on the attention they create and the difference that they make. Peacocks are people-orientated and therefore make great motivational speakers. People in general and learners in particular tend to be very encouraged by peacock teachers.

Table 8.2 General characteristics of peacocks

Mature characteristics	Immature characteristics
Extrovert – loves people	Feels rejected when relationships fail
Likes to be with people	Weak willpower
Can influence people positively	Undisciplined
Enjoys life	Very emotional, cannot hide emotions
Always interested in people/things	Likes physical contact – can be negative
Cheerful – sings/whistles frequently	Disorganised
Lives in the 'here and now'	Submissive
Usually very positive/optimistic	Not always as confident as he or she seems
Easily inspired	Insecure, needs to feel accepted

Mature characteristics	Immature characteristics
Enthusiastic nature	Usually too impulsive
Doesn't stay angry for long	Fears rejection and failure
If one thing fails, he or she will start again	Tries to please others without thinking first
Strong sense of justice/fairness	Doesn't like routine
Makes new friends quickly	Uncontrolled rage
Makes a great first impression	Egocentric, attention-seeking
Very tender, compassionate and loving	Seldom plans ahead
Respects other people	Talkative

The conflict-management style of the peacock

The typical style of the peacock is to negotiate, which is obviously the best way of solving any conflict. Peacocks don't like conflict, because they don't want to become unpopular, as the essence of their being is that people should adore them at all times. But they would also not be peacocks if they let an opportunity pass to state how they viewed the conflict situation. They are very assertive during conflict, although they might focus too much on emotions rather than the matter being discussed. They also like to fight other people's battles for them. The reason why this conflict-managing style works very well is that it *gives* and *takes*. In conflict peacocks express what they genuinely believe, but at the same time, they are open to other people's feelings, ideas and solutions. In a nutshell: being able to engage in conflict with confidence and to listen to others is the secret of a successful conflict-management style.

Eagle – choleric

Eagles often say: 'For me, only the best is good enough. Winning is everything.' As a teacher, the eagle always wants to be 'the best' – whether it is his or her class that has to win every competition or achieve the best results in the subject.
Eagle teachers are natural leaders who like to give instructions and expect other people to follow. In the classroom they are normally strict and task-driven.

Table 8.3 General characteristics of eagles

Mature characteristics	Immature characteristics
Very good self-discipline	Can be hostile towards people
Great determination, goal-orientated	Cannot control anger
Excellent self-esteem, not bothered by others	Sarcastic
Ambitious/optimistic/likes challenges	Untactful, insensitive
Practical/doesn't waste time/natural organiser	Not always in control of words
Always sees the bigger picture	Not very affectionate
Strong, natural leaders	Shows little/no emotion
Can take charge quickly and positively	'My way or the highway'
Good at evaluating people	Impatient
Quick, calm and bold in emergencies	Domineering, makes other people's decisions for them
Extremely hard worker who always completes tasks	Often says: 'Get over it'
Likes 'out-of-the-ordinary' things	Stubborn
Adventurous/not scared of the unknown	Can be too self-sufficient

The conflict-management style of the eagle

A teacher once looked at the characteristics of the four temperaments and remarked that she didn't understand why 'domineering' was a weakness! This indicates the way in which eagles see themselves in conflict. They have to take control before anything can be solved. Taking charge is not a bad thing in a conflict situation. (Somebody has to do it!) What also helps is that eagles are very much task-driven and tend to focus on content rather than on emotions. Of course, they sometimes don't realise that they have said something that could hurt other people.

Some eagles can become aggressive when they are at the losing end. They are very prescriptive and demand a lot from other people. They frequently interrupt people as if it is their right to do so. Naturally, the other party involved in the conflict can feel inadequate, embarrassed and even threatened. Strong eagles may lack certain basic social skills, which can anger the people around them. The most difficult thing for an eagle to say is 'I am sorry', and the second most difficult thing for them to say is 'I was wrong'. Being able to give a sincere apology is the one technique that every eagle teacher should acquire concerning the management of conflict.

Owl – melancholic

As teachers, owls are structured and very observant. Focused, wise, calm and quiet – this is the profile of the owl teacher. They are hard-working, loyal and creative. And they expect other people to respect them and also strive for excellence.

Table 8.4   General characteristics of owls

Mature characteristics	Immature characteristics
Wise	Feels that people don't understand/ appreciate him or her
Multi-talented	Can suffer from depression
Multi-skilled	Can be too much of a perfectionist
Very sensitive	Critical, often pessimistic
High moral standards	Often sees problems that don't exist
Intense and complex	Not easily satisfied
Creative thinker/inventor	Doesn't like sharing
Problem solver	Lacks self-confidence or self-worth
Gives attention to detail	Over-sensitive
Perfectionist	Holds grudges
Analytical/logical	Emotional/moody
Foresees potential problems	Doesn't like to work in teams
Doesn't like the limelight	Insecure
Self-sacrificing	Unpractical
Self-disciplined	Easily withdraws
Doesn't do things in excess	Introverted
Hard worker	Indecisive
Loyal	Suspicious

The conflict-management style of the owl

Based on the sensitivity and humbleness of the owl, one can understand why they withdraw from conflict. It is simply 'not their style' to fight. It should not be necessary to have conflict, they argue, if everybody would just 'do what they have to do'. Because they are so loyal, they cannot bear it when people lash out and use emotions to intimidate or manipulate others. They also withdraw from conflict because they hate it when others are critical of them, although they themselves are very critical and analytical. Sometimes when they do take part in conflict management, everybody is astonished at the insight they reveal and the solutions they come up with. This stresses the fact that the owl has so much to give, even in conflict situations – if only they would give it!

Swan – phlegmatic

Swan teachers focus on interpersonal relations. They always build other people's feelings of self-worth and self-confidence. It is simply not their style to shout and scream. They are gentle and practical and always try to help others. As teachers, they are sensitive to atmosphere and generally try to accommodate others.

Table 8.5   General characteristics of swans

Mature characteristics	Immature characteristics
Calm nature	If not interested, slow to start
A swan 'looks before leeping'	Lack of ambition
Thinker/planner	Doesn't get involved easily
Diplomatic/approachable	Handles stress well by hiding it
Often undiscovered leader/good negotiator	Doesn't confront people
Good sense of humour – dry wit	Avoids conflict
Vivid imagination	Worries too much/anxious
Reliable	Not living up to potential
Level-headed/controls emotions	Frustrates others with calm nature
Loyal	Unmotivated

Mature characteristics	Immature characteristics
Practical/effective	Undecided
Relaxed/peacemaker	Aloof
High standards/neat, hard worker	Sarcastic

The conflict-management style of the swan

While owls do not give enough of themselves, swans give too much. They never stop giving to other people, but also never stop *giving in* to other people. Swans surrender too easily because they overvalue the maintenance of relationships and undervalue the attainment of their own goals. They believe it is easier to put up with the way things are than to face the problem and try to solve it. Because they are pleasers, they argue that they might 'lose' somebody if they displease. Sometimes they come up with the most wonderful ideas to solve a problem, in order to escape the alternative of asserting themselves in a conflict situation. It usually works, because they refrain from becoming emotionally involved or 'taking sides'. Instead, they dilute the conflict between others by 'putting them on a new trail'. They have to be very careful, though, that they are not intimidated or manipulated. They truly believe that other people would treat them fairly, yet if in a conflict situation they experience that others (probably eagles) don't respect them, their self-concept suffers. Sometimes they end up by surrendering with a sarcastic remark such as: 'Okay, as always you are right, we'll do it your way.' This is almost the closest a swan comes to engaging in a conflict.

The four temperaments are not rigid, exclusive categories; you might find yourself having characteristics of each bird! A person seldom has characteristics of only one temperament, but each teacher and learner will probably have a primary and also a secondary temperament. In other words, you could primarily be an eagle, but also show many characteristics of the peacock (your secondary temperament). Try to determine what 'bird' you are dealing with and use this knowledge to understand yourself and your learners better. However, remember that we are all unique and can never be permanently 'caged' in a category.

Not only teachers have certain temperaments; learners too may be categorised. We shall discuss learner temperaments in Section C and also consider an African perspective to personality.

9

Acting *in loco parentis*

Michael Biccard

The Children's Act of 2005 is aligned with section 28 (3) of the Constitution and defines any person under 18 – unless married or emancipated by order of the court – as a child, and any person over 18 as an adult.

Parents and caregivers are responsible for the wellbeing of their children. Once a child arrives at school, the teacher takes over this role. Under South African common law, teachers act *in loco parentis*, which means 'in place of the parent'. For a few hours daily you take over the role of a caring parent, as an unofficial guardian. You have a legal duty to take the same reasonable care of a learner that a parent or caregiver would take and to act in the child's best interest.

While you as the teacher act *in loco parentis*, you have the right to maintain authority through fairness and order in a peaceful setting where learning can take place, but you have the added responsibilities for the protection of learners. You also have the obligation to care for the physical and psychological wellbeing of the learners in your care. If you do not take your responsibilities seriously, you could be liable for damage caused to a learner if it is proven that your conduct falls below the standard of care commonly accepted as being reasonable in a parent–child relationship. There are instances where your specialist knowledge would make you aware of dangers that a parent might not appreciate.

The Children's Act (RSA, 2005) mentions the following duties for teachers:

> *(a) safeguarding and promoting the wellbeing of the child*
> *(b) protecting the child from maltreatment, abuse, neglect, degradation, discrimination, exploitation and any other physical, emotional and moral harm or hazards*
> *(c) respecting, protecting, promoting and securing the fulfilment of, and guarding against any infringement of, the child's rights set out in the Bill of Rights and the principles set out in chapter 2 of the Constitution*

(d) *guiding, directing and securing the child's education and upbringing, including religious and cultural education and upbringing, in a manner appropriate to the child's age, maturity and stage of development*
(e) *guiding, advising and assisting the child in decisions to be taken by the child in a manner appropriate to the child's age, maturity and stage of development*
(f) *guiding the behaviour of the child in a humane manner*
(g) *maintaining a sound relationship with the child*
(h) *accommodating any special needs the child may have*
(i) *generally, ensuring that the best interests of the child are the paramount concern in all matters affecting the child.*

It is clear that you have a duty to protect the child from emotional and moral harm, to protect the rights of the child, and to guide and advise the child in educational matters and decisions that have to be taken by the child. To achieve these ends, you must nurture a sound relationship with the child so that the needs and best interests of the child are met.

The *in loco parentis* duty is clearly an important responsibility you take on, even as a novice teacher. When the parent, as primary caregiver, hands over to the school or teacher, you have an essential, legal and contractual duty of care towards the learners entrusted to you as caretaker parents. This duty suggests that you have an obligation to 'accept responsibility for the safety and wellbeing of the learners' for as long as they are under your care.

The standard of care is the application of the ordinary skills of a competent professional and what can be expected of a reasonable person, for example a class teacher acting within the constraints of the circumstances. Your duty to care may be influenced by, amongst other things, the subject or activity being taught, the age of the children, the available resources and the size of the class.

One may ask when a teacher's duty to care should begin. There are no set times. If the child arrives at school within what could be seen as a reasonable time, the school gates are unlocked and the child is allowed to enter the premises, then the school and the teacher's duty to care begins. A reasonable time (depending on the school's circumstances) could be half an hour before the first period begins.

When does our duty to care end? The learners need a reasonable time to leave the premises. If the school has a rule that the children must leave the premises within a certain time frame, then it would be unreasonable to expect the school and the teachers to be on duty for longer than about 30 minutes after the children are expected to leave. It is unreasonable to be expected to wait around until the last learner has left.

Furthermore, you have a duty to act while taking care of children at school. It is not enough to simply warn learners of potential dangers. You must ensure that no harm comes to learners while they are on the school grounds. The Children's Act defines the duty of care to mean that a person with care of the child may do what is reasonable in all the circumstances for the purpose of safeguarding or promoting the welfare of the child.

Being *in loco parentis* has many facets, and you will have to achieve teaching aims and maintain order by means of the school's Code of Conduct and within the bounds of the disciplinary policy of the school – and all this needs to happen within a safe and caring environment where quality teaching and learning can take place. To fulfil your duties, it is essential that you know each learner and endeavour to guide and to protect all learners by ensuring that their rights are not violated, while looking after any special needs they may have. You could be found guilty of negligence if learners are injured and there is evidence that you did not fulfil your role of care towards them.

What constitutes negligence? Negligence means not taking reasonable care. It also means not acting when you should. As a teacher, you should warn learners against dangerous games, places or actions. Continually remind them of school safety rules that are in place. You should also report any dangerous objects or areas to the principal. You should not leave learners unattended in class or during extramural activities. Injuries from a broken window or fist fight in your absence have dire consequences for you and the school. Your school should also give clear information to parents regarding the opening and closing times of the school.

For you as a teacher to be found negligent in the event of an accident, it will have to be proven that you could have foreseen the accident but failed to take reasonable steps to prevent it. You could also be found to have acted negligently if you did not try to prevent a child being hurt physically or psychologically through the acts of a bully. In most instances of negligence, the questions 'Did you care?' and 'Did you act?' – as a reasonable care-giving adult would – will be asked. A teacher (or school) can only be held liable for damages if the teacher (or school) did not act with caution or breached their duty in an unreasonable and guilty manner.

If you apply your professional judgement, training and experience to situations in a reasonable manner, seeking to promote the best interest of the learners in your care, you would have met your professional obligations.

When acting *in loco parentis*:

1. The teacher has an autonomous right to maintain authority whilst on duty in order to create a learning environment that is orderly, co-ordinated and harmonious, where quality education can take place. For this to happen, the school has a legal obligation to draw up a Code of Conduct and policy for disciplinary practice. In all instances, policy should be implemented in a way that is firm and fair. The rights of all participants should be protected by fair measures to maintain the teacher's authority. Discipline should be directed towards correction and not retribution.
2. The teacher is obliged to care for and supervise the psychological welfare of the learner as an impressionable, immature person.

10

Taking care of yourself

Sarina de Jager

Teaching is a demanding profession, and any teacher will tell you that it most certainly is not a 'half-day job' with plenty of holidays. Teachers play many roles, including that of parent, coach, counsellor, doctor and social worker. No wonder they often refer to the teaching profession as a calling rather than a career. Teaching places a heavy physical and emotional demand on teachers each school day, and for some teachers even their weekends are filled with hours of marking or extramural school activities. This, at times, leads to an unsustainable pace, and it is easy for teachers to become burned out. This is when you become completely exhausted of physical and/or emotional strength and lose your motivation, usually as a result of prolonged stress and exhaustion. This is why you must make time to consciously take care of yourself in body, mind and soul. Self-care is not something optional that you do when you have time. For a teacher it is the foundation that allows you to give your learners the focus and energy they deserve.

You are a complex being with various facets. Commonly we refer to our physical health, mental and psychological strength, and spiritual wellbeing. Each of these components requires attention and maintenance. Wellbeing is generally defined as being healthy and happy. In this section we will discuss how to maintain wellbeing and avoid burning out. Or, as the saying goes: to burn bright but not out!

Looking after yourself physically

Your body needs good nutrition and exercise to stay healthy and balanced:

- A balanced diet consists of nutritious meals that include fruits, vegetables, protein, fat, carbohydrates and milk and dairy products. It is to your advantage to take the time to prepare meals and snacks that provide you with the energy required for teaching every day. A packed lunch of fruit and sandwiches is a healthier and cheaper alternative to a pie and soft drink bought at the tuck shop. You also need to drink sufficient amounts of water regularly. Stay away from fast food and too much sugar, alcohol and caffeine.

- You need to rest your body too. Make sure that you get at least seven hours' sleep each night in a warm, comfortable and well-ventilated space. You may find you need to take a nap each afternoon too or just spend a half-hour lying quietly on your bed! If you are feeling tired and listless, check your diet, as you may need more minerals. Ask your pharmacist for a supplement, and if the fatigue or listlessness persists, consult a doctor.
- Teaching generally requires that you move a great deal, but sitting down hunched over your planning or marking affects your posture and makes some muscles lazy. Exercise moderately by taking brisk walks each day. Do some light exercises to stretch and relax your muscles and maintain your suppleness and strength. When you exercise, you release endorphins (happy hormones), which improve your mood and motivation.

Looking after yourself emotionally and spiritually

As a teacher you will be confronted with learners who exasperate you and increase your blood pressure. Dealing with this type of behaviour on a daily basis can be exhausting, and it is therefore essential that you take care of yourself emotionally.

A good place to start is by becoming self-aware. Keeping track of your feelings and thoughts and acknowledging your emotions can help you notice the red flags of burn-out before it is too late. Let's talk about the red flags and the green flags, red being warning signs you need to look out for and green flags being things that you can do to remain balanced and well. Red flags you need to look out for inlcude:

- changes in your appetite and sleeping pattern, for example eating too much or having no appetite, sleeping more than usual or not sleeping at all
- fluctuations in your mood, for example crying more than usual or feeling emotionally numb, having aggressive outbursts or acting out of character
- feelings of hopelessness and worthlessness; these feelings could also be accompanied by scary thoughts like hurting yourself or ending your life
- feeling panicked and out of control, or unable to breathe, or feeling unsafe or scared most of the time
- isolating yourself and avoiding people.

These flags need to be taken seriously and you need to seek help as soon as you identify them. Seek help by talking to a psychologist, a counsellor or a spiritual leader. The most dangerous thing you can do is keep quiet.

How do you keep balanced in a profession that is so demanding? Have a look at the following green flags:

- Nurture healthy relationships and surround yourself with positive people. Make sure you spend quality time with family, friends and those who form part of your support structure.
- Have hobbies or activities outside of the school context.
- Be involved in your community. For example, join a club, church or charity and spend time giving back to society.
- Practise mindfulness. This involves making time to focus on your breathing and becoming aware of your emotions (refer to the activity in Chapter 16 on aggression in the classroom for a useful activity in mindfulness).
- Set goals to challenge yourself. This can include pursuing a postgraduate degree, mastering a skill, finishing a project or participating in an event (theatre production, marathon or book club).
- Manage your time well. Remember that when you value yourself, you will value *how* you spend your time, *with whom* and *on what*. Time management is important in a teacher's life, as a lack of time and too many things that need doing tend to catch up with you and cause a lot of stress. Some guidelines to consider when managing your time are the following:
    - Learn to prioritise. Think of your day as packing a jar with rocks: you start off with the big ones (the most important things to do), then the medium rocks and lastly the small rocks (least important).
    - Make your calls in the morning. An early start to the day can relieve you of a lot of stress and even improve your mood.
    - Do not take on what you cannot cope with. It is important to know yourself well enough to say no to certain things. Value yourself and your time sufficiently to spend it wisely. Do not try to please everyone.
    - Learn to distinguish between what is urgent and what is important. Don't keep yourself so busy with less important things that you don't get to the important stuff.
    - Make lists. Make them in a notebook or on your phone. You can even set reminders on your phone to help you stay focused on completing certain tasks.
    - When you have precious hours to relax and spend with friends or family, make sure to commit to the time without getting distracted by work-related matters. (For example, do not answer your emails, be on your phone or work on your computer during this time.) Be present in the moment and learn to enjoy not being busy.

The secret to a healthy and happy life is balance. Look out for the red flags, and keep pursuing the green flags.

> **Mind shift**
> Remember that events like the loss of a loved one, a break-up with a romantic partner, your parents separating or getting divorced, relocating to new place or school, being diagnosed with an illness or having a family member who needs care, a car accident, a robbery, losing your job or any other traumatic event could impact your wellbeing in a significant way. If you are going through events like these you need to seek out support and make sure to keep an eye out for the red flags.

11

Counting your words

Yolandi Woest

All around us, we hear people talking. At airports we sometimes hear different accents, a variety of languages and various levels of excitement or anticipation. At sporting events we usually hear expressions of frustration or cheers of victory. People talk (or shout) when they drive. In our highly technological age, we even see people talking while on their own in their vehicles – and they are not mad!

Human communication includes many modes, but we rely largely on speech. The way in which people talk provides their listeners with a wealth of information. Based on this information, biases develop, prejudices are formed, impressions are created (and first impressions, they say, are lasting!) and expectations are established.

As a teacher, you will talk to different educational role-players: colleagues, learners in your class, learners from other schools, staff members from other schools, parents, district officials – in fact, too many to count. You will need to consider carefully your choice of words as well as the tone in which you interact, as the way you talk affects the response you get.

Since the world of teaching relies so heavily on oral communication, we look now at how what you say and how you say it can work either in your favour as a novice teacher or, if not applied appropriately, against you.

Talking to other novices

At the beginning of each academic year, several new teachers start their careers simultaneously at the same school. These individuals find themselves facing similar challenges, and experience the intricate dynamics of the subculture of a school in much the same way. You may find yourself 'huddling together' and forming a group with those peers.

In those first few weeks, you may feel overwhelmed by countless new observations, impressions, insights, challenges and uncertainties. You will most definitely feel the need to discuss these matters with 'people who understand' – those in your direct, new environment. However, you must be mindful of the way you talk, where you have the conversation and especially the topics under discussion.

Here are a few tips when talking to your peers, i.e. novice teachers starting with you at the same time, at a new school:
- Refrain from discussing other staff members. Although you all may experience similar difficulties with the same colleagues, it is advisable not to bad-mouth them. Some months down the line, you may shift allegiances, but you can never take back those unkind or untrue words. Should you need to express your feelings about a specific staff member, do so in the privacy of your own safe space with a trusted friend who does not work with you.
- Do not discuss confidential matters that learners have shared with you with direct peers. Keep in mind that learners experience their emotions very intensely, but they never last long. Learners might relate an incident to you in tears. This leaves you upset, worried and feeling that you have to sort out the problem immediately. You must talk to the grade head or HoD if a learner has confided something that needs to be reported by law, such as abuse, but these issues do not have to be shared with direct peers.
- For obvious reasons, do not insult or swear at direct peers. Also, be careful of the kind of jokes you make with them. They might seem funny to you, but can be subtly sexist, racist or offensive to others. The fact that your direct peers are as new as you are to the school environment does not mean you can treat them with less respect than more experienced colleagues.
- Do not overly praise when you are not sure of someone's real abilities. Although collegial support is conducive to any working environment, you might be adding to someone's false sense of self. Be very aware of all other developing identities around you and the influence you have on them. In the same way, do not take excessive praise from direct peers to heart – they are as inexperienced as you.

Talking to learners

Apart from your direct peers, you'll be talking to the learners after class, on the playground and when you coach them. Most of these will be informal chats while establishing or maintaining a good rapport, but some will be of a more serious nature and learners may confide in you, with the expectation that you will keep their confidence.

Here are some guidelines for making sure you communicate appropriately with learners:
- Always keep the classroom door open when talking to learners. Other staff members or learners might perceive a closed door differently to your actual intention of creating a safe space where a learner may speak freely.

Rather talk to learners in a group. It is never a good idea to be alone with a learner in any situation, anywhere, ever.
- Channel learners' issues to the correct people. When learners discuss private matters with you that raise serious concerns, you should immediately alert the relevant structures, for example your HoD.
- Keep very accurate records of what learners tell you. Use a separate diary for personal discussions with learners. Write down the time, duration of the discussion and your advice, if any was given. Follow up on these meetings with the learner or alert the appropriate people in time. In terms of the law, if the learner divulges abuse, it must be reported. Never promise a learner that you will not tell anybody; rather promise to tell someone who can help.
- This piece of advice may not be applicable to teachers working in the Foundation Phase, but is definitely key if you intend teaching older learners. Do not touch learners, no matter how well meaning it may be. What you see as a supportive hug can be misconstrued from a learner's (or other observer's) point of view. The general rule of thumb is *never* to initiate contact, even after establishing a good relationship.

Talking to parents

It is generally advisable to communicate with parents in writing. This gives you time to think about what you wish to say. It creates some distance between the two parties and is thus less intimidating, and it also serves as a permanent record of events. Serious disciplinary matters will generally be dealt with by senior staff, but there may be occasions when you need to contact a caregiver or parent about important or urgent matters regarding their children.

If you call a parent, politely introduce yourself and ask whether it is convenient for the parent to speak to you. The parent may ask you to phone back after work or offer to return the call at a more convenient time. He or she may even immediately make a face-to-face appointment with you. If the person takes your call, state the purpose of your making contact briefly. If your call is to raise a concern rather than report misbehaviour, reassure the parent that the child is not in trouble before you proceed to the matter at hand. Parents get very anxious and protective when it comes to their children. Be factual. Only share information that can be backed up by physical evidence or what was observed. Always allow the parent to state his or her point of view. Listen empathetically and try to create trust. Parents need to feel that you are acting in the best interest of their child.

If the call is about a particular behaviour or minor incident that took place, ask the parent questions such as 'Has your daughter ever done this type of thing before?', 'Why do you think that Barisso might have done such a thing?', 'What do you think we can do to help/avoid such a situation in the future?' You will also have to explain what the school's code of conduct says the consequences will be. Often parents become defensive or aggressive. Remain polite. If matters get out of hand, do not proceed with the conversation. Say that you will refer it to senior management. You should do this anyway if the problem with the particular learner arises again or if you cannot get parental support. Never be reluctant to ask for help.

Talking to the press

- Do not talk to the press or media in any form. Usually the school will have a designated person who deals with press releases and media relations. You might be the only witness to an accident involving school learners and whatever you say publicly at that moment can have an immense influence on your career and consequences for your school. Should you be approached by the press, refer them to any member of the SMT. Remember: as a novice teacher you are a 'soft target'.
- Do not make public statements about your school. Any statements about your school, its learners, their parents, the future of education – literally anything you say in public – can have serious repercussions. Do *not* quote any member of staff on any matter, regardless of whether he or she made a statement or not.

Communicating online

Even before we offer advice about your online social presence and communication, we need to warn you about keeping your electronic devices safe. It is your responsibility to ensure that your cell phone and other media devices are password-protected. Keep these devices securely locked away during school hours and do not leave them in your classroom overnight. If learners can access your devices, they could spread literally anything 'on your behalf'. It is extremely difficult to prove your innocence in cases like these. Also ensure that all your electronic devices are safeguarded with effective anti-virus software to protect against the spreading of viruses.

Many of the learners whom you will teach, even those in remote areas, are able to access and use technology with ease. Technological advances have been so rapid that we currently live not only in a global village but also in a borderless and generally faceless society. This new shape of society impacts on the traditional role of teachers, who may need to adapt their social interactions.

Social media refers to 'a set of platforms or tools that foster interaction, discussion and community, allowing users to share information and build relationships' (Cleary, 2014). There is very little control over the subject matter, what is said, who participates and where the communication is directed, making social media platforms very powerful (cf the Arab Spring of 2013 or #FeesMustFall protests of 2016). These platforms are also volatile, changing constantly while new ones emerge.

In the era in which we live, each of us has a digital footprint. You might think the fact that you do not have Facebook or Twitter accounts renders you 'invisible' to the rest of the digital world, but this is just not true. All applications, searches, maps, browser histories – literally anything you do online – is easy to find if someone really wants to learn your whereabouts. The digital world comes with numerous advantages but, as a novice teacher, you need to be responsible and knowledgeable in order to protect yourself from the dangers of the digital world. Did you know that search engines such as Google 'remember' and keep track of your online activity? That is why people receive specific advertisements, suggested pages and invitations.

Currently platforms such as Facebook, Instagram and Twitter are public domains. This means anyone can see and read what you post. Keeping the following guidelines in mind when you are active online may help you avoid embarrassment and, at worst, dismissal:

- Imagine yourself in a public place before you like, share, tweet or disclose any information online. Would you be comfortable laughing out loud at a specific joke in the presence of a head teacher? Would you share a racist, sexist or dehumanising joke with your 12-year-old learners? One could argue that they are not supposed to see it, but the reality is they do. Parents, colleagues and all other role-players can see what you do or say online – especially if they want to find out.
- Think carefully about the reason for creating or joining a particular network. What is the purpose of joining? Will you have time to maintain and update it? Will you be able to keep your social and professional life separate?
- Consider having two email or social media accounts: a personal, private one and the public, professional one you can use for communicating and sharing with parents and learners. Yes, you are an adult and have the right to express strong public opinions on a social platform, or share the fun activities you do, but it is best to plan your profile carefully.

- Consider what you wish to reveal. What do the photos say about you? And the avatar you choose? What are the items that you 'like'? Even the responses that your friends post create a personal image of who you are and with whom you associate. Nowadays many companies (and that would imply SGBs) check out your profile and often make decisions about your application even before paging through your CV.
- Only join closed groups and limit access to your account.
- Do not accept learners or colleagues as friends on social media platforms. Especially at the start of your career, you might feel flattered by suddenly receiving 220 Facebook invitations. However, again the most probable reason for this sudden interest is the novelty you bring to the school environment. It does not imply a trusting relationship or popularity. It certainly does not translate into being a successful teacher.
- Take care of how you formulate responses. Do not post something when you are highly emotional. Wait a while to cool off, re-read and only then press the 'send' button. Once it's out there it cannot be retracted.
- Never speak ill or make fun of people or share deep personal secrets or fantasies on such media.
- Never respond with negative comments or use capital letters.
- Never forward any e-communication indiscriminately. You have no control over where it goes and even a junior IT technician would be able to trace it back to your domain.
- Do not try to be part of every conversation. You may lurk without having to comment on everyone else's piece.
- Do not send or read emails or text messages during class, even if you are only keeping an eye on the class.
- Avoid having your photo taken in compromising poses and with dubious company. Very little remains private today and one Facebook post of a photo or comment may haunt you forever in your career. It has not disappeared simply because you deleted it.
- Think carefully about dating sites. Although it is no crime to join a dating website, keep in mind that older learners (or younger ones posing as old enough) also have access to these sites. How would you react if you were asked for a date by a learner or a parent?
- Pornographic websites? NO. Just NO. Protect yourself by blocking these websites from all your electronic devices as well as your personal Wi-Fi settings at home. There are ways in which you can be added to these sites without your knowledge or consent. It may also have legal implications for you as a teacher.

Using social media or e-communication is often fraught with pitfalls, but these channels can be used effectively and to your advantage. For example, some learners may confide in you via this medium and you may be able to provide support and encouragement without the learner being embarrassed in your presence. Documenting discussions or agreements you make with a learner, colleague or parent may protect you at a later stage when you need to provide hard-copy evidence. Use the new technologies with caution, and responsibly.

Section C
You and your learners

We now turn our attention to some important aspects related to your learners. You may have your lesson plans ready and your learning and teaching support material prepared ... but without the learners you have no one to teach! They are, after all, the real reason you are employed as a teacher. Your relationship with the learners and how much you know about them is important to your success as a teacher. We look at how important it is that your learners are 'ready' for learning and how you can facilitate and focus their readiness. We also provide some ideas for identifying and working with different personalities and temperaments in your classroom. We have also included a simple, fun way of identifying the learning preferences your learners may have. *Remember: this is just a guide and you should not label learners in any way.* Since there are differences in learning styles and preferences, we also look at dealing with diversity more generally in your classroom. We felt the need to add advice on dealing with difficult or aggressive learners because these learners can derail your lessons and negatively influence others' learning. Remember that you should ask for help from your HoD when dealing with extreme cases and always work within the policies of your school.

If you think you are too small to make a difference, you haven't spent the night with a mosquito.
African proverb

12

Equipping learners with 21st-century skills

Rinelle Evans

Regardless of where you start teaching, the learners in your class will be growing up in a world that is fast-paced and changing rapidly as globalisation, economic opportunities, digital communication and technology advance. By the time they leave school, they will face new and different challenges to the ones you may have. They need to be prepared with skills to do so.

In order for a learner to set him- or herself apart from others when vying for a place at university and later in the job market, it will no longer be sufficient just to be literate, numerate and know a few general facts about five or six subjects taken for Grade 12. Even knowing how to operate a computer is not enough. School leavers will need content knowledge, various literacies and proficiencies that prepare them to meet the challenges and opportunities of today's world and enable them to participate fully as adults in society. These skills also need to be transferable to many different situations and roles, as the job market is not stable, and in order to earn a living one may need to change jobs several times in an adult life. Some learners may be fortunate enough to find jobs outside the borders of South Africa. Having many workplace skills increases employment mobility.

Employers worldwide seek employees who have more than just a qualification they may have gained after leaving school. In order for learners to successfully participate in the global economy, we need to teach what are commonly called the 21st-century skills. Some sources even call them survival skills (Wagner, 2008). Some countries consider these skills so important that they have designed pedagogical frameworks within which the skills are taught at school. The success of their economies will be driven by the next generation of young adults, who must be well equipped to deal with the constantly evolving demands of economic markets.

The following skills are not developed in isolation but easily interact with one another, as you will see from our descriptions of each skill. We have added some that we believe are essential for South African learners to master.

It goes without saying that you as the teacher also need to be developing these skills in order to teach them!

Core knowledge

This is the assumed basic knowledge in various fields that any matriculant ought to have acquired after 12 years at school. Furthermore, a school leaver would be expected to be able to reason logically and rationally, read with comprehension, communicate well orally and in writing in at least one language and know how to access valid information.

Collaboration

One of the reasons why the school curriculum includes group work is to develop the skills required to work as part of a team later in life. Teaching learners the processes and practices involved in effectively working as a group is a start to developing turn-taking, active listening, brainstorming, reaching consensus about shared ideas, taking responsibility for sections of a task, learning to accept constructive criticism, showing leadership, being empathetic towards others and in general being able to manage and organise.

Creativity

This skill relates very closely to problem solving or innovation. Being able to look at something and think differently about it often leads to the required solution or an imaginative new creation. This thinking skill is often called 'thinking outside the box'. It involves looking at a situation and asking: How can this be modified? Minimised? Maximised? What can be substituted? What can be added?

Communication

Commonly thought of as a 'soft skill', being able to communicate well – especially face to face – has become very important in a digital world. Someone who can express him- or herself well and with confidence when speaking or writing is looked up to and considered a leader. Competence in English is much desired and if you are able to express yourself in several languages, you certainly have an edge.

Apart from being able to present ideas well, a school leaver ought to be media literate too. This means understanding the various media sources such as radio, social media, press or television. You should teach learners how to access information via these means and also to interpret the information in order to make knowledgeable judgements about its validity, source and creators.

Learners will not only be consumers of information but will also need to be skilful producers of information.

Cultural awareness

Especially in a diverse country such as South Africa, learners firstly need to understand and know their own history, culture and heritage in order to place into context the history, culture and heritage of the various people with whom they will interact later in life. Being cross-culturally aware implies an ability to recognise, interpret and appropriately react to people or situations in order to avoid misunderstanding or offence.

Citizenship

A citizen is generally defined as someone who has official rights and can claim protection from the government of the country in which he or she lives. These may be birth rights or based on the length of time someone has lived in the country. Being a good citizen implies civic literacy and social responsibility. It is far more than not littering or obeying the rules of the road. It is linked to living morally and acting ethically in all respects. It entails responsibility and respect towards your community and environment, as well as having integrity.

Critical thinking

This thinking skill is related to several of the other skills already discussed, such as problem solving, accessing and analysing information or creating something new. It also has to do with making well-reasoned, appropriate decisions in a particular situation. One should not just accept at face value all information or arguments that are put before one. Ask for evidence that supports others' claims. Challenge with questions such as 'How do you know that? Who said that? What is the alternative?'

Computing

Currently, information and communications technologies (ICTs) include devices such as computers, laptops, tablets, digital cameras, scanners, cell phones, electronic games, audio devices, global positioning systems, electronic whiteboards and the internet, while even more will be added to this list as our world develops technologically. Being literate in ICT means being able to use these devices correctly in order to use and create textual, numerical, visual and aural information safely, responsibly and ethically. Creative and critical thinking skills are key to becoming ICT literate.

Career and learning self-reliance

You may recognise the characteristics of this skill as those of being a lifelong learner. Employers will expect the people they appoint to be self-directed, productive, independent and accountable employees. In order to become this, learners will need to understand the importance of finding solutions themselves, learning more about things on their own, being able to adapt to a new responsibility even if one has not been trained for it and, above all, displaying enthusiasm for learning. Not all learning leads to a formal qualification and you will need to teach learners how to find the answers from a variety of sources.

Cash competence

Not all learners will be able to gain a post-matric qualification allowing them some form of job stability in terms of income. Furthermore, the instability of our country's economic climate does not guarantee a job for life. We thus believe all school leavers should be equipped with the basic skills for earning an income by knowing how to be a successful entrepreneur. Cash competence also implies managing your income successfully, which includes knowing how to manage the money you earn, buying the best deals, shopping around for bargains and so on. Pointing out the snares of materialism may also help school leavers prioritise and rethink their values. See the section on earning, saving and spending (Chapter 37 in Section E) for the issues you should be teaching learners about.

Curiosity

This means having a strong desire to learn or know something. Curiosity carries a positive connotation and differs from being inquisitive, which means wanting to know more about other people's business when it's none of yours! When you are curious, you wish to learn more about something or better understand why certain things work the way they do. Curious people love gaining knowledge and often actively seek out challenges and new experiences to broaden their horizons. Curious people are able to make connections and see relationships between pieces of information. This skill is also linked to others we have already explained. Imagination is generally stimulated by being curious, and this leads to deep learning.

Caring

In this very fast-paced and – for many – harsh world we live in, showing concern for or kindness to others is often neglected. This skill is applicable to the environment, living creatures and intangibles such as one's heritage, but is mostly person-centred and cuts across culture, age and gender. Having empathy for others, trying to 'walk in their shoes' and being less self-centred are traits of a mature citizen that we should teach our learners. Showing them how to help in the community in small ways develops social responsibility and leadership skills.

Knowing facts is still significant, but not sufficient. In each of the lessons you teach, you should try to include more than just your subject's content knowledge. It should be clear from our discussion that school leavers (and you!) should be developing skills that go beyond the curriculum currently required to pass Grade 12. As a novice teacher you ought to assist in developing a well-balanced, involved citizen who is able to progress well in the job market.

13

Identifying your learners' temperaments

Philip Mirkin, Alta Engelbrecht and Chantelle de Wet

In your career you will work with a range of people. Each culture, gender and age group requires us to modify our approach in order to interact with them in appropriate and helpful ways. In this section we help you to recognise and manage different learner behaviours appropriately. In many classroom situations, you rely mostly on your intuition to guide your actions and decisions. Knowing a bit about basic temperament types, as already explained in Section B, may help you be more tolerant of the behaviour and responses of your learners. Please note that these temperament types are contested and not accepted by all educators, and they should not be used as definitive boxes into which we put our learners. They are, nevertheless, a simple means of identifying some personality traits and also understanding the behaviour of learners in our care.

As humans we tend to categorise the world around us so that we can control and understand our contexts better. Because we so easily categorise and label each other, we also tend to think that behaviour or thinking that differs from ours is disrespectful or even abnormal. One way of categorising human nature is by our basic temperament of choleric, sanguine, phlegmatic and melancholic.

You will have a preference for working with one or another temperament, but no one temperament is any better or more useful than any other. They are all natural and healthy in their own way and together they make for a balanced human being. It is our task as adults to become balanced in all four and to encourage children to develop the mature characteristics of their natural temperaments. Although we may display several characteristics related to two or more temperament types, we generally have one or two that are dominant. Once you can identify a learner's dominant temperaments it will help you to manage him or her, and your expectations of him or her, with greater ease. Each learner is an individual who will need to be addressed as such, but his or her basic nature will fit within these groupings.

Basic nature: Introvert/extrovert

Extrovert learners are the ones you will generally notice first. They are loud, volunteer to help, constantly get up out of their seats, tell others what to do, or clamour to answer questions and tell stories. They tend to live in the moment and react or respond rapidly to things that happen around them. They may seem overconfident or even cheeky, but all this outward activity is just the extrovert showing that he or she continually needs interaction with the outer world to feel okay.

Introvert learners are generally quiet and tend to withdraw into themselves to feel okay. They do not need the outer world to give them confirmation of their worth. You may take a while to notice the introverts in your class, as they often hide in the corners or even up front. You may also need to draw them into class discussions by asking them questions, but be careful that you don't expose them to the careless comments of the extroverts. Introverts internalise feelings, and can be deeply hurt if they are forced to expose themselves. These learners take a while to trust the outer world and may experience extroverts to be childish, careless and superficial. Introverts tend to mature more quickly than extroverts, simply because they do more processing of their experiences.

Managing introverts and extroverts

All learners, especially young ones, are by nature immature, which means they are focused on themselves; everything is about them. Your task is to help them gradually shift their awareness to others. In the immature state the extrovert can be very domineering and selfish. The immature introvert, on the other hand, takes everything personally and thinks that life is unfair. By being brought to an awareness of the needs of others they will both modify their temperament and be useful members of the class community.

All learners need to feel valued. You can use extroverts to do various tasks, such as handing out books or helping out in other ways. The introverts feel their value by caring for others in more personal or nurturing ways, such as making a card for someone who is sick and asking the rest of the class to sign it. You could also help them to be responsible for watering the plants or keeping the classroom clean and tidy.

Because extroverts attract a lot of attention to themselves, you can position the loudest of them in the front middle section of the class. When they make a joke or attract the class's attention to themselves, it is easier for you to shift the attention back onto the content at hand. Be aware that some introverts hate to be moved or disturbed in any way. If you have introverted learners seated in the front you may first need to negotiate with them about where they would like to sit, should you need to bring others to the front. If you get their agreement first, they will feel acknowledged and be willing to help. Introverts will often be good leaders in ideas and activities in class and can be a great asset in organising events and materials.

Refer to Chapter 8, 'Determining your personality traits', in Section B, which outlines the characteristics of the four main personality types: sanguine, choleric, melancholic and phlegmatic.

Extroverts are generally sanguine or choleric learners. Extroverts are quickly stimulated by new things and can create an interest for other children with their enthusiasm. Their greatest gift is the ability to make things seem interesting when they are involved.

Sanguines are light and bubbly children, but are easily distracted, or cause distractions of their own. If they are not well managed, **choleric** children can be very domineering and destructive. They generally have strong opinions and are not slow in putting them into action. If they are able to use these gifts to the benefit of the class, they will learn to value their temperament and know how to use it to help others.

Melancholics and phlegmatics are generally classed as introverts. The **melancholic** learners are often delicate children and can be very deep thinkers who take their time before making decisions. When still in the immature phase they can be oversensitive and take things personally. A good way to bring them out of themselves is to make them aware of others whose suffering is worse than their own. Once comfortable, they are very organised and pay great attention to detail. They can become the person you can go to if you want to know if anyone in the class needs help. They can also help others in one-to-one situations.

Sleepy **phlegmatics** – the slow and steady learners – seem to eat and sleep through much of life until they have a task to do. Then, if they say they are going to do something, you can leave them to get on with it, confident that the task will be done well. They are your most stable and reliable learners, but may need a firm push to get started. They are very dependable and are not often absent from school. You can use the sanguine learners to excite and awaken them by seating them next to each other; the phlegmatics will, in turn, help to calm the sanguine children.

Drawing on the bird metaphors used on pages 38–45 of Section B, learners too can be classed as peacocks, eagles, owls and swans. Their behavioural patterns may not yet be as fixed as those of adults, but their emerging temperaments can be spotted by teachers who make an effort to know their fledglings.

13 – Identifying your learners' temperaments

You will soon realise that you do not respond to all learners in the same way and that showing respect for different temperament styles will gain you the trust of the learners. The characteristics shown in Table 13.1 may help you recognise a learner's temperament.

Table 13.1   The four basic temperaments and how teachers should respond to them

Peacock child (sanguine)	Eagle child (choleric)
■ Sociable ■ Talkative ■ Lively ■ Emotional (up and down) ■ Enthusiastic ■ Can't focus on one thing for a long time – gets bored quickly ■ Interrupts people while talking ■ Dress code – fashion ■ 'What friends have, I want too' **Teacher** ■ Celebrate their input. Use their humour and love of play to enliven your class. ■ Use stories to capture their attention. ■ Gain their co-operation through directing their imagination and attention. ■ Provide them with social responsibilities. **Teach/practise** ■ Teach them perseverance, to finish a task, by making a game of it. ■ By welcoming their input, you diminish the possibility of them creating negative group pressure. ■ Help them to manage their emotions with relevant stories and guidance. ■ Help them to be calm and to think before they act or speak.	■ Competitor ■ Organises friends and home ■ 'Today we're starting to practise' ■ Assertive ■ Physical aggression (boys) ■ Domineering ■ Always wants to be the leader; 'My word is law' **Teacher** ■ Teach the learners elements of teamwork and how to negotiate agreement. ■ Show them that winning is not always everything. **Teach/practise** ■ Teach them to be patient – it's fine to make mistakes; we learn from mistakes. ■ Teach them to say: 'I'm wrong' and 'I'm sorry' by showing them the 'big picture' and broadening their understanding of the situation. ■ Teach them to recognise other people's emotions and show empathy by guiding their attention to the melancholics. ■ They should not get their own way if it's not in the best interests of the class.

Owl child (melancholic)	Swan child (phlegmatic)
- Very sensitive - Talented, but humble - Can take a long time to make decisions - Deep and strong feelings - Often an only child (this can be bad for them) - Questions everything – analytical - May easily lose trust in others - Be careful that child doesn't 'disappear' **Teacher** - Don't shout and surprise them unexpectedly. - Ask them questions in class; ask for their ideas; make sure you listen to the feelings behind their answers. - Value and acknowledge them and their input in class. - Be cognisant of possible pestering by cholerics or sanguines. - Use examples of the suffering of others to draw them into discussions. - Care, and often tell the learner that you care. **Teach/practise** - Talk about emotions. - Teach them to not always take things personally. - It's fine to be alone; they don't always need to be part of a social group. - Give a lot of love and appreciation.	- Calm - Afraid of scolding or punishment - Reacts well to positive awards - Even-tempered; not often up/down - Giver/pleaser - Willing to help – even at their own expense - May lose on purpose to make others feel better **Teacher** - Consistently show appreciation for little things that the learner does. - Often convey to the learner that you care about him or her. **Teach/practise** - Teach them assertiveness by giving them small repetitive responsibilities, such as emptying the rubbish bin. - They should learn to display their feelings.

The temperaments are only one way of looking at the human personality. In considering an African perspective of personality, we note that the development of one's personality within the African culture is holistic in nature, and strongly influenced by culture. As Ramokgopa (2001: 109) states, 'it is geared towards the fostering and enhancing of altruism, which in turn, prepares individuals to collectively face the challenges of life'. The learners in your class will have differing combinations of temperaments. If a learner is repeatedly showing a negative attitude in class, it may be due to a clash with a neighbour. Putting the learner next to a learner with a complementary temperament may encourage him or her to present a more positive attitude.

Another important consideration is that we change as life goes on. Younger learners have not yet developed a *set* personality. As a teacher you need to consider different personalities and prepare for a diversity of learning styles, responses and interactions in your classroom. You will also need to be constantly aware that your own personality differs from many of the learners' and that you need to make allowance for this, at times even working to change it.

14

Identifying your learners' learning styles

Annelize du Plessis

When we step into our classroom, we meet between 30 and 40 learners with diverse learning needs, and every learner learns differently. How will we be able to help them achieve academic success? The answer lies in that besides being knowledgeable about the content of the curriculum, it is essential that teachers have a basic understanding of how learners receive and process information during learning. One way of accomplishing academic success is through simultaneous multisensory instruction (SMI).

SMI challenges both teachers and the learners in our classes. It allows teaching and learning activities to be not only creative and active, but also most enjoyable. It engages all the learners with their diverse learning needs in the learning process, keeping their attention and boosting achievement and self-confidence (An & Carr, 2017).

Let us look at how SMI can be successfully and creatively utilised when we prepare lesson activities.

Transformed teaching is possible if one facilitates and assesses in a multisensory way. This means that we use as many senses (sight, hearing, touch, movement, taste, smell) as possible to process information. This is also referred to as SMI (Eloff & Swart, 2018) or the VAKT (visual, auditory, kinaesthetic and touch) learning styles profile. Smell and taste as senses are included but used infrequently in the learning process. We do, however, acknowledge their importance in the learning process. Once again we emphasise that the teacher will have to be very creative and innovative in the way he or she presents and facilitates content and assessment tasks. SMI is fun and the learners enjoy the creative activities. In order for us to utilise SMI, we first need to find out *how* our learners receive and process information. This is the first step in the process of successful learning.

The following is a description of an activity that you can do with your learners to explore the way they receive and process information. This exercise is not costly and will take roughly five minutes of class time.

14 – Identifying your learners' learning styles

It makes use of the infinity sign, ∞, which learners draw on a blank piece of paper (De Jager, 2009).

> **Did you know?**
> Among other things, the infinity sign symbolises eternity and empowerment. Infinity derives from the Latin word '*infinitas*', meaning 'unboundedness' or a number with no end. The latter was discovered by John Wallis in 1655 and it symbolises an infinite sum in mathematics.

Follow these steps in order to carry out the exercise:
1. Show the learners what the infinity sign looks like.
2. Hand out a blank A5 sheet of paper to each learner and ask him or her to place the paper in a landscape orientation. Then ask the learners to write their names at the top of their pages.
3. Get the learners to draw an infinity sign in one single action. The infinity sign should lie on its side like the numeral 8 that has fallen over, as shown in the example. The infinity sign can be any size, as long as it is drawn in a single action and the lines all meet (i.e. there are no gaps or crossed lines in the sign).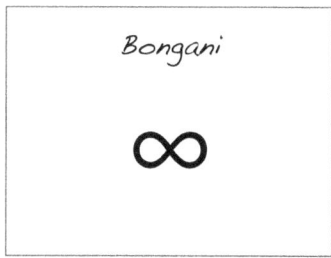
4. Ask the learners to use a ruler to draw a horizontal line through the infinity sign where the lines cross right in the middle.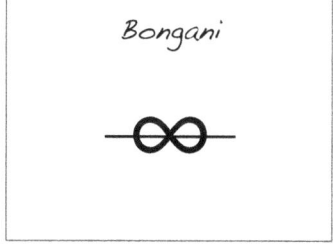
5. Now let each learner determine which section of his or her symbol is the largest.

If the section of the infinity sign **above the line** is the largest, it indicates a preference for taking in information visually.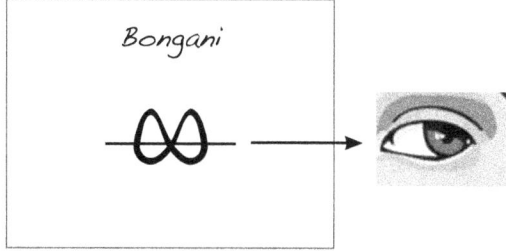

Learners who are predominantly visual prefer to observe rather than having the work explained to them verbally. These learners will remember what they see and recall information by looking upwards. In most cases they have vivid imaginations and may have photographic memories. Visual learners should preferably be seated in the front of the classroom so that they can see everything. If learners are predominantly visual, try including some of the visual modes shown in Table 14.1.

Table 14.1 Examples of visual modes to be incorporated in the lesson for visual learners

pictures	flow charts
colour	making notes, handouts
PowerPoint presentations	highlighting work
posters	YouTube videos, films
models	flipcharts
diagrams	tables and graphs

If the sections of the infinity sign **to the sides** are the largest, it indicates a preference for information in an auditory form.

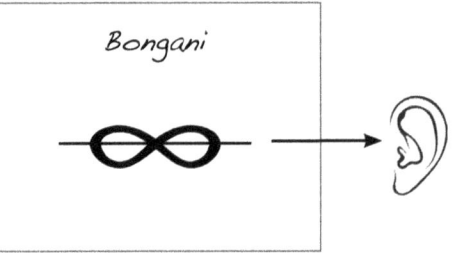

Auditory learners use their advanced listening skills to receive and retain information. They prefer content to be explained orally. Whilst studying, they tend to talk to themselves and repeat learning content out loud. Auditory learners enjoy talking in the classroom, discussing relevant topics (especially in groups), and prefer verbal instructions to written instructions. They move their eyes back and forth before recalling information. They should preferably sit in the middle of the classroom and it is not necessary for them to maintain eye contact with the speaker at all times.

If your learners are predominantly auditory, then you may include some of the auditory modes shown in Table 14.2 in your lesson plan.

14 – Identifying your learners' learning styles

Table 14.2   Examples of auditory modes to be incorporated in the lesson for auditory learners

oral presentations and discussions	debating
stories	radio
music	discussions
rhymes	note-taking

If the section of the infinity sign **below the line** is the largest, it indicates a preference for kinaesthetic, practical and experience-based learning situations.

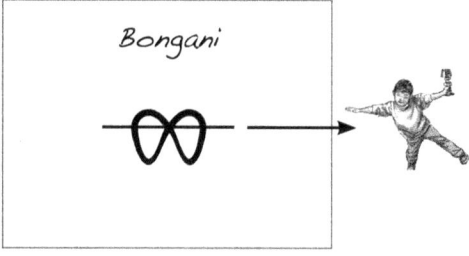

Kinaesthetic learners learn best through hands-on activities. This assists them to retain information because they are actively involved. They enjoy a tactile component as part of the learning process, which means that they love to touch things like clay or media.

You will easily recognise a kinaesthetic learner when such a learner rides on his or her chair, or is constantly busy fidgeting with an object. Of course, these learners love music and dancing, role-play and moving around during class time. These learners recall information by looking down and they should preferably be seated at the back of the classroom where they can cause minimal disruptions. If your learners are predominantly kinaesthetic, then you may include some of the kinaesthetic modes shown in Table 14.3 in our lesson plan.

Table 14.3   Examples of kinaesthetic modes to be incorporated in the lesson for kinaesthetic learners

movement	contact
group work	touch
demonstrations	building things
active learning	drawing
dancing	role-play
rapping	

Finally, collect all the infinity signs from the learners and plot the different learning styles in each of your classes. This will help you plan your lessons accordingly and purposefully introduce ways of accommodating each learner's learning style.

The example class list in Table 14.4 indicates that we need to plan mostly for activities that accommodate learners with a visual preference (YouTube videos, PowerPoint presentations, pictures) and for learners with kinaesthetic/movement preferences (role-play, group discussions, building models).

Table 14.4 Example extract from class list: Summary of learning styles

Name of learner	Visual	Auditory	Kinaesthetic/tactile
Bongani	✓		
Lerato			✓
Peter			✓
Catherine	✓		
Katlego	✓		
Lindulile			✓
Jackson			✓
Reagon	✓		
Kensane		✓	
TOTAL	4	1	4

As a novice teacher, you should now be able to discover how your learners, each with their diverse learning needs, receive and process information. We also suggest creative and innovative tasks that you could use to enhance the process of learning. By utilising SMI, we deliberately involve each learner. Lastly, if our learners cannot learn the way we teach, we have to teach the way they learn.

S M I [l e] ... is my learners' learning style

15

Readying the learner for learning

Philip Mirkin

As a novice teacher you may be under the impression that your job is to get your learners to learn what you want to teach them. This is a misconception. Your job is to get or keep them learning-ready. Until they are learning-ready, their learning will be slow and frustrating – for them and for you. Getting them learning-ready is what this section is about. Let's see what learning-readiness looks like.

Learning-ready learners

- **Have what they need in the right place at the right time**

Learners who are immersed in their task have everything that they need. They are not thinking about anything except what they are involved in and the others who are with them. The boundaries between themselves, others and the task they are involved in disappear and learning and productivity are at a peak. Even difficult and demanding tasks become easy and quick to the minds of children in such a state. You will know that this is true when discipline problems disappear, and when the bell for the end of the lesson rings, they let out a cry of disappointment.

- **Are present, open and positive**

Learners demonstrate the joy of the moment in action. Children are naturally able to enter this state of openness and positivity given the right environment. Negativity in any form may separate the child from the learning process. Even the act of being objective, of thinking or reflecting rationally about the situation can create a break in the learning-readiness of younger children.

- **Are not easily distracted**

When learners are ready to learn they choose where their focus will be directed. It is not easy for them to be distracted. On the contrary, their focus and intention to learn becomes contagious and can help to draw other children's attention into the learning process. This is true for all learners, but if you can engage the sanguine and choleric learners, they can help to draw the introverts into the work too.

- **Maintain focus for long periods of time**

Time seems to be of no consequence when children are in the middle of their learning process and totally focused on the activity at hand. It is often disappointing for children when their challenge comes to an end and they feel that they must leave this focused state. This state is sometimes referred to as 'flow' or the 'zone'.

- **Ask questions**

Social and cultural status and authority barriers disappear when all members are engrossed in the learning process. They will ask questions of each other and work respectfully with others who are 'inside' the learning zone as equals. Even the teacher is simply another source of potential help.

- **Do individual research within their interests**

Learners will carry their learning-readiness into other domains outside of the classroom. This is characterised by a pursuit of their interests outside the classroom through reading and discussions in their free time.

- **Do not need teacher supervision**

The sense of engagement and their valuing of what they are doing is enough to keep learners focused and on track. The role of the teacher becomes one of facilitator and support, and not supervisor or authority. Learners will ask for clarification when needed and may lose their state of learning-readiness if they experience a conflict of priorities or if they lose trust.

- **Check for appropriateness and direction**

Once your learners are mostly learning-ready, you can simply direct their attention to the tasks and activities that will take them to success in the subject you teach. Be aware, however, that redirecting their attention can cause a shift from the learning-ready state and you may need to get them actively occupied in the new work again.

- **Are proactive**

The proactive child is your greatest ally in the class. He or she is ready to be given a task and can be trusted to work out the best way to accomplish it. These learners are also a great help in assisting with learners who are struggling with work or in getting the class ready for a change in activity.

When a learner is not learning-ready, learning is slow, hard and someone else's fault. Learners who are not yet learning-ready:

- **Have no direction**

They are easily distracted and cause distractions. These children are open to influences around them, but because they do not have a direction or focus of their own, they will usually look for the fun and distracting elements in the environment. The 'TV child' is always waiting for something to catch his or her attention in a way that requires no inner participation or effort. This passivity is one of the greatest barriers to learning-readiness. Moving such children into a learning-ready state is often a daily task for the teacher. Giving these learners things to do and getting them active is usually an effective strategy.

- **Do not know what they need**

Passivity and hyperactivity breed a lack of self-awareness. Learners' lack of inner activity also makes them reliant on outer stimulation, but they will be unwilling to respond to anything that requires effort. Having enough children in the class who are learning-ready will provide the best role-models for such disengaged children. Once they become engaged themselves, they can begin to appreciate the feelings of accomplishment associated with completing something that is meaningful, and that adds value to others as well as themselves.

Passive children may 'wait to be interested' before being moved into action. This often does not happen because they have trained themselves to rely on a strong external stimulus to push them into action. A high-sugar diet can be just as responsible for making children become hyperactive or passive as TV watching or other inwardly passive activities.

- **Have damaged engagement**

The natural interest of a child can be easily lost through simple matters such as being tired, stressed, hungry, depressed, having too much exposure to electronic media and so on. These are often factors that come from a learner's home life and are out of the teacher's control. Up to a certain age the child will not be able to make the needed changes without his or her parents' support. However, by engaging the learner's goodwill, you will be able to determine the source of the problem and be a partner with the child in addressing his or her challenges. By giving the learner repeated experiences of being in a state of learning-readiness he or she will naturally gravitate towards it. Hopefully, in time these learners will find the reasons and strength to address and overcome their challenges.

Drugs, abuse and similar problems are usually too big for a child to address without professional intervention. If such intervention is not available or wanted, such children may never become learning-ready, and inevitably develop secondary symptoms such as a lack of self-esteem or self-belief. Very often such children lack meaningful adult relationships. You should report such cases to senior and/or support staff. Do not engage too deeply with such troubled learners while you are still learning the ropes of your new profession and school. Such learners are often masters at manipulating situations, having had to navigate many difficulties in their past, and you may find yourself in a situation that will compromise your position.

16

Managing aggressive behaviour

Sarina de Jager

Learners acting defiantly, blatantly ignoring instructions, verbally abusing teachers or their peers or even getting physically violent in the classroom are part of the day-to-day reality faced by teachers around the world, very often seen on video clips that go viral here in South Africa.

You may already feel anxious just thinking about having to deal with such a learner. Because aggressive learners tend to make the people around them feel anxious or frustrated, you as a teacher might find it difficult to feel sympathetic towards these individuals or to try to see their point of view. You will more likely feel like punishing them, ignoring them or not getting too involved in the issue. So how should you as a teacher act responsibly and effectively in challenging classroom situations, especially where learners' behaviour is disruptive or disrespectful? In this section, we discuss a few keys you can use to unlock the challenge.

> **Mindshift**
> Using labels such as 'difficult learner', 'aggressive learner' or 'the depressed girl in Grade 11' could allow us to think that these individuals *are* what their labels tell us about them. How do you think the labelled person would feel about him- or herself if he or she overheard you? Consider a gentler way of referring to learners by foregrounding the person rather than the problem, for example 'the learner who has difficulties' or 'the girl in Grade 11 who is experiencing depression'. When we talk differently about our learners, we help them and ourselves understand that one is not *defined* by the difficulties or challenges one experiences. In the words of Dr Seuss, 'There is no one alive that is Youer than You.'

Key 1: Thinking about how the learners think

To understand learners who are acting out in your classroom, we might ask the question, 'What are they thinking?' Siegel and Bryson (2012) talk about the *mental staircase*. Imagine that your brain is a school building, with an upstairs and a downstairs level. The downstairs level refers to the part of your brain responsible for basic functions such as breathing and blinking and strong emotions such as fear and anger. Whenever a learner in your classroom is acting out in an aggressive way, he or she is making use of the downstairs level of the brain. The upstairs brain is made up of the cerebral cortex and its various parts. Imagine climbing up the mental staircase of the brain and entering the upstairs library, full of books and maps, a space where good decisions can be made and you are encouraged to think about things. Where the downstairs brain is driven by emotions and reactions, the upstairs brain is in charge of higher-order and analytical thinking.

Both these parts of the building are very important. We need to feel and we need to think. However, when we get stuck in the downstairs part, feeling overwhelmed by emotions and reactions, we struggle to make good decisions or find solutions.

Key 2: Helping the learner get 'unstuck'

Once you understand that learners who are acting out have become stuck in the downstairs level of their mental state, you can show them how to climb to the upper level. There, in the upstairs brain, they can apply some strategies to manage their emotions.

Now, you may be asking, 'How do I get them to climb the stairs?' Let's look at the following case study.

> **Case study**
> Lerato is a Grade 10 learner. She is known around school as a bully and gets into regular fights on the playground during break time. During a Tuesday morning Life Orientation lesson, Mrs Chambati talks about bullying in the classroom. A group of girls start giggling and point to Lerato when Mrs Chambati mentions the characteristics of a bully. Lerato sees this and flies up from her chair, knocks her table over and starts swearing at the girls. Mrs Chambati engages with Lerato by asking, 'Lerato, I can see that you are angry and frustrated right now. Would you like to take a walk to the restrooms and come back, or would you like to sit down and rejoin the lesson?' Lerato decides to sit down and Mrs Chambati goes on with the lesson. At the end of the period she asks Lerato to come and see her during break to discuss the way she is feeling and what happened during class time.

The first step in guiding a learner to move from the emotional level to the thinking level of the mental staircase is that we have to *acknowledge* what he or she is *feeling*. Lerato might have expected her teacher to firstly focus on her unacceptable behaviour and chase her out of the classroom. However, Mrs Chambati first acknowledged how Lerato was feeling at that moment. Lerato was probably very angry with the other girls, but she was allowed to decide about her next action because her feelings rather than her behaviour were noticed. The teacher had encouraged her to move from the lower level (emotions) and climb the staircase to decision-making (cognitive reason).

> **Mindshift**
> When we acknowledge the emotions of the learner who is acting out, we are not condoning his or her actions. Acknowledgement simply creates capacity for the learner to make better decisions.

Key 3: Giving the learner a choice

Once we have acknowledged the way a learner feels, we can guide him or her to climb to the upstairs brain where he or she can think about strategies, doing things differently, and understanding why his or her behaviour might not be acceptable. Mrs Chambati empowered Lerato by giving her a choice about her behaviour: leave the room to cool off or sit down and be part of the lesson again. The teacher could also have asked Lerato to help her with an activity in the classroom.

When learners are being difficult or aggressive, their initial reaction might come from a place of feeling trapped, helpless, misunderstood, frustrated or stuck. By giving them a choice about their actions, you are helping them move away from helplessness and feeling stuck to feeling empowered and in control of their circumstances.

Key 4: Doing it differently next time

Lerato's behaviour is unacceptable in a classroom context. However, Mrs Chambati understood that her distressed outburst meant Lerato would be too emotional and irrational to discuss her behaviour. Give the learner who is experiencing aggression time out to climb to the upstairs brain before trying to deal with the problem. Once a learner has had time to cool off, a calm conversation can help the learner think of ways to react and do things differently next time. Some questions and ideas to explore with the learner could include the following:
- In what way could you have acted differently today?
- Let's think of strategies that can help you stay calm next time you feel like

acting out, for example breathing exercises, mindfulness, walking away, talking to a teacher.
- How has what happened today helped you understand yourself better?
- What makes you angry/sad/happy/scared?
- What advice would you give to someone angered by another person who has made an unnecessary or offensive comment?

With these four keys in hand, you will hopefully gain more confidence in dealing with learners who are aggressive and difficult in the classroom. The key sentence to remember is: 'Engage, don't enrage.'

Steer clear of the following behaviours when dealing with aggression in the classroom:
- Do not get angry (never counter aggression with more aggression, or, in the words of Margaret J. Wheatley [2005: 19], 'aggression only moves in one direction – it creates more aggression').
- Do not try to engage in a rational conversation right away; speak to the learner later in private. You may also be upset and need to calm down and recollect yourself.
- Do not enforce a punishment or consequence immediately. This may just escalate the situation. You need to calm things down first.
- Avoid touching the learner who is acting out. A well-intended hand on the shoulder could be experienced as threatening and might worsen the situation.

Classroom interventions

Here are a few strategies to apply in the classroom context to encourage self-awareness and self-regulation and therefore avoid aggressive behaviour:
- Teach learners the three-seconds rule: When confronted with a difficult emotion, person or situation, count to three before reacting or engaging.
- Before starting your lesson, do a breathing exercise. Learners can stand or sit for this activity:
  - Ask learners to put both hands on their stomach. They should close their eyes, or look down at their hands.
  - Ask them to take three slow, deep breaths. Ask them to notice whether they can feel their hands being moved in and out.
  - You may like to count '1, 2, 3' for each breath drawn in and '1, 2, 3' for each breath exhaled.
  - Encourage learners to think about how the breathing feels, answering the following questions for themselves (silently):

- Can you feel your hands moving in and out?
- Can you feel the air moving in through your nose?
- Can you feel it moving out through your nose?
- Does the air feel a little colder on the way in and warmer on the way out?
- Can you hear your breath?
- What does it sound like?
- Guide learners through a body-scan exercise, facilitating awareness of how their bodies feel at that moment:
  - Ask learners to take a deep breath in and out.
  - Guide them to focus on how their bodies feel at that moment. Start at the head and move to the neck, shoulders, arms, chest, belly, back, legs, feet and toes.
  - Learners do not have to comment on what they are feeling. The point of the exercise is for them to become aware of how their bodies are feeling.
  - End with a deep breath in and out.
- When discussing the classroom policy at the beginning of the year, make the acceptable behaviour clear, explain the routines you expect and include how we deal with aggressive behaviour in the classroom. Get the learners' input and have an open discussion about it.
- Sometimes a group or a whole class can act aggressively. In such cases it could be helpful to engage with the 'ringleaders' – those who initiate the behaviour and from whom the rest of the group take their cue. Building a trusting relationship with these individuals and expressing genuine concern about their behaviour could go a long way in changing the tide for the whole group.

> **Mindshift**
> What do I encourage if I yell at learners or act aggressively towards them? What atmosphere do I create? Do I need to be more self-aware? How can I manage my own aggression, anger or emotional triggers?

Remember that you are the agent for change in your classroom. You can create a classroom atmosphere that is tolerant of expression and openness. Each child is dealing with his or her own circumstances and feelings. By acting in the correct way towards difficult behaviour, you can add calm to their chaos.

17

Working with linguistic diversity

Rinelle Evans

South Africa has always been an exceptionally diverse country, both geographically and ethnographically. Our rich cultural diversity is manifest not only in colourful dress, interesting foods, songs and dance, or religious practices, but also most audibly in the variety of languages heard on every street corner.

The insistence on English as a language of teaching and learning by some parent communities has created many academic difficulties, not only for learners whose strongest language is not English, but also for the teachers who very often are also not proficient enough in English to use it as a medium of instruction.

Few learners would have had a solid grounding in their primary language when they enter school; most would not have ever been exposed to, let alone mastered, English. Teachers are thus faced with a group of varying proficiency levels and some learners who understand nothing of what the teacher is saying. The teacher then needs to spend a great deal of time helping individual learners catch up. Please note: these learners are lagging behind because they do not understand *English*, not because they are not clever enough to cope. Teachers sometimes put foreign language speakers at the back of a classroom and work with those who seem to understand better. This only increases the children's sense of isolation and difference, especially in the large classes our country allows. Unfortunately they often encounter serious academic hurdles that may hinder them throughout their schooling. This situation is bad for the teacher as well, especially when she has no knowledge of the learners' language(s) and cannot communicate more effectively. It may be helpful (although not always practical) to ask a parent or older sibling to sit in on the lesson and act as interpreter until the learner has gained more English. It definitely requires more of the teacher to also prepare vocabulary lists, graded worksheets and find various strategies to ensure that the learners with limited English are not lost completely. This same situation may occur in any class where a learner is not familiar with the language used for teaching.

In high school, what is misleading, however, is that some learners sound fluent when they speak English and do not struggle to express themselves. We say they have acquired BICS – basic interpersonal communicative skills. They appear to understand everything the teacher says because listening and reading (receptive skills) are the easiest to develop. However, when required to use the written form to express themselves, it is evident that their vocabulary is limited and their sense of grammatical structure is seriously lacking. Extended written passages are generally poorly structured and incoherent. It is thus wrong to assume that being fluent in spoken English means a learner can function optimally in an academic environment.

A young learner requires a level of mastery in the language of instruction that will enable him or her to engage in sophisticated language functions and to deal with language in abstract, context-reduced forms. We call this CALP – cognitive academic language proficiency. This is a specific form of academic language essential for learners to succeed academically.

Another big challenge a teacher faces is her own lack of fluency in the medium of instruction. Not being able to praise or reprimand a child appropriately, not being able to follow up on questions or barking single-sentence instructions because one is not fluent in what we call classroom English adds a great deal of stress to a teacher's day, to say nothing of compromising the learning opportunity.

Here are some practical suggestions for dealing with language and ethnic diversity in your classroom, especially where the language of instruction is English:

- Reflect deeply on how you could harness all the linguistic potential to make each lesson meaningful and exploit the rich variety of language available in your classroom.
- Spend your first lesson getting to know your learners. Have them draw up their own language profile. Ask them to bring examples of text (adverts, books, poems) in their own languages to class and to share them. Encourage them to take pride in their languages. Show a genuine interest in their lives outside the classroom and use what you learn about them as individuals to link their world to the learning opportunities you prepare.
- Ensure that your own proficiency in the language of instruction is close to native tongue competency, but beware of using language that is too sophisticated in an attempt to suggest authority/superiority.
- Use and allow code-switching when necessary as a teaching tool, but avoid letting the learners become dependent on it. This means that you should not insist on your learners using English all the time. Often concepts are better

explained by peers in the first language than even a simplified explanation in the language of instruction. In view of the additive bilingualism approach officially advocated at present, consider allowing learners to use their own languages for group work and discussions. This will help the task to be completed more successfully. The oral/written report back will, however, be in English or whatever the language of instruction might be.
- Give clear, chunked instructions in simple language.
- Allow for 'think time', i.e. learners need time to think about their answer and then also to translate it into English.
- Avoid putting pressure on reluctant speakers. Try to ease their feelings of inadequacy about using English by speaking to them alone rather than addressing them in the group.
- Create an atmosphere conducive to experimentation where learners feel confident enough to try, even if they make mistakes. Tell them that failure is an acceptable part of the learning process.
- Acknowledge the reality of different languages in the same class and be on the lookout for any high stress levels related to racial interaction.
- Create opportunities for learners who are not proficient in the language of instruction to demonstrate what they do know, even in another language.
- Adopt a supportive attitude to learners and encourage learners to offer peer support.
- Tolerate grammatical or pronunciation mistakes that do not hinder comprehension. Initially, fluency is more essential than accuracy. Errors, whether spoken or written, that do not interfere with communication are not corrected. What is being communicated is more important than how it is said. Error tolerance should be high, since making mistakes is considered a natural outcome of skills development. Learners may have limited linguistic knowledge but be successful communicators; you could guide them gently with the view to achieving greater proficiency.
- Make learners aware of the appropriate socio-cultural language forms, for example polite forms of address, changes in inflection or other paralinguistic features when speaking to adults, taboo forms and so on.
- Since learners come from such diverse geographic and cultural backgrounds, it is possible that few share a standard accent when speaking the language. As the target language (probably English) is only a vehicle for communication, an accent that does not impede comprehension is acceptable. With regard to English as a first language in South Africa, we have traditionally accepted the British spelling and pronunciation as the norm. The other national languages would, no doubt, have their own point

of reference for what is acceptable expression, both in writing or speech. The language class is a vital means of teaching learners tolerance and respect for each other's ways of expression.

- Capitalise on your learners' knowledge of their own languages. Get them to explain concepts to classmates in their own language. Let them write words in their vernacular on the board, which the rest of the class could add to their 'word bank'. You could also introduce language awareness activities by comparing the features of different languages. Mother tongue support (rather than the effects of its interference/influence) is being increasingly endorsed.
- Demonstrate or find/draw pictures of concepts that your learners may possibly find foreign in their own context. Visual representations usually clarify such concepts easily. This includes writing down words on the board as you explain things. Remember your own English accent may be foreign to their ears!
- Teach general vocabulary as well as subject-specific jargon early and often.
- Compile a compendium of activities you could use in the classroom to promote respect for all languages while developing English. Consult relevant websites and books. Collect ideas from other teachers as well. Your repertoire will be useful as you try to meet the demands of a multicultural classroom.
- The classroom is a wonderful milieu for developing respect for diversity. Even if you teach a homogeneous group you should be sensitising your learners to the fact that we need to respect all languages and cultures and ought to get to know and understand them better. Respect for each learner's language enhances the status of that language and its associated culture and also reinforces the learner's self-worth.
- Learners should be encouraged to mix with speakers of other languages in order to gain respect for those languages and cultures and also to help them realise that their peers have proficiency in at least one language. The realisation of their deficiency in other languages may even spur them on to learning more about that language.
- Projects such as a 'Voices of our Land' day, where learners present items in their various languages, encourage respect and show learners that each language has a vital function and is important. Such projects also encourage acceptance of difference. Each item could be preceded or followed by a brief translated explanation.

- The fact that a learner's personal, intellectual and material growth is dependent on his or her proficiency in English cannot be denied. However, you must be very sensitive that you are not subtly transferring the notion that since English is so widely spoken in the world, it is superior to other languages. You need to take extreme care to explain that it has become the most common vehicle for international communication purely for historic and technological reasons and that it is the common denominator in our own multilingual situation for historic reasons, just as many former colonies still speak the language of that era, for example Portuguese in Mozambique, French in Algeria and the Democratic Republic of Congo and, to a lesser degree, German and Afrikaans in Namibia.
- Bear in mind that humour is very often culture-bound. Jokes, comic strips and even satire in text can be misunderstood or not comprehended at all. Be especially aware of this when selecting passages for comprehension.
- If you have no knowledge of the language most widely spoken in your area, consider taking a basic language course so that you may be able to introduce some of the vocabulary and grammatical aspects into your teaching of English. A teacher with a high degree of CALP in many languages would be invaluable in teaching a variety of subjects across the curriculum.
- Plan a class project that highlights each learner's mother tongue to celebrate International Mother Tongue Day on 23 February annually.
- It is useful to individualise tasks where possible and to use group and pair work. For such tasks, mix less proficient learners with stronger ones for most activities so that the former gain from the latter. Try to encourage the less able ones to contribute by giving them the opportunity to take responsibility for some task in the group. Try to establish which skill they are better at and design their task round that.
- Establish good rapport and a workable communication system with parents and caregivers, some of whom may be truly illiterate or not able to read and write in English. Value their input and consult with them about their children.

Many South Africans have welcomed the changes that have taken place in our country; others have found them unsettling. As a teacher you need to challenge your own biases and perceptions so that you can deliberately help learners function effectively in a complex, diverse society using as many languages as they know.

Section D
In the classroom

Since this section deals with a number of specific classroom matters, it is a long section. We have organised it in what may be a logical sequence for those of you starting out your teaching career. We look at the stresses and concerns around that very first day as a teacher. Irrespective of the day, we cannot emphasise enough the importance of being prepared for each and every lesson. Although you will eventually settle into a routine with your classes, we provide you with some guidance on starting out with a new class. Your university course may have prepared you well for lesson planning, but have they pointed out the importance of lesson preparation? We provide some tips for the smooth flow of a planned lesson by thinking about lesson preparation. You may have been advised that group work is important for learning (and it is), but we suggest that you first work with learners in pairs before tackling larger groups. We have provided you with some ideas around how to get pair work going in your lessons. We have then included some specific discussion around homework, managing marking, how to teach sensitive topics and how to teach Physical Education (PE) (which can be challenging if you have not been specifically trained for it). Many issues around discipline may arise from large, unmanageable classes, so we help out with some practical suggestions for managing large classes. We also provide a good example of a discipline system that you can adapt for your own classes, but remember: with any discipline system, consistency is the key. You may realise that a significant part of teaching is about establishing and maintaining good communication with your learners. We assist you by discussing questioning skills and general communication skills that you need as a teacher. We conclude this section by presenting two extremes: classrooms where you will be able to (and expected to) integrate technology into your teaching, and classrooms where you may need to make your own resources or even have to recycle items to make resources. Both are possible and rewarding!

If you are planning for a year, sow rice. If you are planning for a decade, plant trees. If you are planning for a lifetime, educate.
Chinese proverb

18

Creating a meaningful, safe and optimal learning environment

Hannelie du Preez

Learners spend most of their day at school within the four walls of a classroom. During this time they learn important subject matter and acquire valuable skills that they will need in their adult lives.

Later in this section, you will read more about the hidden curriculum: the unofficial, unwritten and unintended messages, values and perspectives you may be conveying without knowing that you are doing so. The classroom as a *communal learning space* also sends a particular message: the learners are not even aware of, but react to. When the atmosphere, ambience or classroom culture encourages and strengthens learning, the learning that takes place is consolidated. What you teach (subject matter) and how you teach (pedagogical approach) can be influenced by the physical environment. Your classroom can thus either reinforce and strengthen your expertise or it can contradict or enfeeble what you hope to achieve. In summary, your knowledge, pedagogy, professional conduct and identity should be in accordance and intentionally aligned with the look and feel of your classroom. Let's explore this communal space, which ought to be conducive to teaching and learning.

The classroom whispers

Have you ever noticed that when you enter a room it somehow 'speaks' to you? As soon as you enter the door, the room tells you how to behave without anyone being present inside it. This notion also applies to classrooms. As the learners step into your classroom, their perceptions of your classroom set the tone for the learning experience. They will react to this environment cognitively, socially, emotionally and even physically.

Every classroom sends a different message. This message is determined by your unique personality, your decorating preferences, the subject and age group you teach, as well as your pedagogical approach and teaching philosophy.

Practical Guidelines for Novice Teachers

> Hey you, happy to see you! Please come in so that we can start learning!

> Don't worry about your wheelchair; you belong here and we'll make space!

> Wow, you are a big bunch. My classroom may be filled with bright decorations and feel overwhelming, but don't stress: we will squeeze you in.

> Please come in. I may not have plenty and diverse resources to offer, but it is organised, clean and tidy.

> Oh good, plenty of people! Time for group work!

> Oh, it's you. I didn't really have the time to get everything in place but sit anywhere you like. I hope there is enough space, though.

> This classroom has strict rules. Don't move anything. Don't touch anything. Don't say anything. To obey is more important than to learn!

> Smart kids in front! Those who struggle, please sit together at the back.

> Wow, this room yells distractions of every kind!

> Come in so that we can get it over and done with. Not sure what we will learn, but I'll think of something.

The kind of message that your classroom conveys depends on you! Your classroom tells the learners what you think and feel about them and, most importantly, what is expected of them socially and academically and if they will succeed or fail. Your classroom can either support or hinder the learners' ability to engage, focus and learn.

Setting up a communal learning space is not merely clustering desks together, hanging up posters or putting a pot plant somewhere. Rather, it requires careful thought and planning. You need to think about sensory integration, as your senses are the receptors of the stimuli. You also need to be practical about decorations or the arrangement of furniture. You need to create a classroom that says, 'Welcome everyone! I am your teacher and I am passionate, prepared, excited and committed to helping you flourish! Let's get started!'

Sensory integration and behaviour

Sensory integration is a specialised field within occupational therapy and neuroscience. In short, your brain makes use of complex neurological processes to organise the information and sensation your body retrieves from the environment. Your brain interprets sensory stimuli and informs your body how to effectively react within the environment. This process of sensory integration draws on information from your seven senses (see also Chapter 14). Yes, that's right! We have seven senses and not only five.

The seven senses
1. Touch – tactile
2. Sound – auditory
3. Sight – visual
4. Taste – gustatory
5. Smell – olfactory
6. Movement and balance – vestibular
7. Joint and muscle – proprioception.

You will have learners in your class who are sensory seekers and others who are sensory avoiders, and you need to strike a balance between these two groups, from both a sensory and a practical point of view, when setting up your classroom.

The environment we see with our eyes

The ability to see is a great privilege, because most things we learn and experience are expressed visually, for example numbers, words, shapes, colour and movement. The following sections discuss some visual aspects that may hinder or cause physical and or emotional discomfort for learners when they look at the layout and appearance of your classroom.

Glare and flickering lights

The sun is a natural source of light while fluorescent lights provide quality and intensive light. Sometimes overhead fluorescent lights or data projectors cause a glare or flicker. Such an intensified light is excessively bright and causes discomfort or distortion that affects a learner's ability to see properly. The best option is to determine the source and cover it. You can do the following:

Figure 18.1 Glare

- Hang sheets, curtains or blinds in the windows. If the school has funds available, you can also tint the window or paint it with a light colour. If you have creative posters, art or butcher's paper you can also use this to cover the windows. Just be cautious that you do not block the air from flowing freely or that the room does not becomes visually cluttered.
- Change the globe or tube when it starts to flicker. You could also install filters or covers that are safe and fire-resistant.

Visual clutter

Visual clutter is a type of sight pollution, as it provides too much visual information. Such clutter can easily distract learners, whilst those who are visually sensitive can experience discomfort. To prevent overwhelming visual clutter, you can do the following:

- Group posters or pictures that belong together and display them on a simple solid background colour. This is called visual blocking.
- Avoid hanging up too many posters or objects. It is advisable to rotate posters or art work regularly to retain learners' interest. With regard to decorations, more is not always better.
- Try to keep one wall completely empty.
- Should you wish to paint the classroom walls or floors, first obtain permission! Stick to pastel or soft colours such as light green or only have one bright undecorated focus wall.

18 – Creating a meaningful, safe and optimal learning environment

Ambience and line of sight

Ambience is another word for atmosphere, and it signals the mood or setting a learner will associate with a communal space. Create a straight line along which you have unobstructed vision. To create this you can do the following:

Figure 18.2   Ambience and line of sight

- Mount mood filters over the light source to make it tolerable for learners who are light-sensitive, especially in a reading or music corner. This creates a subdued and relaxed atmosphere.
- Carefully plan your layout and set-up so it creates an inviting mood that reduces behavioural issues and promotes academic engagement. The line of sight is important here. For example, create age-appropriate and accessible shelves, cabinets, theme corners or areas where material and resources are stored and related content areas can be grouped together.
- Install cabinets or shelves (with curtains) close to the ceiling that are out of reach of the learners. These can serve as an additional storage space should you have limited floor surface.

The environment we listen to with our ears

The ability to hear is a complex process that brings much joy and is also crucial for learning and keeping us from harm.

Every minute of the day, a school is filled with noises and sounds, both within and outside the classroom. Some of these sounds are irrelevant or incidental but unavoidable and can cause much distress to an auditory-sensitive or -avoiding learner. You

Figure 18.3   Sources of noise in a classroom

could help lessen the effect of sound by doing the following:
- Use an electronic clock that does not make a ticking sound and regularly check anything like a fan that causes 'white noise'.
- Adopt the correct grip and pressure when writing on the board with chalk to avoid the screech of the chalk scratching the board. Avoid using old chalk that has hardened, or break it in two and write with the softer edge.
- Fit tennis balls to the feet of desks and chairs to minimise the harsh, scraping noise when chairs are pulled out or moved around.

- Discourage learners from using a pen or stationery that makes a 'click' sound.
- Place a carpet on the floor to muffle sounds. If the school has funds, sound-absorbing materials could be fitted against walls that are close to a playground, tuckshop or busy road. Otherwise, using free-standing screens or cork boards to block sounds from different directions is also a viable option. Even covering a wall with empty egg boxes could help.

The environment we feel with our hands, feet and body

We use our skin to touch. We can feel contours, pain, pressure, shape, temperature, tension, texture, vibrations and weight. Most learners want to be actively involved in what they learn, and the classroom becomes a space full of tactile information waiting to be explored. For young learners, movement, i.e. being able to use their joints and muscles, is part of learning. We need to be sensitive to learners who avoid or seek any form of touch and movement. To stimulate the proprioceptive system you can do the following:

- Allow learners to use unobtrusive tactile tools such as DIY fidget toys, fidget cubes, tactile discs, stress balls, pipe cleaners, play dough or clay, or elastic string.
- Provide flexible and textured seat surfaces, weighted toy objects, beanbags, exercise balls, scoop chairs, footrests, standing desks or elastic bands around the feet of chairs for learners to push against.
- Permit learners to use oral chew tools such as pencil chew toppers, chewy tubes, chewy sticks or a necklace chewy.

Ready, set and go

Perhaps you are a novice teacher and it is the beginning of the year in an empty classroom, or you have decided your classroom needs a 'makeover'. Regardless of whether you are starting from scratch or only making improvements, spend some time critically thinking about how the communal space might represent the intentional and hidden curriculum. The following sections discuss some general matters to consider.

Seating arrangements

Seating arrangement refers to the way in which the learners' seats are arranged in the classroom. This plan is influenced by the size of the classroom, the type of furniture and the number of learners you are teaching. Find a layout that best suits your own and your learners' needs. Tape down the aisles and blocks on the floor so that you have a 'master template' of your floor plan.

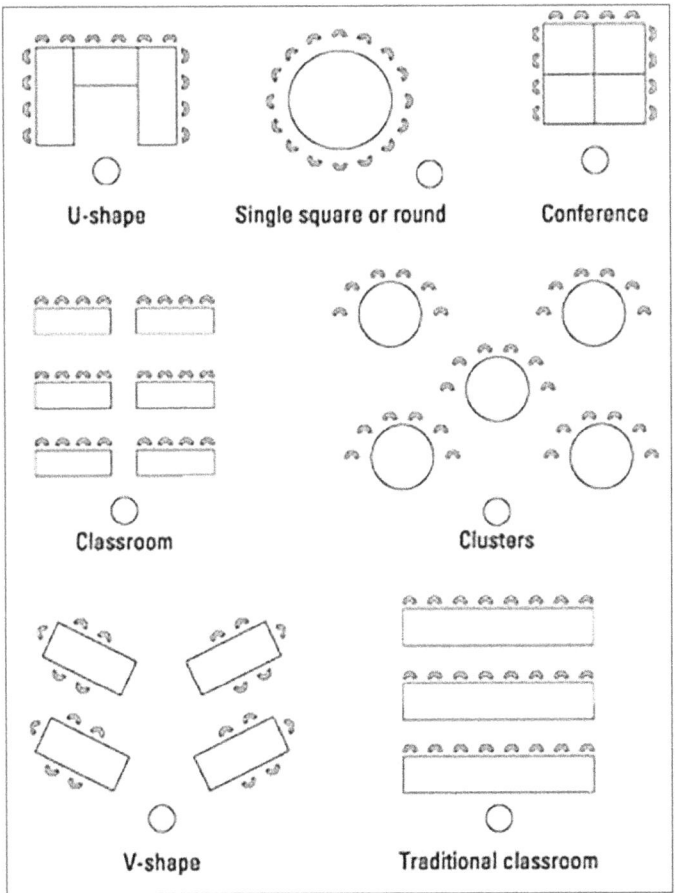

Figure 18.4 Seating arrangements

Practical Guidelines for Novice Teachers

Designated areas

In a differentiated classroom, each learner has different needs that must be met, often at the same time. Designated areas are distinct parts of the classroom where learners can develop, practise and improve their social and emotional skills. Some teachers create calm-down areas, silent/individual corners, group areas (areas for multimedia or experiments), exhibition/theme areas, resource boxes, or trays where learners can place their belongings.

Figure 18.5 A classroom with designated areas

Safety concerns

With so much happening in a classroom one should not ignore safety issues. Here are some tips that you should keep in mind:

- All windows and door exits should be clear of clutter and obstructions.
- Decorations, posters, light fixtures or technological devices must be fitted properly and not block any learner's view of you or the board or screen.
- Hazardous materials such as cleaning supplies and chemicals used for instruction should be properly labelled and securely stored. Also, do not paint walls or furniture with lead-based paint, as this is a toxin quickly absorbed by one's skin.
- Anything that you or a learner could trip over should be removed or carry a clearly marked warning, for example 'Mind the step'. Electrical cords must never run across high-traffic areas, walkways and doorways. Do not cover these cords with rugs or mats.
- Electrical circuits should never be overloaded. Be careful how many devices you are plugging into one outlet.
- A written plan with illustrations on how to evacuate the classroom should be placed close to the door and referred to regularly.

Think of your classroom as a welcoming educational space in which you and the learners would like to spend time. If you walk into your own classroom and you feel agitated, tense or that something is wrong, you should immediately act on it. Regularly ask yourself, a co-teacher or, more importantly, the learners what message the classroom is conveying to them.

19

Surviving the first day

Rinelle Evans

For some, the reality of starting their career kicks in upon receiving an official letter of appointment. For others, it may only dawn on them once the festive season is over. No matter when you realise that you are no longer a student and have a new routine to get used to, you cannot be unprepared. Start planning for that first meeting with your learners as early as possible!

The first day of a new school year is like going on a blind date or chatting to a stranger on the internet. There is a great deal of apprehension, as well as excitement! It is also the beginning of a long-term relationship with your learners. It is an extremely important meeting, as it sets the pattern for future interactions. It shapes learners':
- attitudes
- behaviours
- expectations
- interest levels.

This first meeting may determine how easily you will be able to motivate the learners to become interested in the content you teach. You should plan this first meeting carefully, as it may often last a full school day or the first couple of days of the new academic year. Use the first meeting with your learners to cement the three Rs – no, not the traditional reading, writing and arithmetic, but *rapport, routine* and *rating*. Whether you are dealing with your home room class or each group that will be taught by you, these three objectives can be applied.

Create rapport

This means starting that close connection between yourself and the learners: a bond that becomes a solid, happy working relationship as the term goes on. You need to feel in control of the classroom, but learners ought to feel relaxed enough to ask questions and enjoy their learning experience. Here are some ways to start off well:
- Try to get a class list well before the class is due to arrive. Practise saying the names. Get help with pronouncing the names if they are in a language

not your own. In a class of 40 learners, you'll want to use a name to get attention and call the learner to order, but it is also an excellent way of personalising the classroom, as each learner has a unique face and name – two very important possessions. Show your learners you care by learning (and using!) their names as quickly as possible. Knowing the names and then matching them up with faces helps you remember the learners more easily. Capture photos of individual learners on your cell phone or have each row cluster together in a group to remember their names.

- Do not listen to other teachers' views about how 'naughty' or 'cheeky' a particular learner is. Tell the class that everyone starts with a clean page and that they determine how they fill their page. This is especially important when you have been teaching for some time and are working with the same group for a second year. Do not drag past baggage along.
- Avoid comparing siblings to each other or referring to personal matters if you happen to know the learner or the parents.

Establish a routine

In an educational context, the word 'routine' has a distinct meaning. It refers to a particular response to a teacher's call for action and is repeated with consistency each day. Without routine, the class is never sure what to do, and is usually noisy and unsettled. Plenty of teaching time is wasted as the teacher shouts and nags the learners into some semblance of order. The behaviour in any classroom is determined by how much you let learners get away with.

From the very first moment that learners enter your class, they need to know what you expect. Do not just announce the rules. You need to explain the purpose of the routine. For example, why do you want learners to stand next to their desks or cover their books in a certain way? Drill them about safety procedures in a science lab or using equipment, for example in a kitchen or when playing sport. You will also need to practise the desired habit several times until the learners do exactly what you want them to do. Be patient. It takes effort, but the smooth management of your class is worth the effort and establishes an environment conducive to learning and teaching. It may take you as long as a month, or maybe even the whole of the first term, to establish the routines. Learners and your colleagues will take you seriously once you have succeeded. Investing time in the teaching of classroom procedures saves you teaching time and emotional energy.

Think about your class policy: How will you deal with absentees? How will learners be expected to cover their books? What will you do if a learner is late or has not done his or her homework? Will you allow code-switching? How do you want to manage the administrative matters each morning? Negotiate a contract or class code of conduct, with fair consequences when a learner transgresses it.

Rate/rectify/remedy

The first day is usually hectic and very little learning takes place. You should plan a simple task that could serve as an ice-breaker and help you get to know your learners. You could also use the task to assess the learners' knowledge of your subject and thus get a sense of where you will start teaching them. A short questionnaire or oral task may give you useful information on the learners' background knowledge and attitude towards your subject.

Plan the first lesson and manage it in such a way that the learners know what to expect and you feel confident and in control of the situation. A key question to ask yourself is: Have you prepared for this first lesson in such a way that the learners will want to come back?

> **Dress code and appearance**
> Most schools have a dress code. Find out in advance how you are expected to dress. Government schools are generally conservative and may expect men to wear a tie. You may not be allowed to wear T-shirts, flip-flops or even denim jeans. It is wise to show as little skin as possible. Dressing more formally during the first few days helps establish the required distance between a young teacher and the class. You will feel more confident if you know that you look smart, but make sure the outfit is also comfortable. Choose your shoes wisely. You will be standing in them for a very long time each day. Classrooms are notoriously too hot or too cold; some are also very dusty. Have a sweater in your class to put on when necessary and avoid white, as it quickly looks grubby. Take a close look at your hairstyle – you may need a good hair cut. Practising good personal hygiene is key when working with people.

20

Planning, preparing and starting your lessons

Piera Biccard and Philip Mirkin

This section focuses on preparation (and not the written planning) of your lesson. Your preparation really tells the class how organised you are. The learners will pick up very quickly whether you know what you are doing. Being properly prepared means really knowing what is going to happen during the lesson and how it is going to happen. You should be able to write down the flow of the lesson in 'steps'.

Let's imagine you have planned a lesson on the water cycle for Grade 5 learners. Although you have written down your aims and objectives for the lesson and you know what the learners are going to do as well as how you are going to assess their learning, have you really prepared for the flow of the lesson? It's a good idea to write down exactly what is going to happen during that lesson and what preparation you need to do for it.

Let's look at a typical lesson and the preparation that you should be thinking about:

- Greet the class. Settle them down.
- Introduction. Let's say you *planned* to get learners' attention by pouring water from a jug into a glass. Are you *prepared* for it? When will you put the jug of water and glass in your classroom? If the jug and glass are not ready and available when you need them, you will spend some time trying to get them. You may have to turn your back to the class to find the bottle of water in your bag and this may give learners the opportunity to become restless. Or you might send a learner out to fetch it – now you have the class becoming restless while you wait for this learner to return. Do you see how even though you *planned* a good introduction, you did not *prepare* for it?
- Learners write down all the things they use water for (2 minutes).
- Get learners to share with a partner (2 minutes).
- Learners read page 114 of their textbook. Have you stopped to consider where the textbooks are? Do the learners have their textbooks? Where are they – in their bags? Are the bags outside the classroom? Now you have

to deal with the disturbance of asking learners to fetch their textbooks in their bags outside. Perhaps the textbooks are in the cupboard and the cupboard is in the back corner of the classroom, but the classroom is so full you have to ask learners to move their desks so that you can get to the textbooks. In those few minutes, you create an opportunity for learners to be idle and disruptive. Rather, make sure you know where the textbooks are and *prepare* to have them ready before the start of the lesson.
- Learners work in groups. You give them cards that they arrange to place the water cycle in the correct order (5 minutes). The learners use the cards and the activity goes really well. At the end of the lesson, the learners return the cards to you … but now they are all mixed up because you didn't have individual envelopes or plastic bags for the cards. This means that you have to find some time before the next lesson to sort out the cards! The planning was good, but the fine detail of preparation can derail your lesson.

We are sure you get the idea. Sometimes, however, you may spend a great deal of time preparing an item that you need for your lesson. Give very careful consideration to how much time you spend in making your own learner teacher support material (LTSM). There is so much that is readily available online for you to use. Instead of spending many hours looking for a picture of forests in books or magazines, you can use resources such as Pixabay or Pexels to source free-to-use pictures. If you do not have access to online resources, use what you have. If you want to discuss the school uniform, you don't need to spend hours drawing it – simply ask one of the learners to stand up.

There are other areas where lesson preparation can help you maintain good discipline and good timing. The time that learners spend lined up outside your classroom can be used productively to give one or two instructions, such as, 'You will need to take out a pencil once you sit down' or 'Do not take anything out of your bags today.' If the learners get to know that you give important instructions at this time, they may settle down faster.

Another tip is to explain to learners how long they have for each task you expect them to do. In our example above, you will see that there is a time allocation given in brackets. You should prepare your written lesson plan with specific timing included. Also tell the learners about the time allocation. Tell them: 'You have two minutes to write down all the uses of water you can think of' – and then stick to it. If, however, you see that many of the learners have not completed the task, give them a little bit longer. At the start of your career you will not know how long learners take to complete certain tasks, so monitor the time they take carefully. At the end of the lesson, compare your expected time to the actual time the task took. This will help you to prepare more accurately for the next lesson.

Let's try to imagine that our water cycle lesson is well prepared. As you write this down, try to visualise each phase as it would happen. Imagine yourself teaching at each phase of the lesson and what you will need to organise so that the lesson flows smoothly, and so that you can be fully focused on the class.

Table 20.1   Lesson preparation

Lesson phase	Preparation needed
Line-up.	Ask learners to take out their NS textbooks. Check that each learner has one as they lead in.
Greet the class. Settle them down.	
Introduction.	Jug, water and glass ready before class starts.
Learners write down all the things they use water for. (2 minutes)	Correct exercise books.
Get learners to share with a partner. (2 minutes)	
Learners read page 114 of their textbook.	Learners have own textbook.
Give them cards that they arrange to place the water cycle in the correct order. (5 minutes)	Each group's cards in numbered envelope.

For this lesson, you need to get the jug, water and glass ready, remind learners to take out their textbooks at the line-up stage and place the cards you made in numbered envelopes. Now you have a well-planned and prepared lesson.

It may seem really time-consuming to do this, but it will mean that your lesson flows smoothly and that you limit the possible disruptions or opportunities for the learners to become disruptive. This will really help your self-confidence as a teacher. It is so important that the learners trust you. They will trust you when they feel that you really are in control of the classroom. As your confidence grows, so will your ability to try new ideas in your classroom. Eventually, this type of preparation will become second nature to you.

20 – Planning, preparing and starting your lessons

Right, so you have spent several hours planning and preparing in private for your public presentation: the lesson! So what happens now?

Learners will arrive at your classroom from assembly, the playground, a home room period or another teacher's class. You need to give clear signals regarding the new environment and what you expect of them. If you do this consistently with them, then the simple act of lining up outside or standing at their desks should get them into the state of learning-readiness that you expect of them.

At the door

Each school has its own system of managing learner movement and behaviour. You may have to enforce it or you may have some leeway in how you choose to have learners enter and leave your classroom. Consider asking the learners to line up outside your door and be quiet before they enter. Choosing how to manage their arrival and readiness for your lesson sets the tone for an effective learning opportunity well before you start.

This is also the time when you can identify those who may become a challenge once they enter the classroom. You could keep those individuals outside for a quick chat to help them become learning-ready. This is a good way to establish a connection with a learner who may not naturally or easily connect with teachers or adults. Sometimes a young learner may need to sit quietly and be left alone during the lesson, or perhaps the learner needs to sit close to the teacher for a sense of comfort and protection. All of these things can be identified by the observant and creative teacher, who can then provide the support needed.

Entering the classroom

Brief contact with the learners to re-establish a connection as they enter the room can help them to remember your expectations and to become ready to be the person that they need to be in your class. Greet them by name whenever possible. You will notice a lot about their personality and state of mind in this moment. This is also the time for the learners to give you information (for example, 'I was absent yesterday') so that there are fewer disruptions during the lesson.

Opening address

Wait for silence or use a signal such as a small bell to gain learners' full attention before greeting the class formally. If you have previously set clear expectations for them, they should be settled and ready to learn once they get to their desks. If they are tired or distracted, you may want to do a simple activity to get them going. A quick overview of what will happen in the lesson that day and how it relates to what they were learning previously will help them to orientate themselves for the lesson.

Getting them going

You could recap previous work, present new content, conduct an investigation, start group work, hand out worksheets, assign exercises, assign reading or encourage note-taking while you are explaining or demonstrating.

Sometimes a quick quiz or random questions about the previous work will help those who are still asleep or not ready to engage to wake up to what is happening. The trick is to get them active as soon as possible. If you give a long introduction where they remain passive, those who tend to be non-learning-ready will simply fall back into that state. Even a fun little game related to your lesson can do the trick.

Every new class will give you a honeymoon period of around three to five lessons in which they will be well behaved and follow your instructions without too many questions. If your expectations are very different from what they are already familiar with, they may need to ask you lots of questions to find out exactly what you expect of them. During this honeymoon period they will be more focused and responsive than they will be later, so use it to set very clear expectations and boundaries and be very fair and consistent with them. This will help the learners to trust you. Once this period is over, you will have become familiar to them and they will start behaving more comfortably towards you. They will need reminding of how you expect them to behave, but will be co-operative if they trust you. If your expectations were not clear and consistent, then their behaviour will reflect this.

In the odd case where a class does not give you this honeymoon period and learners are already disruptive from the start, you can know that the culture of this group, or perhaps even that of the school, has not trained the learners to behave appropriately. If you are a teacher of learners in their first year of school, you will have the particularly challenging task of familiarising them with the expectations of being at school. Set clear expectations for the learners from the start, in a simple and fun way.

21

Managing large classes

Piera Biccard

An unfortunate consequence of addressing past imbalances in South Africa is the lower funding per capita, resulting in an unfavourable teacher-learner ratio. Teachers already in the system are struggling to teach groups far larger than their experience or training has equipped them for. You may find yourself facing a class of up to 50 learners and you will certainly have to develop ways of coping with mixed-ability groups as well.

Problems related to class size are complex and differ from context to context, so 'large' can mean different things in different circumstances. When you read articles that refer to classrooms in the United States, 'large' could denote about 25 learners. When we think of the reality in South Africa, especially in government schools, 'large' could describe up to 80 learners. Unless you are at a private school, you are most likely to be teaching classes with more than 35 learners. Although this is not ideal, there are some strategies you can use to cope:

- *You* seat the learners. Perhaps arranging them alphabetically is useful initially until you get to know them better. Do not let them seat themselves – show that you are in control of *your* classroom. Make a seating chart and display it. This means you can learn names faster and do not have to repeat the seating each lesson.
- Time all your activities. If you have asked learners to write down five sentences, tell them how long they have to finish it. Stick to the time and then move on to the next activity or phase of your lesson.
- Use group work or pair work to help you manage feedback and discussions.
- Try to learn as many of the learners' names as possible. This helps you with discipline and getting specific learners' attention.
- Try to arrange your classroom so that you 'can get everywhere' during a lesson. Move unnecessary furniture outside. Move around the class when talking. Perhaps learners can leave their bags outside (if it is safe and dry). You may want to mark where all the rows start with chalk or masking tape so that learners can leave the class the way they found it.
- Have definite procedures for leading in and out. Also plan for how equipment or textbooks will be handed out. You may want to elect a group

- representative who will collect and distribute materials – this will mean fewer learners are getting up or walking around in the class.
- Have a 'no walking around rule' (unless the lesson requires it).
- Try to find an alternative venue for some lessons (for example, the school hall or field). Ask the SMT for permission and only use these areas if the lesson task allows for it.
- Noise is going to be an issue. Ask learners to speak at half-volume. Have some way of getting their attention after group discussions (for example play your ringtone or switch the lights on/off).
- Once you know the learners, rotate them so that they all get a chance to sit near the front or at the back (unless you have identified reasons, such as poor eyesight, to keep them in front).
- Do not start the lesson until *everyone* is quiet. Give them a few minutes to settle down. Rather spend five minutes waiting for silence than the rest of the period repeating instructions because you were not heard the first time.
- Give one instruction at a time. If possible, write these down on a chalkboard for everyone to see (for example, the textbook page number). Use simple language and short sentences. Break your instructions up into manageable chunks.

Large classes are not ideal, but they are a reality in South African schools. You need to ensure that you have a plan for how to tackle some of the organisational issues, as well as some ideas for allowing smooth teaching and learning. Try different approaches to formative assessment since this is vital to learning and can often become problematic in large classrooms. Work smarter – not harder!

Working in pairs

One way to help you deal with large classes is to let learners work in groups or pairs. In this section, we look in more detail at how to work with pairs in your class.

Group work really has become a buzzword in education. It is a teaching method that is often valued because of its links to more modern educational theories (social constructivism and African-based pedagogy). But just how can you use it in a classroom and still be smiling at the end of the day?

We are going to suggest that you take some 'baby' steps towards group work by using pairs. Using pairs makes a few things more manageable. Firstly, there is no movement of learners or furniture. Secondly, the noise level will remain within a reasonable range and thirdly, you should be able to see if the pairs are not working more easily than if five or six learners were sitting in a group.

From the learners' perspective, working in pairs allows them to practise their language skills (even in a Mathematics class this is very important). They learn how another learner understands the concepts. They may feel more confident than when working in a large group. Occasionally, change the pairs so that learners can work with a new partner, or swap learners when you find combinations that are counterproductive or negative.

The first thing you need to consider is what you are teaching and how group work will help the learners with the topic or concept. Let's imagine you are teaching a Grade 6 Mathematics lesson on adding fractions. An important concept in this topic is that the fractions must be written with common denominators. Often, finding the correct denominator is not as difficult as converting the numerator. So you would want learners to be supported when they work on converting the numerators in the equivalent fractions they write.

Once you have introduced your lesson you can get the learners to first work individually on a few problems (finding a common denominator) and then to work on converting the numerators with a partner. In this way they get to explain their reasoning to a peer and they may benefit from a peer tutoring them. Often, learners who are working in pairs will have the courage to ask you to assist them (when individually they may have been too shy).

You could also ask the pairs to work together from the beginning on a few problems. You could follow this up with a whole-class discussion and clarify any misconceptions. Then, you could ask the learners to work individually once they have been supported through pair work and your follow-up discussion.

Pair work or group work should have a very specific purpose. The task should never go on too long. Use the pair work as a way to support learners before they work on more challenging work individually. Make sure that the pairs know exactly what they have to achieve. For example, 'Read page 13 of the textbook and write down what you think are the five most important points.' Do not give an instruction such as 'Discuss in your groups' without telling them what they should achieve. For example, you could say, 'Make a decision on ...' or 'Provide three suggestions to solve the problem' or 'Draw a mind map'.

Be sure to tell the learners how much time they have for each activity. Keep the time frame short but reasonable. While the pairs or groups are busy, walk around and listen to what is going on. This is not the time to have a cup of coffee or check your email! If you are not involved, you will lose out on a lot of learning that is happening, and if the learners pick up that you are 'busy' with something else, they will start misbehaving.

Perhaps the following questions can assist you in deciding when and for how long to use pair or group work. Remember to include individual work and whole-class discussion as part of the lesson.

- What is the most difficult or critical aspect of the concepts learners must learn today?
- When would they need the support - before working on their own for a while or after working on their own?
- When should I come in and get feedback from the pairs to discuss with the whole class?
- What part do I want them to do on their own for assessment?
- Will the task need more than two people?
- What specific question or instruction will I give them? (Not 'Discuss ...')
- What will the pairs or groups produce after they have worked together? (A list, a table, a diagram?)
- Are there individual learners who should not work together?

In each lesson, try to think of a task for:
- the teacher alone, for example explaining or demonstrating
- the learners alone, for example reading or writing
- learners in pairs or groups, for example discussing, role-playing, sharing, showing
- the teacher interacting with learners, for example discussion, report back.

Then arrange these in a sequence that makes sense for the topic and grade you are teaching. Remember, the lesson does not have to start with the teacher explaining something. Make sure you shift these tasks around in your lessons. Your lessons must not become predictable. If the learners are interested during the lesson, it does help with discipline too.

A lesson where you read from the textbook and learners listen to you and then answer questions individually should not be the norm in your classroom. There are times when this will happen, but you should integrate different activities and different groupings of learners so that you enhance learning.

If you would like to read more about pair and group work, we suggest you perform an internet search for the 'Think, pair, share' co-operative learning strategy developed by Frank Lyman and Arlene Mindus in 1977 for more ideas and advice.

Teaching large classes effectively remains a challenge for all teachers. Success depends on your personality and your ability to manage and motivate the learners in front of you. There is no recipe for success. We have shared our experiences with you and some methods that you can try. With careful planning you should find large classes easier and just as rewarding.

22

Giving homework

Nhlanhla Mpofu and Mncedisi C. Maphalala

Homework is an essential part of every learner's holistic educational experience. Some teachers refer to it as 'home learning'. While other teachers call this 'supplementary work', we refer to it as the work that learners practise at home to reinforce skills and concepts learnt in class. Although some educationists contest the value of giving homework, others claim several pedagogical merits of homework. You may teach in a school that has a particular homework policy and may thus not have a choice in this. You may want to reflect on your own opinion currently and test it once you have been in the classroom for a few weeks.

The purpose of homework

Homework is educational work given during school that is intended to reinforce or practise skills in other environments out of class hours (Emami et al, 2014). Homework assignments could also be given in advance as preparation for a particular lesson.

Homework prepares learners for learning and scaffolds them to integrate new knowledge. According to Carr (2013), homework reinforces subject knowledge and understanding by offering learners opportunities to apply, practise and revise skills and concepts at their own pace. It also promotes self-regulated learning and assessment by providing time for learners to review classroom materials. By completing homework assignments, learners internalise study research, time management and independent thinking skills, which are life skills they will require as they progress in academia. Homework extends learners' knowledge sources by allowing parents and guardians to become an important aspect of the learners' everyday learning experience. Homework establishes a learning network for the learner that involves the teacher assigning homework, the parent providing conditions for the learner to complete the assigned work and the learner successfully completing the assigned work. Such a network scaffolds and stimulates the learner beyond the classroom environment.

Characteristics of a good homework assignment

Effective homework does not happen by chance; it needs to be planned by the teacher. A good and meaningful homework task deepens the learners' subject knowledge and builds essential skills. Homework tasks need to be carefully thought through. You cannot merely say, 'Finish Exercise 4 from 5 to 12 for tomorrow.' Before assigning homework, ask: What did the learners learn today? What can they do to practise this new knowledge? What type of task would best support their learning? In explaining the importance of a good quality homework task, Heitzman (2007: 41) states that it is wise to:

- assign homework that varies in difficulty and is challenging
- explain carefully how the homework should be done
- allow sufficient time for learners to do the homework
- provide timely feedback on the assignment.

Doing purposeful homework should contribute to learning.

Vatterott (2010) provides five similar considerations a teacher should take into account when giving homework:

- **Purpose** refers to the relevance of the homework as an extension of work done in class or preparation for the next lesson. Homework should not be assigned as a routine but an integral part of learning and reinforcing skills and concepts. Learners must understand the purpose of the homework, or this academic tool becomes counterproductive.
- **Efficiency** refers to the time that the learners spend completing the homework. Carr (2013) found that learners who spend more than 90 minutes doing their homework in grades 6 to 8 perform poorly. A general rule for high school learners is no more than 30 minutes per subject per day.
- **Competence** is the learner's ability to complete the homework task on their own with limited or no assistance from others. Where possible, homework assignments should address individual learners' needs.
- **Ownership** happens when learners feel connected to and challenged by the content. This cognitive bridge between home and school helps learners take responsibility for their academic progress, as they are aware of the merits of doing some work at home. Such tasks are also age-appropriate.
- **Appealing** homework assignments are clear and inviting to complete. They are also generally visually attractive and written in simple language.

Types of homework assignments

According to Cooper et al (2006), homework assignments serve different purposes. Most relate to the consolidation of instruction, whereas some may be legislative requirements such as Grade 12 portfolio work. The various types of homework assignments are discussed below.

Carry-over from classwork

This happens when a teacher decides that learners need more time to complete work that was started during class. The learners must, however, already understand the concepts or skills required to complete the task on their own.

Reinforcement homework

This is usually a task in which learners apply or practise what they have learnt during a lesson in a new context. Completing the homework successfully implies that the learners have mastered the content. If a teacher notices that learners are struggling with a topic, he or she might give homework that provides them with more independent practice in order to reinforce the acquisition of the skill, competency or concept.

Preparation homework

This is homework that a teacher assigns in advance of a lesson so that learners have sufficient background knowledge when the lesson starts. For example, a teacher could ask the learners to read the autobiography of a famous statesman in order to understand the social impact of a historical event. The purpose of the preparation homework is to provide learners with prior experiences of an event of which they have limited knowledge and which is uncommon to their daily activities. You may want to do some reading about what is called the 'flipped classroom' for more ideas.

Research homework

Through research homework, learners are given an opportunity to obtain knowledge from sources other than the school. The teacher provides guidelines and rubrics on how the research homework should be written and assessed. The learners use sources such as the library, the museum, oral history and interviews to complete the research homework. Such a task requires careful planning and sufficient time for the learners to gain the maximum benefit from completing it.

Revision homework

This type of homework is done to prepare the learners for tests and national examinations. Tasks similar to those anticipated in the exams are given so that learners independently revise key concepts and skills of the course while they prepare for summative assessments.

> Some **practical matters** to consider about homework include the following:
> - Learners need to be taught how to do their homework. This involves skills such as organising, prioritising, managing time and locating information.
> - Establish a homework policy. This should include what consequences there are for not doing the homework or handing in work late. Remember to also reward exceptional responses. An essay could be read to the class or displayed on a wall; you could hand out a reward, such as a sticker or star. All learners – regardless of age – appreciate a written comment praising their work.
> - When assigning homework, take the learners' daily schedule into account. Some learners may have domestic chores to complete, take a while to travel home by public transport or participate in extramural activities. It is always wise to negotiate realistic deadlines with learners, especially those in senior classes. Also involve the learners in determining the amount and type of homework. If possible, suggest a school policy so that learners are not overburdened.
> - Assign work of an appropriate level and that links to the work done in class. It ought to be an extension of the lesson outcome and prepare the learners for the assessments. It thus needs to be relevant.
> - Provide a realistic time frame for each homework task, for example: 'This task should take you 15 minutes if you focus on completing it.' The younger the learners, the shorter the task ought to be.
> - Avoid assigning homework that costs money, requires devices not all learners have access to or demands a great deal of parental involvement. The work ought to be done independently by a learner using material easily obtained or provided by you.
> - Give clear, concise instructions, preferably in writing. You may want to dedicate a space on the board or near the exit where you can post the homework. If your classroom has an eye-level window facing the corridor, you could even paste the homework up there so that learners can read it from outside the class.
> - Consider giving the homework list for the week/cycle to the learners in advance so that they can pace themselves.
> - Show examples of work done by learners in previous years so that learners get a sense of the standard expected as well as how to prepare for larger assignments.

- Establish a routine for checking homework. You do not want to waste time. Use this section of the lesson to consolidate or revise the work. Also ask the learners for feedback on the tasks. What did they like/dislike?
- Homework should never be given as a form of punishment.
- Checking homework needs to be done as a daily routine before the actual teaching starts. Appoint a monitor in each row to move from learner to learner checking the books/worksheets. They are not expected to reprimand their classmates, only to indicate whether the work for the day has been done.

Homework is essential as a continuation and reinforcement pedagogical tool for content learnt in class. What educators give for homework and the purpose for which they give it needs to be valued in terms of how meaningfully it helps to achieve effective learning. Learner academic achievement can be greatly improved by assigning meaningful homework aligned to the classroom activities. Homework is a great way to individually strengthen the learning done in the classroom, allowing learners to see their classroom activities from a holistic perspective. When applied correctly, homework enhances the process of inquiry and the understanding of subject knowledge. Overall, beyond academic outcomes, homework develops skills in learners such as time management, self-efficacy, motivation and self-discipline.

23

Keeping up with the marking load

Piera Biccard and Rinelle Evans

The demands made by the curriculum and general school policy often dictate that learners are assessed more frequently than teachers can really cope with. It has become necessary for teachers to negotiate and plan their marking very carefully so they do not overburden themselves. Marking (or rather, not keeping up with it) can really spoil things for you as a new teacher. With proper planning and smart use of time, you should manage. Start off by investing in a few red pens and a date stamp.

Firstly, you should be busiest during class time – not at 11 pm at home! This means that you should use every minute of class time, and that includes making time for marking. We do not mean that while the learners are working you sit down with a pile of books and start marking while ignoring the class. No, mark the work of the class in front of you by going around the classroom or calling two or three learners to your desk. Start the year by moving around the class and visiting learners at their desks. This serves two purposes: it shows the learners that you are present and can assist (this can keep them from misbehaving) and it allows you to explain, discuss and clarify matters with the learner while he or she is with you. It doesn't really help if you are marking books at your kitchen table late at night and you find that *all* the learners have totally misunderstood something!

We mark learners' work to:
- establish whether they understood the task
- see whether they have met the learning outcome
- check that they have completed the task
- provide useful feedback
- motivate and encourage them.

It is important that you apply *stratified* or *selective* marking to your subject. You will need to decide which written tasks you are only controlling (checking that it was done). Some tasks you will mark for formative assessment and you may only write a comment. Then you must decide which work needs to be intensively marked. Furthermore, *how much* of this work should be marked intensively? If learners have written an essay, are you going to mark the introduction intensively (because writing introductions was the aim of the lesson) or are you going to mark spelling and punctuation for the second and third paragraphs only? If you narrow down the marking in this way, it is a good idea to reflect it in a rubric that the learners will paste into their books. This will explain to an 'outsider' (parent, district official and so on) what your assessment intention was.

When marking Mathematics, for example, once the learners are working, call them to your desk (two or three at a time) and mark their books. Spend time marking one activity. Provide verbal or written feedback. If a learner has really not understood the concept, provide a worked example (in your handwriting) in their books. This shows the support you have given the learner. Most books will take you a very short time to go through. In each class, there will be only four or five learners who need your intensive support. Once you get to know the class, you can call these learners to your desk first.

If you are marking Social Sciences or another subject where you need to concentrate on the answers and explanations, you can still go around the class and sign and date the books. This will save you at least 20 minutes later that afternoon, as it means you can open them up and focus on marking the content. You could also ask the learners to leave their books open on the page where you want to mark. If it takes you 10 seconds to find the correct place in each book and you have to do that for 100 books, well that's 1 000 seconds – about 17 minutes – saved that afternoon! Also ask yourself: What has to be marked? For example, if you have given learners six questions for Social Sciences, are all questions equally important? Could you intensively mark two questions and provide a detailed memorandum for the others? Your HoD should be able to give you good guidance in this regard.

If a section of work such as a project or essay is going to take you a long time to mark, perhaps you could get the learners to complete it on a separate piece of paper instead of in their books. Learners can continue working in their books in the coming days while you are marking, and it is a much lighter load for you to take home than a pile of exercise books. You will need to ensure that these loose pages are pasted into the learners' exercise books or placed in their assessment files once you have finished marking.

Spending time designing and preparing a detailed rubric can save you a lot of time during the marking process. The rubric should not be too vague and should consist of all the sub-competencies or sub-skills that you want to assess. A rubric can also provide you with an actual mark, as in the example in Table 23.1. It is a four-point rubric and has five different criteria or descriptors that you choose to mark – so the final mark will be out of 20.

Table 23.1 A four-level rubric

Criteria/descriptors	4	3	2	1
1.	✓			
2.		✓		
3.		✓		
4.			✓	
5.		✓		
Total	15			
Comment				
Signature				
Date				

Sometimes it is easier to design a five-level rubric, as shown in Table 23.2, because there is a middle point where you can describe what the average indicator will be.

Table 23.2 A five-level rubric

5	4	3	2	1
Describe exceptional performance or competency that has 'that something extra'.	Describe above-average competency or knowledge demonstration.	Describe what the average performance/knowledge/competency is. You could use your curriculum document to specify the minimum that is expected for the grade.	Describe below-average or missing elements of the competency. If you are not sure what these missing elements could be, leave blank lines that you can write on here.	Describe knowledge or competency that is well below the average or where there are areas of concern or where the learner really struggles.

If you are using a rubric for marking, get the learners to paste it in their books below the work you want to assess. Or you can have loose blank ones with you that you fill in and then ask learners to paste in below the relevant work the following day.

Another idea that can help you keep up with the daily marking (not the intensive marking) is the RAG123 (Lister, 2013) system. This is a system where learners are involved in the preliminary thinking about their work and rating it on a scale of red, amber (orange in South Africa), green and 1, 2, 3, as illustrated in the marking guide in Table 23.3.

Table 23.3 RAG123 marking guide

Marking guide	Teacher says	Learner says
Red	Unsatisfactory amount of work done Poor presentations No workings shown	I wasn't really trying today. I let things distract me. I need to make up for it.
Amber (Orange)	Satisfactory amount of work done Acceptable presentation Some/most workings shown	I mostly concentrated today. I could have tried harder. I didn't really push myself.
Green	Excellent work All workings shown Clear diagrams and labels Extension work done	I really tried hard today. I avoided distractions. I pushed my understanding.
1	Excellent understanding	I am confident enough to explain the work to someone else.
2	Good understanding, working at the targeted level	I understand most of this.
3	Working below the targeted level	I really struggled with this – help!

Learners write a code under the work that they have done (using one letter and one number to describe their work, for example A2). This self-evaluation gives you an opportunity to see how the learner gauges his or her work ethic and understanding. You then assess the work using the same coding system. The coding system would be displayed clearly in your classroom and you would explain how it works. Change the wording to suit your needs and your classroom. This is a quick way of assessing globally for completion of work or for understanding. For example, the learner will write A1 under his or her work while you write A2 and give a quick comment about why you say so. This also helps learners improve their ability to judge their own work. Use this system for the work you want to check and comment on and not necessarily mark intensively.

It is possible to do several other types of effective evaluation of either groups or individuals:

- **Self-assessment.** Learners mark their own work from a memorandum and prove their integrity. Explicitly teach learners to assess their own work and provide opportunities for them to do so before they hand work to you. You then assess the work after the learner has made comments and adjustments. Teach learners how to proofread and edit their own work effectively.
- **Peer marking.** Teach learners to mark each other's work using assessment criteria. Ensure that work marked by a peer is clearly signed. Learners can learn a great deal from critiquing each other's work. They also learn to offer and accept constructive criticism.
- **Swap and mark.** Where appropriate, let learners mark each other's work in class. This reduces the amount of time you need to spend on each piece and it also has the advantage of immediacy, which increases effectiveness.
- **Check drafts.** Let learners submit drafts of their work during the process rather than simply the finished product. In this way you can give them feedback while they are working on the task, reducing the amount of work you will need to do once the assignment is completed. Give learners templates to follow that demonstrate their thinking along the way. Ensure that the process is about improvement, not about a grade.
- Consider **team marking**, where colleagues responsible for other grades help you out and the favour is returned when their load mounts up.
- Devise a system of **credits**, where each learner starts off with, say, 100 marks and then subsequently loses marks for tasks not done or handed in late. This method eases the burden of marking, but implies a fair amount of accurate and regular administration. Its downside is that learners do not receive individual feedback. Use this system for homework assignments and class work, as the task is glossed over and merely checked for completeness. It is also easy to gauge whether this is the learner's own work. Motivated learners seem to favour a credit system, as they know that shirking one's duty is penalised. The marks that are left after the deductions (if any) at the end of each term are calculated as part of the continuous assessment mark on a report. It is also possible to gain credits for exceptional work.

- When **comment-only marking**, the teacher gives feedback in three key areas:
  1. what the learner has done right
  2. what the learner could improve on
  3. what the next step/s should be to improve performance or understanding.

Just giving a mark in itself does not help learners to understand how they might improve their work. Formative comments have greater impact.

Practical suggestions

Here are some ways to survive the sets of scripts piled on your desk:
- Plan submission dates carefully and stagger them so that you can keep the turnaround time as short as possible. Take in written work from different classes at different times.
- Individual teachers differ in how they prefer to tackle the task. Some sit down and get the job done. Others dedicate their full attention to marking 10 scripts and then do something else. There is no best way, but any systematic approach will help you accomplish more in a less mind-numbing way!
- Plan a marking schedule of x number of papers per day or hour and be disciplined about sticking to the plan. Create incentives for yourself and reward yourself when you have accomplished your goal.
- Invest in a marking pen that writes smoothly and at any angle.
- Create a neat, quiet place where you can work. Having to clear up and pack out your memo and papers each time also gobbles away at the minutes.
- Work systematically by first refreshing your memory regarding the memorandum, criteria or rubric descriptors. Monitor your judgement by regularly going back to the memorandum. Also revise the first script you marked once you have completed the batch.
- Do not look only for errors and weaknesses. Point out strengths too. Indicate areas that need improvement, but offer encouragement as well. In order to save time, some teachers create their own type of comment list or checklist and then tick off the relevant statements.
- Comments that praise, question or offer suggestions are more useful than a mere 'Good!' or 'Improving!'

Although marking is tedious and time-consuming, it is an essential part of evaluating the learning taking place. *You cannot sow and then not reap at harvest time!*

24

Making your own inexpensive resources

Piera Biccard

Unless you really are fortunate and you have a classroom that is extremely well resourced, you will find that you need items to enhance your lesson or items to help organise your classroom. Even if you do have access to excellent resources, there are a number of cheaper items that you can use for your classroom and your teaching. Recycling household items is a simple way to save costs when making resources. In fact, recycling is something that you should practise as a teacher.

McCaughy (2010) suggests the following affordable, yet essential items you should have:

- **Good quality scissors.** Remember to keep your pair of scissors in a safe place.
- **Paper** – all sorts: lined paper, blank paper, construction paper, newspaper, etc. You can cut paper into the right size for an activity, for example flashcards, writing down a question on the day's topic, or doing a class task.
- **A timer.** It helps to set a timer when you want to time an activity. You could use your cell phone if your school allows cell phones in the classroom.
- **A bell or buzzer** to get learners' attention (similar to the ones used at business counters). This helps to get the learners to focus on you again if they have been involved in a noisy activity or group work. Use it sparingly – you should not use it to get their attention every two minutes or every time the class is noisy, because eventually they will become so used to the sound that they won't respond to it anymore.
- **Coloured markers.** You can make posters of the day's vocabulary or the day's important concepts. You may need to glue two or four sheets of A4 paper together to make a poster that everyone can see.
- **Sticky putty or pegs** to display your posters or learners' work. If learners have done something on a loose piece of paper, display it. They love to see their work!

Check with your HoD regarding a budget that may exist for your own classroom and for your subject. Follow the correct procedures when using school/state money for purchases. Depending on your own financial situation, you may find useful items at second-hand sales or charity shops, such as cheap magazines (check that they are suitable) for finding pictures or mosaic work in Art, stuffed toys for puppets, and so on. Be on the lookout for sales at stationery stores or subscribe to their mailing list to see special offers that may interest you. Specialist plastic/cardboard warehouses or factory shops sell a wide assortment of plastic tubs/boxes or sturdy cardboard boxes at a very reasonable price – especially if you buy in bulk.

Ideas for items that you can make from recycled materials

You will be spending a great deal of time in your classroom, so it is important that you make it as appealing as you can. You also need to make sure that your classroom is organised and functional. If you were not given any shelves or cupboards, you can make a plan. Approach places like your local grocer or supermarket for empty boxes. You can use these for storing all sorts of items. With a little creativity you could make a bookshelf out of empty boxes, even if they are different sizes.

Figure 24.1 Vegetable box drawers

From your own home (and ask your family and friends to collect for you), you could bring food boxes or containers. These can be useful not only for storage, but for reading cards or Mathematics. For example, nutritional information lists on food packets contain many numbers that you could usefully work with.

The following items from your home may be useful in making resources for learners or resources for your own use in your classroom:
- ice cream containers
- toilet roll inners
- yoghurt containers
- tins (be sure that they have been cut with a rotary tin-opener so that the edges are smooth and safe)
- plastic bottles (milk, dishwashing soap, etc)
- egg boxes and many more.

24 – Making your own inexpensive resources

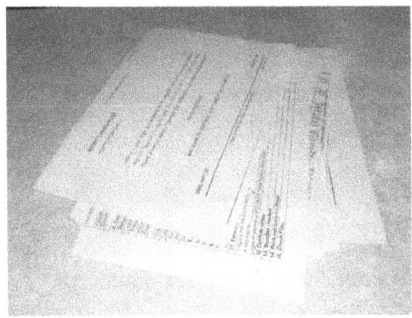
1. Start with some scrap paper. Make a neat pile by aligning the edges.

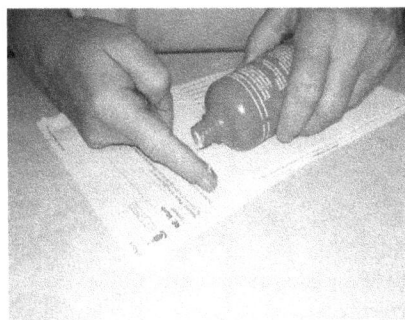
2. Smear wood glue along the one edge, ensuring that all pages get glue.

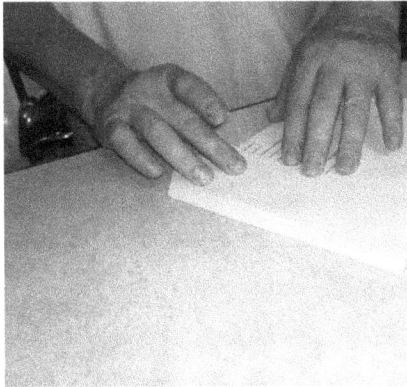
3. Hold it all in place with another sheet of paper.

4. Place a heavy weight on top and allow to dry.

Figure 24.2 Making your own pad of paper

We hope that Figure 24.3 on the next page will give you some ideas of items you can make for your classroom, whether to help you organise equipment or to make items that your learners can use. You just need some time to collect items, and creativity!

1. Use egg boxes as paint holders.

2. Secure boxes to make storage space.

3. Use milk or juice jugs as stationery storage.

4. Use milk or juice jugs for book holders.

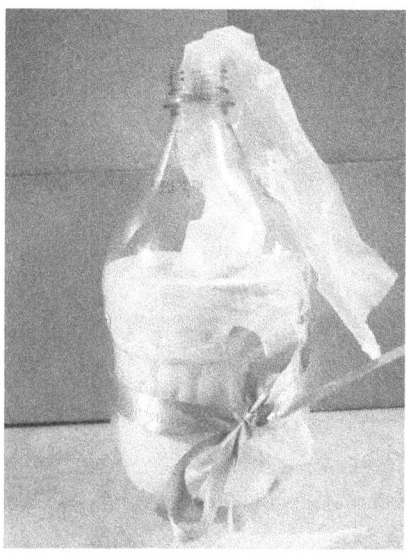
5. A roller towel dispenser

6. Use toilet roll inners for germinating seeds.

7. Use clean and safe egded tins as group stationery holders.

Figure 24.3 Classroom resources made from recycled everyday objects

24 – Making your own inexpensive resources

In the above photos we show you some ideas for recycling household items for classroom purposes.

Egg boxes can be used to hold paint or small items such as paperclips or beads. Vegetable and fruit boxes that are sturdy and strong can be used for storage space. Please ensure that you do not stack them too high, in case they fall over. Plastic milk or juice bottles make good stationery or small book holders. If you are using tins, please ensure that they were cut open with a rotary tin-opener and that the edges are absolutely safe. They can be glued together or nailed onto a wooden plank and used to store resources or stationery for a group. Toilet roll inners also serve several functions, such as a small germinating holder for seeds. A few glued next to each other and painted can also be used to store stationery. You can also make a roller towel dispenser by using a 2ℓ plastic bottle and toilet paper that you feed through the top. If you use a coloured bottle, no one will notice that it is toilet paper.

To make a fairly inexpensive write-on board, place a piece of paper or cardboard inside a plastic sleeve. Use the normal whiteboard markers and a tissue to clean it.

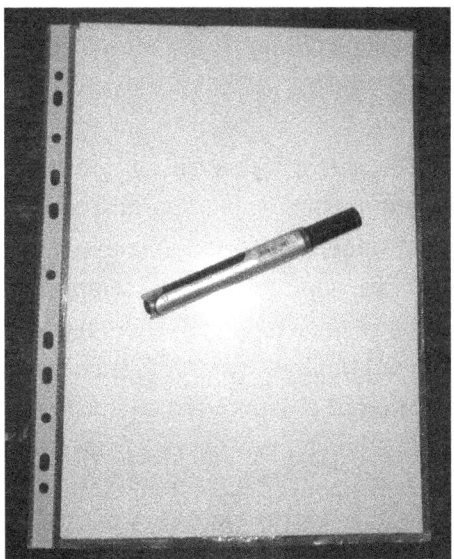

Figure 24.4   A homemade 'whiteboard'

25

Using digital tools to enhance your teaching and learning environment

Candice Livingston

You may never be fortunate enough to teach using expensive technology. The learners in front of you may never even have owned a cell phone. It is, however, important that as a novice teacher you are aware of the myriad digital tools that you or your learners could use to develop digital literacy and integrate e-learning into your lessons. You are limited only by your imagination, and we suggest you think of ways to adapt our examples to your own context. Consult Appendix D for many more digital resources you might find useful.

Let's look at some social media tools that are not commonly used but that are easy to include in your teaching.

Voki

Voki (http://www.voki.com/) is a free Web 2.0 tool that allows teachers and learners to create talking, customisable characters or avatars of themselves in order to present biographical information, express an opinion or read a poem. Users can customise characters to resemble living people, animals and cartoons. All that learners have to do is record their voices via the microphone on a laptop or telephone, which is then uploaded as an audio file. Alternatively, typed dialogue is converted to speech by the Voki software. Completed characters can be shared via social media, email and embedded code. With free Voki accounts, users can create unlimited characters.

Learners often lose concentration in the classroom and the teacher's voice starts to fade into the background. Introducing an avatar for some lessons can get learners' attention and make it a little more fun. Choose a quirky and interesting avatar – not just one that looks like you. Use it for particularly dry discussions and incorporate it into an interactive presentation. Learners will feel like they're watching a show – and they'll be learning at the same time.

These online avatars can be used by the teacher to explain difficult pieces of work or to give extra information, or learners can create them to do a presentation and practise fluency.

> **What is an avatar?**
> In computing, an avatar is the graphical representation of the user or the user's alter ego or character. It may take either a three-dimensional form, as in games or virtual worlds, or a two-dimensional form, as an icon in internet forums and other online communities.

The following sections discuss examples of ways that Voki can be used in the various subjects.

Language teaching

Learners create avatars to read their poems, practise their reading fluency, pronunciation or present a speech. You may be able to read extracts from a novel that is rich in dialogue or in the particular dialect of an area in an expressive voice. Not having to read the same passage to several classes will also save your voice from fatigue.

History

Classroom biography study offers high-interest reading with a purpose, as learners begin with inquiry and research, then summarise and organise their information, and finally prepare oral presentations to share with the class. Learners collaboratively explore a number of sources to create a biographical timeline about a selected person. They resolve any conflicting information they may have found during their investigation. Learners then create avatars that resemble these famous people and present their information to the class.

Geography

Each learner chooses a different country and does further geographical research on that country:
- Where is it located? (Which continent? What other countries does it border on?)
- How large is it? (Square miles/kilometres? Population?)
- What is the climate like?
- What are some of its major landforms? (Mountains, rivers, seas, etc)

Learners then create a Voki character that relates to the country or continent they have researched. This character is used in an electronic presentation (of three to five slides) to present the information to the class. They may use images downloaded from the internet to enhance their presentation visually.

Mathematics

A Voki character could guide learners to solve mathematics problems step by step.

Life Orientation

Learners could create avatars to introduce themselves to the class, while any awareness campaign (regarding AIDS or bullying, for example) can be supplemented with a Voki presentation.

Science

Who are the people behind the world's greatest inventions? Learners read the biographies of inventors and create presentations that highlight how these inventions from the past have influenced the future.

Biology

A Voki character could describe any biological function or explain how to label a diagram or discuss problematic terminology.

Instagram

Instagram is a free mobile app and an online mobile photo-sharing, video-sharing and social networking service that enables its users to share pictures and videos either publicly or privately on the app, as well as through a variety of other social networking platforms, such as Facebook and Twitter.

There are many ways to include photographs in the teaching and learning process in your classroom. You can use Instagram to showcase learners' work or progress. Snap pictures of learners' artwork and other special projects to share on a private Instagram account only accessible to families and others in your school community. Snap photos of projects, class outings or other milestones and share them on a class page. Instagram can also be used to feature a 'Learner of the Week'.

You can use Instagram to capture field trip memories. Invite a learner volunteer 'archivist' to take photos on your field trips, camps and school outings or during class parties and share those on your Instagram account.

The true potential of the use of photography can be realised in specific subject areas, as illustrated in the examples discussed on the following pages.

Geography

Ask learners to photograph local geographical features or create a class project where weather patterns are documented in digital photographs over a specified period of time.

History

Have learners browse historical photos and create a bulletin board or poster display showing Nelson Mandela's or Mark Shuttleworth's Instagram feed. Challenge learners to find and photograph locations tied to local history.

Languages

Imagine what a favourite character would post. Challenge learners to find photos that would appear in a literary character's or writer's Instagram feed. Invite learners to snap photos of their favourite books and then browse the photos in your feed for more ideas on what to read. They could be invited to share their reading recommendations.

Snap photos of a learner's writing at the beginning and end of the year to show progress. Take 10 photos that could serve as a prompt for writing, for example an empty bird's nest, a 'For Sale' sign and a broken doll. Or ask your learners to write an essay based on a sequence of photographs – in essence, you would be asking them to become photojournalists.

Daily journal writing is an excellent way for learners to practise their language and composition skills. However, coming up with fresh topics could be made easier by creating a variety of visual images that can be used as writing prompts. Try close-ups or different angles of common objects. You can ask learners to free-write on the image or use a caption to ask a question or offer a fill-in-the-blank sentence. Photo prompts can also be used as an interesting lead-in to essays in other subjects. For example, distribute photos of topography for learners to identify before writing a geography paper.

Science

Record progressive steps in a science experiment. Watch as a plant unfurls or a chemical compound slowly changes colour, and preserve these changes on Instagram. Remember to add a caption with instructions for each step. Then upload the images to the class page so learners can follow instructions from anywhere.

Art

Take a picture of learners re-creating a famous piece of art. Arrange the learners with or without costumes and set pieces, and have them add their own twist to the artwork. This works for just about any medium depicting people. You can also record the steps in their art production for future reference.

Mathematics

Set a project that would require the learners to find and photograph geometric shapes in nature. This is a good method for teaching Fibonacci's sequence and Pi.

> **To remember when using social media applications**
> - Make alternative arrangements for learners who do not have access to smart phones.
> - Instagram limits registering accounts to those aged 13 or older.
> - Before posting any photos of learners, be sure to get permission from the parents and the school first.
> - Get your headmaster and HoD on board before you begin with any social media project.
> - Set your privacy settings so only approved users are able to access your class photos.
> - You must engage with the learners' postings. This takes time, but inspires the learners to write.

Other photo-sharing apps

Snapchat is another photo application through which learners can share personal photos and videos with friends. Snap a photo or a video, send it to your friends, and it will instantly disappear after they view it. Learners could respond orally or in writing to the photo. As the teacher, you will need to ensure some learning takes place and that this is not just a fun time for the learners. Flickr also allows users to take stunning photos and instantly share images with groups on platforms such as Facebook, Twitter and Tumblr. You can enhance your photos by using built-in filters, editing features and geo-tagging. Photobucket and Shutterfly both allow you to personalise and create photo books, photo cards and stationery (which can be ordered online) and still share it with your friends and family. Google+ is an online photo editor that allows you to apply special effects, manually (with Android) or automatically, often using multiple sequential shots. Effects include composite motion in a single image, short animation, photo-booth style and high-dynamic range rendering. Google+ is also integrated with all the Google apps, so it can be used interactively in the Google classroom.

Blogging

A weblog (or blog for short) is generally defined as a website containing a writer's own experiences, observations and opinions. It often has images and links to other websites. This is a form of journaling and is easily created and updated without any knowledge of HTML. Blogs that are specifically aimed at education are called Edublogs. What makes a blog so effective is that it becomes the intellectual property of the writer, who creates an online identity.

A blogger's voice is unique and a well-written blog will engage the reading audience. One of the best parts of blogging is that bloggers don't have to be trained writers. Most blogs are written in a conversational tone, which is warm and inviting. Blogging allows the educator to guide the growth of a learner's digital footprint, with advice about the correct use of language and safety precautions for the use of the World Wide Web.

The key features of blogging are:
- the reverse chronological order of posts
- an easy-to-use hyperlinked post structure
- an open-to-anyone nature
- a comment option that fosters feedback and interaction.

From an educational perspective, blogging with these features has the potential to support learner interaction, enhance learner engagement and provide an environment for collaboration and knowledge creation. Blogging is regarded as a natural tool for writing instruction and, as research has shown, it fits very well with the principles of the process approach to teaching writing.

No matter what subject you teach, reflective practice (metacognition) is something you can use to encourage learners to write and think about their learning. Blogs also allow learners to express themselves creatively, to connect with people, to learn, to make a difference and to establish themselves as an 'expert' in their field. However, the secret to blogging success is that learners have to write often and be passionate about what they are writing, love to read and be willing to learn.

A teacher's enthusiasm is often the driving force in determining the success of an assignment of this nature. Group work can be assigned to learners and the groups can post summaries of the content they generate. Learners can do their writing assignments in the form of blog posts. Another option is for peer assessment to take place, where learners comment on each other's posts and provide feedback on the work that has been generated. You need to give your learners as much guidance as possible. An assignment ought to be effective if it has been well-crafted and extends over time. For example, you could create an assignment for which learners are expected to write one blog post a week for six weeks.

Since blogging is a writing application, various types of writing can be assigned. The use of argumentation also flourishes in a blogging context. Learners can write an opinion piece so that all learners then engage with each other's topics, permitting lively discussions to arise from the opinions shared on the blog. More ideas include learners sharing various stories in the news, and writing reviews of books, television programmes, fashion trends and more. They could create how-to lists of subject-specific content. They could write about success stories or heroes in your subject field. They could also write reflective pieces on people that they have interviewed. The list is endless. If there is a writing assignment that could be done on paper, then it can be converted into a blog post with the added benefit of multiple people being able to read the post and comment on it.

> **What are the challenges of blogging?**
> As with all online applications, there are a number of challenges involved with using social media in the classroom, but none of these are insurmountable.
>
> ■ **Maintaining online anonymity and privacy issues**
> Your learners must be made aware of the dangers of posting personal information online. It is always advisable to create an anonymous blog when you start out to ensure the safety of the learners in your class.
>
> ■ **Time commitment**
> Writing takes time, and good writing takes even more time. It is important to impress this aspect of blogging on your learners. Even though a blog uses conversational and colloquial language, the content of the post needs to be planned and researched before writing can begin. The audience needs to be considered. And what you want to say must be communicated in a manner that is interesting or unusual.

■ Technological demands

The technological demands of creating a blog page and writing numerous blog posts can be offputting to learners and teachers alike. Not only is a certain 'tech savvy' required to blog well, learners need access to computers and the internet, which might not be available to many learners. You could collaborate with the computer teacher to create an integrated assignment that incorporates cross-curricula outcomes.

Exposing learners to online web applications is invaluable in developing 21st-century literacies. We are no longer living in a world where we just access information. Instead, we too participate in the creation of information. As a teacher you may need to develop pedagogy that includes teaching learners to use technology effectively to communicate. In addition, they need to know how to safeguard themselves against online predators. Learners also need to be taught to distinguish between false and credible information.

By bringing the digital world into the classroom, teachers are able to extend the sphere of knowledge and in many cases link learning to a digital world learners know well, allowing them to develop their unique digital footprints in a responsible manner.

26

Eliciting positive behaviour

Michael Biccard and Philip Mirkin

'Discipline is about positive behaviour management aimed at promoting appropriate behaviour and developing, in learners, self-discipline and self-control' (Joubert, 2008: 5). The focus should not be on punishment or fear. Let's look at the difference between negative and positive discipline in Table 26.1.

Table 26.1 Differences between negative and positive discipline

Negative discipline	Positive discipline
Reactive	Proactive
Punishment	Positive behaviour management by raising learners' awareness of the consequences of their behaviour for their chances of success or of disrupting others
Demerits, detention, daily report, disciplinary hearings	Applying a policy of Assertive Discipline and explaining why the discipline is needed
Punishment focuses on misbehaviour and may do little or nothing to help a learner behave appropriately in the future	A teacher-directed activity whereby we seek to lead, guide, direct, manage or confront a learner about behaviour that disrupts the rights of others
Requires control through punitive measures, where discipline is equated with punishment	A process through which learners learn control, direction and competence as well as a sense of caring
The adult who punishes the child teaches the child that the adult, rather than the child, is responsible for the way the child behaves.	Good discipline is a process, not a single act. It needs to be purposefully planned. The ultimate goal of discipline is for learners to take charge of their own behaviour, take initiative and be responsible for their choices, and respect themselves and others.

Adapted from Joubert (2008)

Perhaps you will find that the discipline you were subjected to was a negative type of discipline. Think to yourself: Did it work? For everyone? Is there a different and better way of disciplining? Let's look at one positive model of discipline, called Assertive Discipline.

Assertive Discipline

The aim of the Assertive Discipline (Canter & Canter, 2001) programme is to teach learners how to make the correct choices when it comes to their behaviour. In so doing, their self-esteem is raised and thus their academic success will be boosted. The programme is based on consistency, follow-through and positive relationship building. The key is the belief that teachers have the right to teach and learners the right to learn – thus all who are concerned are being empowered:

- Teachers, through established rules and clear routines, leave learners no doubt as to what is expected of them at all times.
- Learners are rewarded for following instructions through supportive feedback.
- Firm disciplinary boundaries are secured within the classroom, which encourages a secure learning environment for all. With this sense of security comes academic success.

The classroom management plan

- Your commitment and responsibility as a teacher is to have a classroom that is safe and orderly: a positive learning environment for the learners and a positive teaching environment for the teacher.
- The classroom management plan has rules for behaviour, supportive feedback when learners follow the rules, and actions that will correct the behaviour of learners who choose to break the rules.
- The management plan is made up of three components: The rules, corrective actions and supportive feedback.

The rules

The body of rules is agreed upon by all through consultation. Spend some time talking to your class about the rules they think are important. Perhaps the school you are at already has a short list of rules. The rules should be displayed on the classroom wall and referred to all the time. These rules apply to behaviour and focus on the required behaviour before real learning can take place. The following example covers almost anything that could happen in a classroom.

Five rules that the learners will abide by (Canter & Canter, 2001; LRPS, 2018):
1. Follow instructions.
2. Keep your hands, feet, objects and unkind words to yourself.
3. Listen while somebody else is speaking.
4. Look after all property.
5. Behave appropriately.

Corrective actions
1. Learners deserve structure, and they deserve limits. There is nothing more harmful to learners than allowing them to misbehave.
2. Corrective actions are consequences. Explain to the learner what specific behaviour has led to corrective action being taken. Also explain that the corrective action is to help him or her as well as the class to learn.
3. Corrective actions must be things that learners do not like, such as apologising to the whole class. Corrective actions must *never* be physically or psychologically harmful.
4. Corrective actions do not have to be severe to be effective.
5. Corrective actions must be appropriate to the learners and easy to implement, for example time out and written assignments. It should also be appropriate to the situation. Being rude may require an apology rather than writing out lines.
6. Check the school policy for corrective actions approved by the school.
7. *No* corporal punishment is allowed in any South African school.

Keeping track of corrective actions
A tracking book is one way of recording corrective actions. You could use a file with class lists or a book with a page for each learner. The tracking book allows you to record incidents that you may need to refer to later when meeting with parents or the SMT. Write the date, a short description of the event and the action you took.

Serious misconduct must be reported to your grade leader or HoD.

Supportive feedback
Supportive feedback is the sincere and meaningful attention given to the learner for behaving according to the teacher's expectations.

Supportive feedback is a system of rewarding learners when they follow the rules. Try to think of supportive feedback that is appropriate for your school and grade. Stickers, stars on a chart or a certificate to take home could work.

How to handle difficult learners

A small percentage of learners will probably fall into the category of difficult learners. The challenge facing us is how to deal with them effectively (Canter & Canter, 2001):

- **Build positive relationships.** A special effort needs to be made to establish positive relationships with difficult learners. The time before learners enter your classroom is a good time to make contact and briefly discuss your expectations for the lesson. If you feel able to negotiate these expectations and give them some choice, the learners will feel respected and will be more likely to stick to the agreement. It also helps you to remind them should they forget the agreement during the lesson. The difficult learner needs to be shown that the teacher cares for him or her as a unique individual and that the teacher is 'on his or her side'. Treat learners the way you would have wanted to be treated in school.
- **Conduct a one-on-one problem-solving meeting** with the learner to discuss specific behavioural problems. The interview includes reaching agreement on a course of action to be taken to remedy the problem. Often a public 'shouting at' and handing out of punishment does not assist the learner to change his or her behaviour.
- **Develop an individualised behaviour plan.** The purpose of this plan is to help the learner behave responsibly and to help you develop a positive relationship with each learner.
- **Gain support from parents and administrators.** The support of parents and the SMT for the learner's individualised behaviour plan is critical. Personal contact with the parents is vital.

The following is a summary of how to establish assertive discipline in your classroom (adapted from Canter & Canter, 2001):
1. Have a classroom management plan.
2. Clearly display the 'rules' poster on the classroom wall.
3. Establish corrective actions and inform the learners of these.
4. Keep track of corrective actions.
5. Give supportive feedback.
6. Teach responsible behaviour.
7. Handle difficult learners firmly but with respect.
8. Prepare your lessons.
9. Reward/acknowledge good conduct.
10. Establish routines.
11. *Be consistent!*

The naughty class

Dealing with a learner on a one-to-one basis regarding discipline is one thing, but when you have a difficult class, there is more you may need to consider.

Children are very intelligent and creative. They may not use all this intelligence to do work, but instead to have some fun or simply to get attention in negative ways. If you can remember that no child is naturally rude or disruptive, then you are already much closer to finding a solution strategy. Children who have not learnt appropriate ways of getting what they need and children who do not believe in the education that they are getting can easily become bored or frustrated and begin to act out negatively in class. All these are simply signs that the learner is having a problem engaging positively with the work. Do *not* take this personally. The sooner you realise that nothing is personal in the classroom (even when their comments are personal), the better.

If the class becomes difficult to manage because of a few learners, do *not* try to solve the problem with the whole class. In particular, do not mete out punishment to the whole class. There will always be those learners who are not responsible for the chaos and you may lose their goodwill if they get punished because of the others.

The ringleader

Your primary objective in such a situation is to form a respectful, working relationship with each learner in the class, but focus initially on the ringleaders. The ringleader may take centre-stage in bad behaviour, but may also get others to do things while he or she hides in the crowd. It is usually easy to identify these ringleaders because the other learners tend to look at them to see their reaction when something happens. Ringleaders are usually highly intelligent and resourceful children who are using their skills and abilities in negative ways. If you can get them to see that you have respect for them and their genius, that is usually enough to begin a rehabilitation. You can use the time before class or outside the classroom to form a respectful relationship with the most disruptive learners. Humour and genuine warmth towards them are often your most powerful tools to help these learners realise that you are a human being with whom they can work.

If the problem has continued for a long time, or was even established before you came along, you will need to call in the help of a more experienced teacher or the learners' parents. If you can't form a respectful relationship with such learners within three lessons or one week, you must call in help.

At the start of your career you have enough to focus on without having to learn the difficult task of knowing how to manage difficult learners without help.

With the learner

Stay connected and ask questions. If you are truly interested in the learner, he or she will sense it and be more likely to be honest and open about his or her challenges. Whatever the difficulty, the basic need of being human is to be seen, heard and accepted. If you make this your priority, the learner will be more open to any suggestions for change in behaviour that you may suggest. If there is no improvement within three such conversations, you must get outside help. In time, you will learn strategies to manage specific types of challenges more directly. If you see each such challenging learner as an opportunity to learn more about humanity, you will have the best chance of success. Trust your instincts, but test them out by asking questions. For example, if you think the learner is lying, ask him or her in a non-threatening manner, 'I will understand if you have been lying. I know that the threat of punishment may be scary for you, but the only way for us to move past this is to be honest. Please tell me, did you lie about ...?'

A powerful technique for building trust with learners is to form an empathic connection. You can do this by checking with them if you have understood them correctly. If you tell them what you think they are saying, in your own words, and ask them if this is correct, they will experience themselves being reflected back through you. This helps them to feel heard and that their views are being respected. If you can accurately reflect back to them the events, together with their feelings and concerns, they will trust you and be more open to possible solutions. An empathic connection is very helpful in avoiding or resolving conflict.

Some practical guidelines that may help you with your general classroom discipline include the following:

- If a learner starts to misbehave and you are busy, you can usually stop the misbehaviour by giving the learner a long, hard look. This will show the learner that you have noticed what is happening.
- Draw the learner's attention to the undesirable behaviour. For example, tell the learners that it is not acceptable to eat in class.
- If some learners are getting restless, you can command them to pay attention. If many learners are getting restless, you may need to ask yourself if you are talking too much and getting boring.
- Draw attention to good behaviour. For example, you could say, 'Well done. Group Yellow is working nice and quietly.'

- Ignore poor behaviour and praise good behaviour. The learners behaving badly should notice this and try to get your approval.
- If a learner is misbehaving while you are teaching, you can move towards the learner; he or she will usually stop the misbehaviour.
- If a learner is not paying attention, ask him or her a relevant question.
- If a learner is consistently inattentive, seat him or her at the front of the class where it is not so easy to misbehave. You may even find that the learner has a sight or hearing problem.
- Encourage groups to discipline by disapproval. If one learner is not working well in a group, the disapproval of his or her peers will usually encourage him or her to do better (Prinsloo & Van Schalkwyk, 2008: 172).
- Your classroom layout is important. Ensure that you can see everyone (and that they can see you). Also ensure that there is enough space so that you can move to all areas of the classroom. You may need to change the arrangement regarding where school bags are left, but check the school policy (and the weather). Moving around the classroom helps you monitor and control discipline. Change where you stand in the classroom frequently so that you can observe all learners. When learners look up from their work to see 'where you are', it is an indication that possibly they have finished the task or cannot continue with the work. Assist them before they find 'something else' to do.

A word of advice on corporal punishment

Corporal punishment is not only about giving a child a hiding with a cane. It is a great deal more and is defined as a deliberate act against a child to inflict pain or physical discomfort in order to control the child. Corporal punishment includes but is not limited to spanking; slapping; pinching; hitting with a hand or any object; denying or restricting the child's use of the toilet; denying meals, drink, heat and shelter; pushing or pulling a child with force and forcing the child to do exercise (as punishment).

Be aware that all forms of corporal punishment are regarded as an act of assault. Assault can be defined as the unlawful and intentional application of force to the body of another person or threat of immediate personal force to another person in circumstances where the threatened person believes that the person threatening him or her has the intention and power to carry out the threat. Therefore, even threatening to assault a person is regarded as assault in terms of the law.

26 – Eliciting positive behaviour

Consequences of corporal punishment

The South African Schools Act, Act 84 of 1996, prohibits corporal punishment and provides for any person who contravenes it to be guilty of an offence and liable on conviction to a sentence that could be imposed for assault.

Corporal punishment and assault become associated more with the fear of power than the respect for authority.

Be warned: touch or threaten a child in any way and you may end up in court!

27

Talking like a teacher

Heather Erasmus and Rinelle Evans

As a teacher, most of your daily tasks centre on talking and listening, and thus these communicative skills need to be well developed. Your primary role is to create an environment in which learning can take place effectively. Each time learners enter your classroom, a communicative episode takes place involving yourself, the subject matter and the learners. Each time you speak, you are sending some message to the learners: perhaps you are explaining complex content or demonstrating a particular skill. Perhaps you are managing behaviour or completing administrative tasks. 'Teacher talk' is *everything* you say when you're in the classroom. It is also a technical term used to refer to the characteristic and often simplified, more focused and deliberate style of speech that teachers use to facilitate their engagement with learners, especially in an instructional context. It includes repetition and rephrasing as well as the typical patterns of interaction with learners, such as posing questions to the class, getting a response from a learner and then evaluating the response.

Teacher talk can also take the form of instructions on how to do a task or correct it. It may consist of feedback on the homework assignment, comments on performance or a summary of a lesson. No matter what message you send, your learners need to understand what you are saying and respond appropriately. If you as the initiator of instructional communication are not clear in your communication and careful in your listening, there is also the potential for misunderstandings to arise.

> **How to communicate effectively**
> - During an informal chat, we usually speak at the rate of ± 130–140 words per minute. You will have to slow down to a more moderate speech rate of ±110 words per minute when teaching. You will need to adapt the speed at which you talk to the level and age of the learners.
> - Speak with confidence so that you sound authoritative but not intimidating.
> - Vary your speed and volume. Use quick phrases, followed by slow, measured speech, repetition, pauses and a low tone of voice. It is monotonous when your voice and speed remain constantly flat and uninspiring.
> - Articulate clearly and pronounce words in a comprehensible manner.

Talking like a teacher generally means that you need to speak more slowly and clearly than usual, repeating the same thing in several ways and using expressions particularly associated with education, classrooms and textbooks.

Proficiency in the medium of instruction

Currently, in South African schools many teachers are expected to teach using a language in which they do not have full proficiency. Based on our country's multilingual nature and various language-in-education policies, this is, increasingly, English. It is assumed that since you speak English socially with reasonable fluency, you will be able to teach content effectively through the medium of English. Being able to speak the medium of instruction well does not imply that you are able to teach comfortably in that language. Yet you will be expected to use the language of teaching and learning fluently, accurately, coherently and appropriately. Not being proficient in the medium of instruction will hinder learners' full participation in the learning experience.

Willis (1985: 5) defines Classroom English as:

> *The specialised and idiomatic forms of the English used when teaching that enable teachers to use English effectively and imaginatively as a means of instruction or as a means of organising a class or even a means of communicating with their learners as individuals about their life outside the classroom.*

(A similar definition would be applicable to Zulu, Afrikaans or any language used when teaching.) See Appendix E for some useful expressions to use during various phases of a lesson.

Your spoken input is particularly important if your learners hear little or no English outside your classroom. In such cases, you are the only source of good spoken English your learners will have. Consult an electronic pronunciation guide or dictionary that has phonetic references when you are unsure of how to pronounce a word. Let's now look at a few common communicative functions that arise in every classroom.

Explaining concepts

When you explain new concepts or content, start by linking the new knowledge or skill to what the learners already know about the topic, and how it relates to their world. It is a sound pedagogical principle to start from the known and move to the unknown and also to work from the simple to the complex. This helps learners as they try to understand the content of your lesson.

Subjects have their own special vocabulary. We cannot assume that everyone in the diverse classes we teach understands all the vocabulary. We may have to code-switch to facilitate understanding – it is your duty as the teacher to ensure that vocabulary is not a barrier to understanding. While you are giving explanations, you need to ensure that what you said was clear. We do this through clarification techniques.

Do not wait for learners to ask you to clarify something. Anticipate that someone in the class may be struggling and either repeat what you have said in another way (rephrase) or ask a learner to explain it to the class. In this way you will see who understood, and also allow those who did not to have it explained again quietly without 'losing face'. We should try to avoid embarrassing learners, by giving them opportunities to learn at a different pace. Never ignore a request for clarification.

Asking questions

Once you have presented the new content, you need to see if the learners have understood it. Most teachers ask questions to check understanding. A question is used when you want to get an answer. It is characterised by a rising inflection in speech, and generally starts with an interrogative word such as 'who', 'when', 'why', 'how', 'what' or 'which'. The basic questioning pattern is that the teacher asks a question, learners answer and then the teacher gives feedback on their responses.

In classroom settings, teacher questions are defined as instructional cues or stimuli that help learners grasp the content to be learnt. Often a great deal of teaching time is spent on asking questions. But not all questions guide the learners to a better understanding of the content. Sometimes teachers keep asking poorly formulated, irrelevant, often unanswerable questions because they do not know how to explain the work.

Different types of questions stimulate different kinds of thinking. Therefore, it is important for you as the teacher to be conscious of the purpose of your questions. Teachers could use questions for the following *purposes*:
- to establish what learners already know
- to encourage learners to become actively involved in lessons
- to stimulate learners' interest in a particular topic
- to evaluate learners' readiness for a learning session
- to check that homework has been done
- to develop critical thinking skills and inquiring attitudes
- to review and summarise previous lessons

27 – Talking like a teacher

- to nurture insights by exposing new relationships
- to assess whether the instructional goals have been achieved
- to improve the quality and quantity of learner engagement.

No matter what question you ask, keep one thought in mind: Does the way I am asking the question allow learners to explore whether they really understand what I have taught them, or are they just repeating something mindlessly? Your questions can be oral or on worksheets. Whichever way you present them, they indicate your skill in allowing learners to show evidence of understanding in their answers.

How to ask effective questions
As you plan each lesson, you should formulate at least three key questions and write these down in your planning. The following points explain the process of asking questions to help the learners to master content and develop critical thinking skills:

- Firstly, pose an open-ended question. Where possible, put the question in writing on the chalkboard or project it on a screen.
- Next you must pause. Allow 3–5 seconds for thinking time. This permits learners to organise their thoughts, and possibly even translate them from their mother tongue into the language used for instruction.
- Now you can call on a learner to respond. There are several innovative ways in which you can nominate a learner without the class knowing in advance who will be chosen.
- Depending on the answer, you may have to rephrase your question, especially if the response is not the one you had hoped for. Another effective way of getting more detail is simply by repeating the same question again.
- You may also have to refocus the learners' thinking, for example: 'That is a good answer but is it related to the next topic?'
- You could redirect the response to another learner, for example: 'Do you agree with that comment?'
- You could also ask a follow-up question in order to reinforce the new concept or information.
- You may need to prompt a learner who struggles to formulate an appropriate answer or who claims not to know the answer. Give a hint or ask another question to guide the learner closer to the expected answer.
- In order to guide the learners to a deeper understanding of the work, you could ask a series of probing questions. This helps the learners offer more detailed and complex responses.

- You may need to ask questions in order to clarify. This means asking the learner to provide more information due to a poorly organised, incomplete answer or when insufficient detail has been provided.
- You may not always have to verbalise a question. Sometimes your body language, facial expression or gestures can elicit a response from a learner.
- As the teacher you need to listen closely to the learner's response to establish that the intended meaning has been received and understood. Ask follow-up questions if the answer is not exactly what you anticipated.
- Value learners' answers, even if they are not quite what you wanted.
- Check for evidence of understanding. Do not just ask, 'Do you understand?'
- Consider your physical position when a learner asks a question. Rather stand further away and repeat the questions so that all the learners can hear the question.
- Look around while you move about. Keep an eye on the rest of the learners when you speak to a specific learner. Someone may give up hope of asking a question if you do not acknowledge his or her raised hand!
- Ensure that your question formulation was correct and precise in order to elicit a correct answer.
- Follow up on a learner's response. Use the answer to lead the learner to discovery (the heuristic approach) and to share incidental knowledge. Use learners' own, rich experiences to complement your teaching. Exploit the learners' questions or contributions. You are not the only source of information.

Giving feedback

This generally takes place after a learner has offered an answer to your question. Feedback is often evaluative – that means you as the teacher assess whether the learner has understood. However, be careful: a learner's response may be very different from the one you expected or it may even be incorrect. If the answer is actually wrong, you probably need to ask more questions in order to guide the learner to self-correction. The way you give feedback can either encourage a learner to thinking differently or it can be demotivating. Imagine that as a learner you have tried to give an answer that you thought was correct and the teacher dismisses your answer and goes on to another learner. Would you volunteer again?

Giving instructions

If you pay attention to your own teacher talk, you will notice that much of the language you use is in the form of an instruction or a command, starting with a verb, for example: 'Look at the board! Open your books on page 3! Take out your exercise books! Keep quiet! Underline the date. Repeat after me!' The tone in which you speak will determine whether the learners experience you as an army commander or a teacher keen to assist them in understanding. Generally, if many learners ask questions or give incorrect responses to a task, you are most likely guilty of giving poor instructions.

Some practical suggestions for ensuring understanding and co-operation the first time round include the following:

- Make sure right from the start that all learners understand the terminology used in your subject, for example 'text', 'passage', 'stanza', 'conjunction', 'milieu'. Also do not assume that they know concepts generally expected of their age in English, for example, 'Line up! Pay attention!'
- Insist on absolute silence and full attention before giving instructions. Maintain eye contact. Use simple language and short sentences. Break your instructions up into manageable chunks. Speak slowly but firmly. Do not rattle on for minutes and expect the learners to remember everything. Check for effective comprehension. Repeat or rephrase the instruction, if necessary.
- Stagger or chunk your instructions and give them in a logical order.
- Where possible, back up instructions with visual material (worksheets/charts/chalkboard). Stand where you can be seen clearly by all. Enlarge your gestures and movements as well.
- Allow for questions from learners before giving a definite signal when to start the task.
- For complicated instructions, call one learner from each row or group and explain the task to them, making sure each facilitator understands fully what is to be done. This lessens the likelihood of learners going off track. You can then move from desk to desk checking whether matters are progressing. Interrupting a learner in order to correct the course of action is far less disruptive than trying to get the whole class to refocus.
- Avoid interrupting tasks with new explanations, announcements or general comments. This breaks the learners' concentration and causes frustration as well as doubt in your ability to organise. Once you give the task, allow the learners to get on with it in peace.

It will be well worth your while to test your skill at giving instructions occasionally by asking a colleague to check your performance or to record yourself, if you have the means.

Praising learners

Effective praise can be directed at an individual learner or the whole class when you want to reinforce a particular behaviour. No matter what the age of a learner, he or she will appreciate being praised for a task well done. In the classroom, praise becomes a powerful motivator and even a tool for improving behaviour. Praise a learner as soon as possible after you have noticed the achievement or progress. Younger learners need immediate encouragement, while teenagers can mostly accept delayed praise. Giving praise effectively is simple:

- Avoid general phrases such as, 'Great work!' or 'Nice job!' Just saying 'Well done!' does not reinforce what was done well. Direct your praise at a particular learner or skill. Your words of praise should be linked to specific behaviours that led to success. Describe what the learner has done well. It may be academically related, an improvement in a skill or just a word of gratitude for co-operation, punctuality or assistance given.
- Show your approval non-verbally too. Make eye contact with the learner. Smile. Be sincere and enthusiastic. Stand near the learner.
- Praise frequently and consistently, but avoid praising trivial accomplishments or weak efforts. Praise must be earned and never be considered cheap.
- Be specific in your praise and state the effort that is evident. Learners need to make the link between input and end results.
- Try to establish what each learner's preference is for being praised. Although most people value public praise, not everyone likes to be in the limelight. Some learners may prefer you to write a comment in their books or to call their parents. Some may even value a wink or thumbs-up more. Motivational stickers and stamps or additions to a chart also serve as praise. Younger learners seem to like public praise while older ones appear embarrassed and often prefer being praised in private. Handing out a reward to someone who deserves it works for any age!
- Do not praise only high marks and academic achievements. Not all learners achieve equally well, since they are not all equally gifted. Praise effort too. An increase from 35 per cent to 40 per cent may be a marked improvement for an immigrant child.
- Look for ways in which to praise each learner: how neatly someone writes, how quickly another completes a task, accuracy, creativity, effort, meeting an outcome, being polite or helpful, accurate pronunciation, correct spelling, using a new word and so on. Keep a conscious account of who was praised each day to ensure no one is left out or over-praised.

- Involve the class in the praise. Consider using silent applause (all children waving their hands in the air without making the noise of clapping).
- Do not combine praise with criticism. This means avoid using the word 'but' immediately after giving a compliment.
- Be sincere in your praise and be careful not to inflate praise.

Generally, praising learners reinforces success, and increases their participation in class.

Code-switching

Although many schools frown on using the mother tongue – in the false belief that hearing English exclusively will help the learners improve their proficiency – there is absolutely no point in using English when the only response you have from the learners is a blank stare or an attempt at looking as though they have understood. It may serve all role-players well if you use the mother tongue or let another learner who has grasped the message explain it to the others in a language they understand. It is morally unacceptable to exclude learners or to allow them to become frustrated and demoralised because they do not understand what is being said, let alone the content. Switching to a common language saves time, and ensures better comprehension and co-operation. Even just translating an unknown word here and there will help learners feel less stupid and engage more with the lesson.

Using silence to communicate

Teachers generally talk too much. Many think that talking indicates they are working. Teachers should not be afraid of silence – a much underrated communication tool – and should use it for effect, to catch their breath, to gain attention and for learners to process the new content. Few realise that silence is also part of fluent speech. Silence is far less confusing than are false starts and verbal mannerisms.

Concentrating on your teacher talk and how you use language will help you use it effectively when teaching. It is vital that you communicate in a clear and simple fashion, as the problems caused by poor explanations or unclear instructions are magnified when a whole class is confused. It is very difficult to rectify misunderstandings and regain order once the learners start looking around agitatedly or asking each other for clarification.

28

Teaching PE when you are not a PE teacher

Elmarie van Wyk

South Africa enjoys exceptionally good weather for most of the year and young children and teenagers ought to be able to spend time outdoors during their leisure hours. We are also a sports-loving country and one would expect learners to enjoy participating in various games or sports. Yet, especially in urban and middle-class communities, children are inclined to spend many hours in front of screens, passively playing electronic games or interacting with their friends on social media. It is also no longer safe for them to cycle or even walk to school, with the result that learners become obese and lack suppleness and are unable to move with ease. Limited movement or motor skills development impacts on other areas of physical development and often affects a child's ability to learn or socialise.

Physical Education in CAPS

PE is currently prescribed as a compulsory topic in the South African Curriculum and Assessment Policy Statement (CAPS) for the subjects Life Orientation (Senior and FET phases) or Life Skills (Foundation and Intermediate phases). PE is deemed so important that it constitutes 50 per cent of the prescribed learning content of Life Orientation per year. CAPS prescribes one hour of practical physical activities and one hour for the other topics per week for all learners. PE is divided into sub-themes that demarcate the type of movement activities prescribed for each school week of the year. This division is called an annual teaching plan and covers the following topics:
- physical and movement development, to help learners gain a variety of motor skills
- numerous games, some with a cultural history, to encourage co-operation and team spirit
- the development of sport skills as well as ethics for traditional and non-traditional sport
- the promotion of indoor and outdoor recreational involvement, aimed at a healthy lifestyle and lifelong participation

- physical fitness education
- rhythmic and dance movement.

(DBE, 2011a–c)

PE is not the same as sports coaching. It takes place during school hours and is part of the formal curriculum. It aims to develop the learner holistically – in body, mind and soul – in such a way that various human movement skills are developed and applied in a playful manner. This subject differs from other school subjects, because here we primarily use the body and physical movements as tools to fulfil prescribed learning outcomes. The benefits of PE include:

- all learners being able to participate regardless of their actual physical abilities
- healthy, physical growth as well as sound social and emotional development
- the attainment of basic sport and motor skills
- possible lifelong participation in movement and recreation
- an awareness of the importance of a healthy lifestyle.

Movement is a necessity while a child is still growing. Developing physical abilities should receive specific attention before the child reaches the age of eight. Children's natural urge for movement and play, as well as the fact that they are less self-conscious, implies that perceptual motor development should start as early as possible. Any strict movement specialisation should ideally only start from the age of 15 onwards.

Even though you may have no training as either a PE teacher or sports coach, you may be expected to assist with this important part of the school curriculum. You may have little affinity for extreme physical activity, but as an adult you ought to understand the importance of caring for one's body through practising healthy habits. You would also recognise that recreation improves social skills, develops leadership skills and even a sense of social responsibility. It must be assumed that the SMT has taken the local climatic conditions into account when scheduling PE periods. You may also be fortunate enough to have another teacher plan the weekly lessons for your grade.

Here are some general guidelines for preparing a PE lesson that learners could look forward to and enjoy:

- Adapt your PE lessons to the available equipment and space. Prepare the space in which you intend to hold the lesson carefully. Create a floor plan to manage activities within the available space. Indicate where to place the

equipment. Make sure that the equipment is ready before the class starts. All other organisational tasks must also be completed.
- Create a disciplined and manageable environment in which to teach. Make sure that learners will be safe and not subject to any injury. Lay down strict codes of conduct and do not tolerate misbehaviour. You are also responsible for the cleanliness and safety of facilities and equipment. You must instruct learners on how to use and handle equipment.
- It is ideal to divide the learners into permanent groups, with group leaders. The lesson should start with learners forming these groups at the beginning of every practical period.
- Where possible, allow learners to wear suitable clothing for PE. If possible, you should also change into appropriate sports gear, such as a tracksuit.
- Endeavour to let every individual learner perform activities and progres in accordance with his or her own ability, gender, interests, culture, talents and knowledge.
- Make sure to plan and prepare activities that include all learners, no matter what their physical abilities. They should all be involved during the lesson and feel part of the group. They should also experience success in what they do. Their confidence should not be shaken. Provide positive feedback and encourage each learner. Adapt or intervene when you see a learner struggling.
- No learner should sit and wait for too long for their turn to participate. Plan extra activities that they can do while waiting.
- Ensure that there is logical progression throughout your lesson, leading towards the desired outcome. Learners must not just be kept busy.
- Learners should only be exempted from participation in the case of medical circumstances. Assign prepared tasks for non-participators.
- Greet your class with enthusiasm. You could perhaps play some up-beat music. Create an atmosphere that is disciplined but relaxed.
- Create a sense of anticipation by linking the purpose of the activity to how it could help the learners' physical development and health. Apart from achieving the prescribed outcome, learners should enjoy the planned activities.
- Make sure that you ease learners into the activity by limbering up. This means slowly warming up the muscles with increased blood circulation and gently stretching muscles. Do not just make learners run around the track or run between markers. A game to push up the heart rate could be used at this stage. Avoid high-intensity activities until the body is ready.

- Maintain a healthy balance between maximum exertion and the correct execution of a movement, especially when new skills are taught.
- Insist that learners adhere to the rules of a game or activity and that they are able to accept defeat or manage victory; this prepares them to deal with similar challenges later in life.
- At the end of the lesson insist that everybody assembles again in their different groups before the class is dismissed. This action restores some tranquility and calms the excited learners before they return to the next lesson or go home.

> **Differentiation in the PE lesson**
> To do justice to each learner and create the opportunity for maximum development and inclusive education, you ought to apply differentiation when planning a PE lesson. By planning differentiated tasks, you will ensure that learners:
> - with talent and interest are not held back or allowed to become bored
> - who are below average or have no experience can be supported without being excluded
> - who do not enjoy movement and sport are not disheartened or discouraged.
>
> So how could you differentiate among learners in the same class?
> - Adapt the steps to be easier for learners who struggle and increase the degree of difficulty to challenge learners with above-average ability.
> - Plan for alternative tasks using the same equipment.
> - Alternate easy and more advanced tasks. Move learners around in accordance with their progress.
> - Sub-divide groups for higher activity levels in your lesson.

It is never easy having to do something that you feel you are not qualified to do. It is a natural reaction to shy away from teaching a lesson that you are not passionate about. Try to think about this aspect of the school week as a broad educational responsibility in the same way as you teach values on the playground or incidentally in class. PE is an important aspect of all learners' holistic development and should lead to the wise use of leisure time and healthy life choices as well as boosting their emerging value system. Make the PE experience meaningful and fun for yourself as well as the learners.

Teaching Mathematics when you are not a 'numbers person'

Piera Biccard

It may happen that you are 'asked' or 'told' by your principal to teach a Mathematics class. This does happen in primary school. Your principal may be left with no other option and his or her reasoning may include that your qualification as a primary school teacher means that you can teach all subjects. Whatever the case, take a deep breath ... you can do this!

Make sure that you have the latest curriculum document and the school's chosen textbook. Fortunately, the latest curriculum document for Grades 4-6 Mathematics (CAPS) has some examples of how to teach the concept or section. Go through the examples carefully and make sure that you understand them. Find the corresponding work in the textbook. Do every single exercise in the textbook. Think of all the problems you had when you worked through the exercises. Your learners will probably experience the same things, so this puts you in a perfect position to understand and explain!

Remember that each Mathematics lesson in the Foundation and Intermediate phase begins with 10 minutes of mental maths. This could be doing tables, bonds or counting exercises. Try to vary the exercises so that your learners do not get bored and so that they can practise many skills. This is the time to get learners warmed up and ready to think mathematically! You could do something called 'number of the day' (see the example on the following page), changing the number each day. The operations you include on the left-hand side should correspond with the grade you are teaching.

An important aspect of Mathematics teaching is that you do not prescribe a method from the beginning. This may be contrary to what you believe Mathematics teaching is and contrary to how you were taught. Give the learners time to think about how they would solve the problem. Encourage them to try their own methods first.

29 – Teaching Mathematics when you are not a 'numbers person'

Number of the day: 20
Add 1
Subtract 1
Add 10
Subtract 10
Divide by 2
Multiply by 3

Figure 29.1 An example 'number of the day' exercise

For example: Ask a Grade 4 or 5 class to solve the problem 18 × 5, and see how many different ways they can find:

```
18 × 5                              18 × 5
 ↓                                  = (20 × 5) − (2 × 5)
= (9 × 5) + (9 × 5)                 = 100 − 10
= 45 + 45                           = 90
= 90

18 × 5                              18 × 5
 ↓                                  = 9 × 10   (halve first, double second)
= (10 × 5) + (8 × 5)                = 90
= 50 + 40
= 90
```

Figure 29.2 Solving the problem 18 × 5

If you think times tables are boring, try this game (Boaler, 2016):
- Give each learner a page with a grid of 100 squares (10 rows and 10 columns). Allow them to work in pairs. Give each pair two dice (one for each learner).
- Each member of the pair gets a turn to roll their die. The learners multiply the numbers and colour in the result on the grid. They try to see how close they can get to filling in the whole block. With older learners you may want to use four dice (two for the first number and two for the second number).

- If you only have four dice, then you roll them and the whole class can work with you on their individual grids. So now they have to add, multiply and then work on where they are going to colour the blocks (area). If you use four dice you can reach 12 x 12 (by using two dice for the first number and two dice for the second number), so you could use a grid with 500 squares.

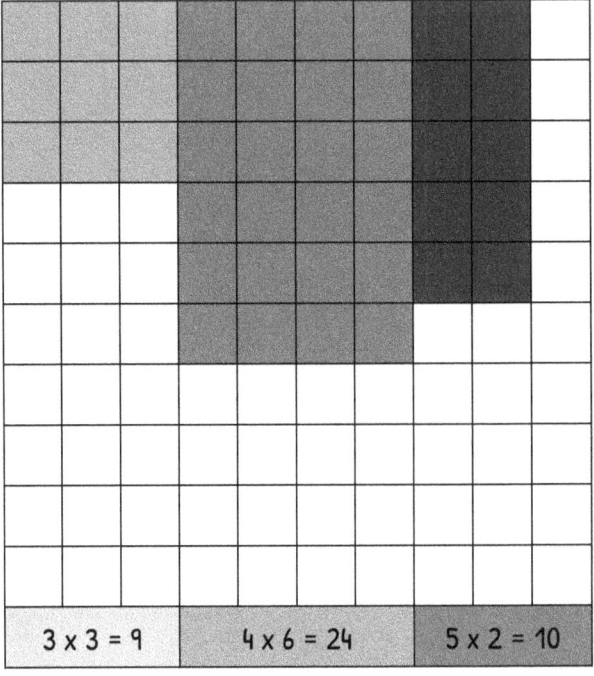

Figure 29.3 The times table game

Allow learners to work in pairs or groups – they learn so much from each other. You will need to tie up the discussions and show how the different methods link to each other. Don't panic if some learners appear quicker or smarter than you. This will happen even with the most competent Mathematics teacher. Use a smart learner's work to check your memo before marking the rest of the learners' work.

Arrange to meet with the HoD each week and check with him or her regarding your teaching strategies. Ask if you can sit in on the lessons of an experienced Mathematics teacher at your school. Ask your school to send you on Mathematics-specific courses so that you can expand your teaching skills in Mathematics. You may find that you are working hard each night before the next day's Mathematics lesson, but eventually you will become more confident and before you know it, you will have been through the entire year's syllabus.

Always try to know more than just what you have to teach. This applies to all subjects, but is especially important for Mathematics. Check the curriculum document and textbooks for the next grade so that you know what is expected in the coming grades.

Be mindful that learners and their parents can be very anxious about Mathematics. You may find that homework is a problem, so never give new work for homework. Rather give tables, or something learners are familiar with that you want them to practise. You may find that you are the most visited teacher during parents' evenings. Every parent wants to know if their child is coping. Prepare to give good advice to the parents of those learners who are struggling. Suggest games that parents can play at home to improve their child's basic counting and times table skills. Sound advice for you as the teacher is not to read out learners' marks or ask them to read out their marks in class, as it places a lot of stress on both the weak and strong learners.

It is important that you understand that Mathematics is not only about following set procedures and that Mathematics lessons are not about you demonstrating a method for the learners to follow. Kilpatrick et al (2001) present five important aspects of Mathematics: conceptual understanding, procedural fluency, adaptive reasoning, strategic competence and productive disposition. As you can see, procedural fluency is only one of five important competencies. Let's look briefly at these five competencies:

- **Conceptual understanding.** Do learners understand the concept – not only a few examples or exercises in the textbook? Can they connect ideas?
- **Procedural fluency.** Can the learners carry out the procedures fluently and appropriately? Do they understand what they are doing when using set procedures?
- **Adaptive reasoning.** Can the learners explain and justify what they are doing? Can they explain what other learners are doing?
- **Strategic competence.** Can the learners come up with different strategies to solve problems?
- **Productive disposition.** Do the learners see Mathematics as something they can construct and understand?

Mathematics teaching is so much more than presenting methods and getting learners to follow these methods. You have to encourage learners to think and reason. You may find that you enjoy teaching Mathematics and cannot imagine teaching a different subject!

30

Dealing with sensitive topics

Johan Wassermann

As teachers we will, at some stage or another, be confronted by topics that we do not agree with, feel embarrassed about, or are unsure of how to engage with. Such topics include race, gender, morality, economics, class, politics, ethics and culture. Apart from your own discomfort with the topic you need to manage the discussion with a class of 40 or more learners, each with their own opinion about it! Remember, too, that many a time you also cause disagreement, not only by what you teach, but also by how you teach it and the teaching and learning materials that you use.

So how would you go about it? Topics are sensitive because some or other aspect thereof might be objectionable or unpleasant to an individual or a whole group of learners. If not well managed, the outcome of a discussion could be that your class becomes polarised by disagreements, with emotions running rampant. This could happen because sensitive topics are in the main multifaceted, have no static point of view and are open to opposing understandings that could test the personal beliefs and values of learners. At the same time you must remember that sensitive topics do not remain constant and depend on contextual conditions. This means that what was considered a sensitive topic 70 years ago might not be one now, and vice versa. Some subjects are considered taboo for particular communities but not for others. It is therefore not always possible to tell when sensitivity will arise. However, unless they are handled well, sensitive topics can spill over and involve the whole school and even the community.

As a novice teacher, you should encourage learners to engage with sensitive issues. You need to guide these young minds to care enough to be inquisitive and to participate in thinking about how topics relate to them and their place in the world. As a result, sensitive topics are generally best taught when learners think of their own allegiances and interests.

You might rightly wonder why you should engage with sensitive topics when they have the potential to divide and disrupt the learning process. The reality is that as a teacher you will find it very difficult to avoid engaging with sensitive topics. Furthermore, there are several reasons why sensitive topics have immense educational value.

First and foremost, the national curriculum expects you to engage with sensitive topics. You are expected to encourage and assist your learners to engage in constructive debates on a broad range of subject-related topics. Very few topics are based on a single truth and learners need to understand that a range of views can exist. The evidence for these topics might also be contradictory. You must thus also teach your learners the skills to constructively engage with such topics. You need to help your learners understand that knowledge can change and that new views and ideas constantly arise. New views and ideas are born when older ones are challenged in a constructive manner with the aim of developing a deeper and more nuanced understanding of a topic. You need to teach your learners to develop a critical mindset with regard to all knowledge and to critically appraise all views, ideas and evidence. This implies that you need to develop in your learners the skills to comprehend that sensitive topics are multi-faceted and complex, as a reflection of the world they live in. Being able to see matters from various perspectives and to evaluate empathetically are skills that need to be taught. So, too, is being able to identify the causes and consequences of actions.

Regardless of the subject content that you will teach, you are preparing your learners to become responsible and thinking citizens of a democratic society. Such citizens need to be able to reflect and skilfully engage with the sensitive social, political, economic and moral challenges that exist in society. Your learners also need to grasp that even when they are critical of a matter, they may experience uncertainty and doubt their own understanding of sensitive topics. This is part of their intellectual growth towards emotional maturity.

Your classroom is thus the ideal place for learners to learn about how to deal with sensitive topics. If they do not learn how to engage courteously with such topics in school they will in all probability never learn to do so. If you do not allow your learners to engage with sensitive topics relevant to their lives for the educational reasons mentioned, you will also lead them to think that school is not the place for engaging with sensitive topics and the related critical thinking.

How to engage with sensitive topics

Now that you have an understanding of why you need to engage educationally with sensitive topics, you also need to consider how to do so. The following four ways will help you in this regard:
1. Knowing yourself as a teacher
2. Knowing the learners in your class

3. Creating an appropriate classroom culture and climate
4. Having an excellent knowledge of your subject.

First and foremost, you need to know yourself as a teacher. This entails knowing yourself emotionally and understanding your ability to manage and debrief your emotions and actions as they relate to sensitive topics. At the same time it is necessary to remember that, as a teacher, you will never be entirely non-aligned, impartial, value neutral and fair-minded. It is therefore vital that you comprehend the influence that you will have on your learners' understanding of sensitive topics. As a figure of authority, much of what you say and do will be regarded as authoritative. You will therefore wield much power and influence over your learners' thoughts and attitudes. You should thus constantly reflect in an honest manner on your own educational practices. Think about the teaching approaches you use, the examples you choose and the likely biases or serious misunderstandings your teaching could cause. In knowing yourself, you should strive towards being open-minded and respectful while adhering to the ground rules for engaging with sensitive topics, as will be explained later.

Should you feel that you want to share your own personal position on a sensitive topic, you should make it clear that other perspectives do exist and that you are not attempting to sideline those. You must therefore allow learners to respectfully challenge your position. This implies that you must know yourself well enough to be comfortable to adopt multiple roles when teaching sensitive topics. You also need to provide a classroom climate and culture conducive for learners to feel able to challenge your point of view. This means knowing where you stand well enough to be a good listener and an impartial judge who acts with dignity regardless of what is said.

Secondly, you should know your learners. You are unlikely to have a homogeneous class in terms of background, class, race, culture, religion, beliefs and values. Consequently, different positions on sensitive topics are guaranteed. By knowing your learners you will be able to work towards pre-empting conflict and recognise misunderstandings and emotional overreactions. This would, in turn, allow you to ensure that the educational value of engaging with sensitive topics is foregrounded and that all learners feel comfortable enough to participate fully in debates, discussions and other educational work.

Thirdly, to create the safe space in which sensitive topics can be discussed, you need to negotiate some rules of engagement with your learners. These rules could include the following:
- Think before you speak.
- Listen to the views and ideas of other learners without interrupting them.
- All views and ideas must receive equal time.
- Offensive and insulting language may not be used.
- Respect and tolerate views and ideas that are different from yours.
- You may not threaten, indoctrinate, stereotype or bully learners who express views or ideas that are different from yours.
- You have the right to express uneasiness about how a debate is taking place and your feelings must be considered by all.
- Ideas and views can be challenged, but you must distinguish between the person and the idea or view proposed.
- Any views or ideas are allowed, as long as suitable evidence is provided in support of the view.
- All evidence presented must be looked at with an open mind in order to find different explanations.

Once agreed upon, these ground rules should be prominently displayed in your classroom. The rules of engagement should allow for a free flow of different perspectives in a supportive and non-threatening learning environment. Under such circumstances your learners would hopefully reflect in a critical manner on the opinions they hold and their consequences by engaging with different perspectives. Without a supportive environment where learners and their thinking are central, meaningful discussion of sensitive topics will not take place.

Finally, you should also have a deep and nuanced content knowledge of the subject you will teach. This includes knowing the intricacies of the sensitive topics that form part of your subject, the different perspectives held and the evidence that they are based on. Your content knowledge base must be underpinned by thorough and methodical planning that aims to expose learners to different and competing views in a balanced and active manner appropriate to their age, as well as their affective and cognitive levels. However, remember that you cannot plan for all eventualities and you will at times be confronted by sensitive topics that you did not anticipate. In such circumstances it is important that you have a sound subject knowledge and appropriate learner-centred teaching methodologies to draw on.

Practical guidelines for teaching sensitive topics

There are many topics that may trigger deep emotions at a very personal level. It may be quite possible that some of the learners in your class have first-hand experience of issues related to topics you address in a lesson. You may be embarrassed or reluctant to address sensitive topics for whatever personal reason. On the other hand, there might be topics that certain learners view as being taboo or sensitive, which you might not realise are viewed in this way. You may need to reflect on your own ingrained or strongly held views.

Common topics that are may be difficult to discuss include the following:

Ethnicity/race relationships	Sexuality	Domestic violence
Gender identity	Mental health	Disability
Politics	Teenage pregnancy/abortion	Rape/sexual abuse
Incest	Paedophilia	Torture
HIV/AIDS	Drugs and alcohol	Death/bereavement
Faith/religion/belief systems	Suicide	Gangsterism/crime

Some learners may express strong and maybe even extreme opinions about a topic. Other learners may be offended or feel so uncomfortable that they do not participate. Some may even become visibly distressed.

- Create a safe space in which learners feel confident to express their views. Establish ground rules that limit turns, and expect reasoned expression and evidence to support an argument. All contributions must be made respectfully.
- Identify topics that may trigger emotions in advance and plan these lessons carefully. You must also research the topic thoroughly. Have a clear learning outcome for the lesson and then guide the learners to achieve this.
- Anticipate the difficulties that may occur in the lesson and think about a way to address them. For example, rather than having a discussion, give learners a sheet of paper on which to write down their views anonymously. These views can be discussed openly without the learners knowing who holds them.
- Define the topic clearly and check learners' understanding of any concepts on which the discussion should be based. Provide key vocabulary or definitions, or use video clips or texts to ensure everyone has similar background knowledge about the topic.

- Identify any topics that you personally may feel uncomfortable to facilitate discussion about.
- Remind learners to focus on the topic rather than on the person expressing an opinion.
- Consider using a signal to interrupt and defuse any situation as soon as you notice a learner's stress. This allows the class to 'cool down' and gives you time to decide how to proceed.
- You may need to debrief the learners so that they can gain perspective and focus on the points of learning.
- Give learners the opportunity to express any concerns they have with you confidentially outside of class. You may need to allow them to stay away. Do not insist on knowing why they feel uneasy about the topic.
- Ask colleagues who have experience of teaching sensitive and controversial issues about their experiences and strategies that have worked for them.

Sensitive topics may vary from school to school as well as age group to age group. In the current curriculum, topics such as evolution (in Social Sciences) or HIV (in Life Orientation) may be sensitive. Other topics such as human reproduction (Natural Sciences) or looking at different religions or child abuse (in Life Orientation) may elicit some discomfort in you, the learners or parents. The Life Orientation curriculum includes issues of age and gender, which may require sensitive navigation depending on your class, school and community. Always keep the discussion age-appropriate – use the parameters of the national curriculum and textbook as a guide. Speak to the HoD before tackling these topics to get some guidance and advice.

31

Revealing the hidden curriculum

Rinelle Evans

In education, we refer to the unintended messages that are sent by texts or teachers as the hidden curriculum. These messages or 'lessons' generally carry negative connotations, as prevailing harmful views about other cultures or subgroups, gender roles and social status may be reinforced. It is generally the dominant culture in a society that dictates what is valued, privileged and shared. In South Africa, currently Western and middle-class ways dominate, and attempts to Africanise and decolonise the way we teach as well as the content we teach are slow. Society in general, as well as schools and textbooks, affect the way children are socialised into a particular way of thinking about, and behaving towards, themselves and others.

The term 'hidden curriculum' was apparently coined by Philip Jackson in 1968. Meighan and Harber (1981: 7) more recently defined this concept by stating that:

The hidden curriculum is taught by the school, not by any teacher ... something is coming across to the learner which may never be spoken about in a lesson or prayed about in assembly. They are picking up an approach to living and an attitude to learning.

These unspoken but implicit academic, social or cultural messages are communicated subtly by posters, the way teachers and learners behave, practices, flags, symbols or statues and even the architecture and maintenance of the buildings. The hidden curriculum has the potential not only to reinforce certain expectations, values or perceptions, but can also be extended to that which is not talked about or is ignored, excluded or ridiculed. For example, insisting that learners speak English during breaks – when everyone, including the teachers, has another language they are more comfortable using – not only strengthens the already high status of English, but also implies that other languages and their speakers are second rate and not important. Such messages, whether intentional or not, result in learners experiencing prejudice or disadvantage and feeling excluded, marginalised and even stigmatised.

The very word 'hidden' implies that you need to look deeply and carefully at long-standing attitudes, beliefs and practices and start to critically question those things that you and others in your community have long accepted. Concealed behind culture and traditions are the foundations of learning particular ways of seeing oneself as well as other people. Most human beings will not question any practice or belief that they are told is part of their culture or tradition; instead they will unquestioningly uphold it without considering its value or relevance. Think of some of the things that you have done or accepted because they are part of the family tradition. Remember all the activities that you have taken part in as a student that you did not quite understand or approve of, but for which defended your actions because you believed they were part of your institution's social or academic culture. The hidden curriculum is often difficult to identify because it is so deeply embedded that we are hardly aware of its presence. It is this hidden curriculum, which is insidiously prevalent in all schools and classrooms, to which we will now turn our attention.

Pay attention to the pictures you put up on your walls, use in your presentations and add to worksheets. What message is being sent? Can your learners relate to these images? Is someone being discriminated against or marginalised even though nothing is said directly in the text? Does a Western, middle-class world view dominate? Critically evaluate the readers, magazines and textbooks you have in your class. Some of the indicators of the hidden curriculum in print material are a disproportionate under-representation of certain people. For example, are the characters representative of the learners in your class? How many ethnic groups are represented? Are most of the characters male? Are characters' roles gendered? Are the female characters all beautiful and sweet while the males are gifted sportsmen or clever scientists? What do the pictures look like? Are they caricatures of certain communities? Do they feed the stereotypical view of 'the other'? Who is portrayed as 'the other', 'they' or 'them'? Often characters that have been identified as black or fat or poor or ugly are marked as different. The hidden message is that if you are different, then you are not like us, and therefore you do not belong. Learners need to experience a strong sense of belonging and any negative associations with indicators of not belonging create emotional discomfort.

Section E
Beyond the classroom

In this final section, we move beyond the classroom to other equally important matters that affect you as a teacher. The topics we present are diverse, but may set you apart from other teachers. We want you to be a great teacher! We all know that teaching extends to your extramural activities, so we look at the role and importance of coaching in your career as a teacher. You will most likely remember your hours on the sport field very fondly when you retire! Ask any teacher and they will tell you that, at one point or another, you will be involved in organising a school function, so we provide you with some structure to organise and plan a school function, whether it is a Big Walk, soccer day or concert. We also remind you that as a teacher, you are expected to be a 'lifelong learner'. We provide you with some ideas and resources for your further professional development, which is very important in keeping you on top of your game, motivated and relevant in today's classroom. You give so much of yourself every day; you need to 'put something back'. Some of you may want to study further or you may be interested in understanding the complexities of learning better. We look at the possibilities of the teacher as a researcher in education. We will provide some advice about saving, investing and insurance and invite you to explore these avenues of looking after your finances early in your career. We conclude this section with some tips from top teachers. This is good advice on a wide range of topics, based on what experienced teachers have learnt from being in the classroom. Take what they say to heart!

Education is the most powerful weapon which you can use to change the world.
Nelson Mandela

The teacher as coach

Elmarie van Wyk

The main objective of coaching sport is to develop learners' skills and help them master the intricacies of the particular sport code. Participating in sport should be about far more than strenuous training for competition or performance. But of course you would like your team to succeed; possibly even win the trophies! Coaching a sport as an extramural activity allows you to get to know the learners on an entirely different level. Establishing a different relationship with learners outside of class often helps with the relationship in an academic context. Encourage learners to participate in sport and enjoy it. Participation is more than competing against other schools or clubs, so even if there are no formal or official opportunities in a league, create the opportunity for those who want to participate in sport even if you have the minimum resources.

Do's of coaching

You will gain respect and endear yourself to learners if you do the following:
- Show them you understand the sport and know its strategies and rules, even though you may not have played it yourself.
- Be well prepared for and enthusiastic about each coaching session.
- Display a positive attitude at all times, even when the team has lost.
- Warm up and stretch your muscles carefully and well. Make this part of the session a fun and interesting one. Avoid doing the same style of limbering up each session. Supervise the session yourself unless you have a responsible captain. Participating in the pre-practice warm-up makes the team respect you and increases team spirit.
- Create a personal relationship with each individual. Acknowledge, accept and respect them for who they are. Define and explain the role that each individual member of the team plays so that they all feel important. Praise all for their effort and participation.
- Try to turn every disastrous move into a learning opportunity. Use humour to alleviate pressure.
- Always place learners' safety and wellbeing first.
- Create short- and long-term goals for each individual and the team.

- Involve the learners in organisational activities for the team. For example, assign some team members to carry the tog bags, others to set up the nets, someone to keep score or bring the water bottles. Sometimes learners who do not want to play sport are also keen to help on the sidelines.
- Always use positive feedback to encourage and improve individual and team skills.
- Create enjoyment using games to teach and apply sport skills.
- Always be an example and provide them with something to strive for.
- Be strict but always consistent and fair.
- Sit on the ground with them when you discuss issues and arrangements.
- Identify and respect their real potential from the start.
- Remember that organised chaos is sometimes fine.
- Use additional activities for improving skills, for example use dance at soccer practice.
- Make the fitness training fun without the learners realising that they are building fitness.
- Before ending the coaching session, make each learner feel that he or she has achieved and contributed.
- Include social events such as eating ice cream after practice to build team spirit, if at all financially possible.

Don'ts of coaching

- It is not acceptable to be late or just not show up.
- Be wary of coaching technical events – such as high jump, shot put, javelin or any others that involve equipment – without sound knowledge of techniques. Don't make up your own – ask for assistance!
- Do not bend your rules.
- Do not criticise or put the learners down.
- Do not favour some team members above the others.
- Do not cancel a practice or postpone a match without very good reason.
- Do not blame your team's lack of success on the learners. Be objective and fair when assessing the reason for a loss.
- Do not give in to parental or management pressure. Stick to principles and measurable reasons why someone is picked for the team.
- Do not be too serious or competitive.

> Consider qualifying as an umpire or referee if you do not wish to coach the sport. This implies that you still get to enjoy being with learners in a different context but as a different type of expert. If you do not enjoy any outdoor activities, start a club or public speaking class. Teaching learners skills that they do not learn in class is a very satisfying experience and adds so much value to your career and a young person's life.

School sport should not be primarily about winning, but about teaching the learners valuable life lessons such as commitment, loyalty, determination, fairness and perseverance. As a coach it is wise to step back occasionally and reflect on why you are coaching. Winning is not everything when working with learners; it is also not always their reason for participating in sport. It has been proven scientifically that constant competitive participation could be destructive. Remember that you are coaching for many reasons besides being first on the league table. Coaching also offers you excellent opportunities for talking informally about making the right life choices, and healthy living. Playing sport improves learners' general wellbeing, may keep them off the streets and out of trouble and is a positive form of socialisation.

33

Planning a school function

Ronél de Villiers and Rinelle Evans

Function halls are usually packed for the traditional end-of-year prize-giving, matric dance or stage performances. Excited children race around backstage; proud parents have fully charged the batteries on their phones or tablets and arrive early to practise tight close-ups of their little darlings. Everyone remembers their first time on stage. Whether it was playing an 'Oompa Loompa' in *Charlie and the Chocolate Factory* or being the lead angel in the nativity play, we still remember the thrill of the lights going down and the excitement of wearing that costume and all that make-up or walking off stage with a trophy or book prize!

As a novice teacher, the roles would have switched, and you will now be responsible for several types of school functions, or at least be working collaboratively on a project with other colleagues and possibly even parents. You will often have the daunting challenge – but also the creative opportunity – to arrange some function or event for the learners and possibly even the broader community to enjoy! It is during the planning of functions that you are able to use your many talents in creative ways.

The key elements of success entail detailed planning of the function or project several weeks before the set date, followed by careful organisation and the actual execution of the event. All this needs close monitoring and checking as the date draws nearer. If you show strong leadership skills, while focusing on detail in the different areas of the process, you will soon be tasked with bigger functions. Be prepared during the whole process for any crisis situations. Teachers are problem solvers! Use creative solutions and develop the skill of thinking on your feet. Tackle any task with a positive, energetic attitude. This definitely makes life easier for those around you, especially when you work together in a group.

All functions, performances, productions or events are temporary by nature; they all have a start and finish date. The main objective is to determine the reason for and purpose of the function and to plan and execute the process accordingly. The sequence of activities that need to take place or get done can be grouped according to four project phases.

Phase 1: Planning

At the start of any planning phase, you need to spend time thinking about the function and do some form of analysis of the event to determine the scale, role-players and general requirements for making it happen. You need to do this well in advance of the set date and should probably have a few meetings at which the team discusses matters and plans on paper. You will need to decide the following beforehand:

- **Why are we planning this function?**

Determine the specific reason why such a function is being considered. For example, the end-of-year concert or valedictory service is an annual tradition, but each year a new theme is chosen or a different guest speaker is invited.

- **What do we want to achieve by arranging this function?**

Perhaps the principal wants every learner in the school to be present on stage at some time during the concert or to sing in the choir. Maybe the school needs to raise funds for a specific project and so a music artist is invited and tickets are sold.

- **Where will the event take place?**

The venue or site of the event determines many other matters. For example, if the function is on the playground, using sound equipment poses challenges and the weather must be taken into consideration. The size of the hall determines how many people can be invited and where guests of honour might sit.

- **When will the event take place?**

The date of the specific function must not clash with other important functions in the community or school. For example, it won't be very successful to host a parents' day on the same date as a huge sports event taking place in the immediate community. It would also not be optimal to have a fun-run during the week. It is key to advertise the event well in advance and have good marketing strategies at hand, to ensure good attendance.

- **Who will be involved?**

If you are the project manager, you need to get a team together. Are colleagues, parents, learners or community members going to help you arrange the function? Select persons who can work together well. You will have to plan carefully and keep your finger on every detail. It is your duty to create good relations with all co-workers, keep the communication flow open and frequent and ensure a pleasant working environment for everyone who is involved.

Appoint someone who can take responsibility for the finances and can draft an initial budget, which needs to be adhered to strictly.

Having decided on the nature, theme and formality of the function, make sure that everyone understands and shares your vision.

Phase 2: Organising

In this phase you will answer the 'How?' question. You will now start putting the ideas you have planned into action by assigning tasks and thus the responsibility to others. We call this delegating. Depending on the size of the project, you may need to form subcommittees to ensure a fair allocation of work. Write down every task that must be completed, write down the name of the person responsible and have a date by which feedback on their progress must be given. Again, planning should be done well in advance. Give yourself enough time to run a smooth operation even if problems arise. All functions strike a hitch; allowing enough time for each task that needs to be completed will take the stress off everyone.

Sometimes the challenge you face means you have to change the original plan. If you do not encounter any serious problems, stick to your original plans; too many changes along the way cause confusion and wastes time.

Phase 3: Execution

Once each person has been assigned a task, they need to start working on it. The following tasks often form part of planning a school function.

Communication channels

The type of advertising depends on the nature and scale of the function. For example, will you use posters, radio news flashes, magazine/newspaper articles, stickers on vehicles, advertisement tricks, or word of mouth?

You will have to organise the designing, drafting, printing, making and duplication of:
- invitations
- directions to venues
- place names
- programmes
- any administrative paperwork.

On invitations and advertisements, clearly indicate the date, time, venue and dress code expected at the function. Posters and copied circulars should be distributed well ahead of time. Provide a telephone number and the name of a contact person in case additional information is needed.

Staff and parents need to be informed of rehearsal dates and starting and finishing times well in advance. They need to be kept up to date about progress. Inform parents of drop-off and collection times for learners. Which staff member will wait with the learners until everyone is picked up? What safety precautions are in place and how will the signing-out procedure for each learner take place? Clearly indicate any changes to everyone involved.

Learners also need to be constantly reminded – over the intercom, at assembly, in register periods – of all the practice and performance dates and times or any changes to the programme.

Flowers/decorations

Decide on the colour scheme and the amount to be spent on flowers. Ask a person who enjoys decorating to take care of the flowers, tablecloths, candles or whatever décor you have decided on. Decide beforehand where the flowers or focus points should be: Foyer? Toilets? A mass arrangement on stage? Only table decorations? What about a bouquet for the guest speaker or adjudicators?

Logistics and technical matters

Arrange with the caretaker or supervisor of the venue about cleanliness and packing out of chairs, tables, umbrellas or sound equipment. Remember to provide enough soap, toilet paper or air freshener for the toilets. Ensure that there are enough dustbins or rubbish bags. Remember to unlock the toilets in time and to lock up after the function.

Depending on the type of function, sufficient staff should be responsible for supervision and control on the school grounds as well as for the removal of people who should not be there. If security staff or car guards are required, they also need to be contracted.

Where possible, enlist the help of parents, teachers or learners who know how to operate microphones, music desks, data projectors, stage lights or whatever mechanical or electronic equipment you intend using. Ensure that the following items are available and in working order:

- Gas, electricity, batteries or generators
- Double adaptors
- Extension cords

- Microphone/s
- Overhead projector/screen/chalkboard
- CD player for background music.

With regard to the lights and electrical power: determine where the distributor board and main switches are located. Be sure that you know whether there are enough power points. Will you need any extension cords? What about adapters, specifically to charge cell phones or laptops from? Check and make sure that all globes/fluorescent tubes are in working order in the venue. Make sure that you have a generator on standby in case of a power failure.

Some events, such as a public speaking competition, may need water jugs and glasses, pens, blank paper, calculators, erasers and pencils.

It is always vital to have sufficient dustbins available for people to dispose of their trash.

The final matter that needs careful organisation is the cleaning up after the function. Determine who is responsible for this as well as who will lock up the venues, store away the equipment and eventually turn off the lights and lock the school yard.

Catering and refreshments

This matter will definitely require a catering committee. Appoint one person who is responsible and who can work under pressure, especially if there are large quantities of food involved. Provide the committee with broad guidelines of what is expected with regard to the:
- type of refreshments or meals required at the function
- budget and expenses
- number of guests
- colour scheme/theme.

The following catering duties also need to be planned:
- Who will buy coffee/tea/milk?
- Who will make and pour the tea?
- Who will provide the eats?
- What type of food will be acceptable? Have diverse dietary requirements, such as vegetarian, Halaal or Kosher food, been taken into account?
- How many cups/side plates are needed?
- Who will wash the dishes?
- Who is responsible for taking out and returning supplies?
- Who will make or rent the tablecloths? And what about serviettes?

Guests

The guest speaker should be invited at least a few months in advance, depending on the importance and size of the function. Decide on the following too:
- Have parking and security been arranged?
- Who will receive the guests and VIPs?
- Where and with whom will guests and VIPs sit during the function?
- Who will take care of the guests and VIPs during the interval?
- Who will accompany them to their vehicles afterwards?

Budget/expenses and sales

Managing money is a very responsible task and you need to be very cautious about who has access to the cash and which claims are being paid out. Appoint a responsible person as well as a monitor to manage all expenses. Remember to arrange for small change if refreshments are sold or the tuckshop is opened. Ensure that till slips and receipts are submitted as proof of payment before any refunds are made. Expenses must be in accordance with the budget to ensure that the anticipated income or profit is not less than planned. Do not deviate from the planned budget. The income from the function should be on target or even exceed it. Being able to raise the target amount will be a good encouragement for future attempts.

Programme: Order of events

Appoint a suitable programme director. This person should be informed about his or her task in detail. Also provide the person with a detailed programme, plus time allocation per item. Give careful thought to how the programme will run. Sequence the items sensibly so that the audience does not lose interest and the flow of the function is not interrupted. If necessary, organise a variety of items to be performed, but select these carefully in order to prevent unsuitable songs, dances or drama performances. Organise piano or keyboard accompaniment if you plan for the school song, national anthem or hymns to be sung.

  Should you decide to hand out a token of appreciation, ensure that a suitable gift has been bought and wrapped. Prior to the start of the function, make sure you have asked someone to hand it over at the appropriate time. Make sure the person also knows where it is available for presentation and at what point in the programme it needs to be presented.

  As project manager, you need to be constantly checking on everyone and making sure that they are on track. Here and there you may need to offer guidance and advice about how to execute the task so that everything runs according to plan and budget. You must have your finger on the pulse constantly.

Remember that you are working with people – unique individuals. Use each and every one according to his or her ability. Make everyone feel needed and valued. Give credit for everyone's contribution. Do not over-plan! Make sure that plans can be changed – leave room for unforeseen circumstances.

Phase 4: Evaluation and feedback

In order to determine the success of a function, it is necessary to receive collegial feedback about the function from all the people who were involved during the process. This can be done by self- and peer reflection using various methods such as:
- verbal conversations between staff
- completing questionnaires anonymously
- having official discussions with the HoD or principal.

Consider having a formal debriefing meeting to tie up all the loose threads. Keep a record of new ideas and improvements to be implemented next time.

A key aspect of being a good project manager is to always thank the people who worked with you to make the function a success. Written letters of thanks should be sent out as soon as possible after the function, even though contributors may already have been thanked verbally. Thank *everyone* – don't forget the cleaners and ground staff or those who washed up.

Make sure that you do not become overwhelmed. Try to relax even when things go wrong. Be adaptable. Enjoy the process of being part of or leading a project. Careful planning, organising and checking ought to ensure a successful event. We have included a planning schedule as Appendix F which may help you manage your project more easily.

Continuing your professional development

Piera Biccard

We are sure you will remember the excitement of your graduation day for a long time. It is really quite an achievement! But is it enough?

You will find that being a teacher involves a lot of 'giving'. You will give your time and energy continually. Eventually, you will find that you need to 'put something back'. Not only do you need to invest in yourself, but many novice teachers will be working towards Continuous Professional Teacher Development (CPTD) points through the SACE.

As a lifelong learner you must continue to acquire subject knowledge and keep abreast of new content developments. This could be done through self-study or teacher development programmes offered by the DBE, tertiary institutions and non-government organisations. Teacher unions are involved not only in the negotiations for higher salaries and better benefits for their members. They are also committed to the improvement of the service that their members deliver to learners. Therefore, they engage their members in professional development programmes over weekends and school holidays. Novice and experienced teachers are obliged to regularly attend upskilling courses focusing on subject content and pedagogy.

As a teacher, you are tasked with continually improving your professional development. The Department of Education in South Africa and SACE have as a requirement for employment that teachers earn 150 PD (professional development) points per rolling three-year cycle (SACE, 2016). The purpose of this is to improve the quality of learner achievements, to contribute to your autonomy and confidence, to revitalise your profession and to establish yourself as a professional in society. The development of professional practices is a continuing process that lasts for the duration of the career of a committed teacher. It is multifaceted, because good teachers learn from many sources: their own life experiences and teaching practice, their peers, the teaching profession at large, their professional reading and formal courses. The underlying principle is that teachers have a high degree of responsibility for their own professional development and the identification of their own professional needs. 'Teacher priority activities' are regarded as professional development activities. These activities include self-study in a subject area, a classroom-based action research project focused on the improvement of teaching and peer group support through a teacher network.

There are a number of options available to you for professional or personal development:

- Your employer may organise workshops and training sessions for you. These will be focused on your subject or specific policies for education.
- Your school may organise something by way of integrated quality management system (IQMS) training. This will be something that has been highlighted by many of your fellow teachers and a need that has been identified.
- Your union will organise and present various in-service training sessions. They will get outside specialists to present various topics to you.
- You can do online courses (some of them for free) through platforms such as Coursera or Udemy.
- You can enrol for short learning programmes at colleges or universities. Make sure that the institution is accredited so that your certificate will count.
- You can enrol for a further degree or diploma on a part-time or distance basis. This takes quite a bit of time and commitment.
- You can diversify and do something totally different, such as cooking lessons or photography. You may find that your first year of teaching is so busy that you have lost touch with your hobbies.
- You can belong to an online group of teachers and share ideas, problems, solutions or motivation.
- You can watch videos on TED-Ed. The topics of these excellent talks range from motivation to helping with discipline.
- There are a number of Open Educational Resources (OERs) available (for free) to you as a teacher. You can search OERArica or SAIDE. Make sure that you understand the CC licence if you plan to modify and reuse the resource. Some you can use, change and share freely. For others you need to reference the source. Some will allow you to make changes and others won't.
- You could start a lesson study group at your school where a few teachers plan lessons together. You then observe each other delivering the lesson and have a reflective discussion afterwards about how learners responded to the lesson.

- If there is an experienced teacher who is prepared to mentor you, ask if you can sit in on his or her classes (when you have a free period). Observe how the teacher deals with discipline and with managing and delivering the lesson.

You can see that there are many options available to you. What is important is that you continue to invest in yourself as a 'lifelong learner'.

Some of the ideas suggested here require that you be visible online. A word of caution: remember that anything you say, do or post online is *permanent* and can be shared with anyone via a screenshot. As a teacher, you will be judged (sometimes more harshly than others are) by the content of what is on your online profile or online activities and comments. Prospective employers can also access your online profile and this could make a difference to whether you get a job or not.

On the other hand, we also need to warn you about stalkers and others who may try to get personal information or banking information out of you. Do not share anything like this online.

From the beginning of your career, keep a detailed list of all the professional development, training, workshops and so on that you have completed. Be sure to keep all the certificates and even the training manuals. You will be able to refer to these when you work on your CV or apply for a promotion.

It is very important that you keep informed of the latest policies or laws regarding education. You may want to find a book regarding education and the law in South Africa. Do not rely only on your colleagues to tell you what is acceptable. Keep up to date with your subject too. Find new ways of teaching the more difficult sections. Do not merely follow a textbook day in and day out. Use the textbook as a resource, but teach the best possible lesson that you can. Keeping up to date will ensure that you are enthusiastic and motivated. As a teacher, you should never be bored!

35

The teacher as reflective practitioner

Rinelle Evans

Teachers spend a great deal of time assessing and evaluating their learners, but seldom think about evaluating themselves! Being a reflective practitioner means that you should spend time each day thinking critically about your day's work – whether that be thinking how the class behaved, or evaluating the outcome of a lesson; even discussing problems or successes with a colleague is a form of reflection. Try to schedule a few minutes after each lesson for this feedback to yourself.

It is best to practise structured reflection. Structured reflection requires you to critically evaluate your own practice with the aim of improving it. One way of keeping track of your observations and evaluations is to keep a research journal.

After the actual presentation of a lesson, you should spend a few minutes thinking about the process and outcome of the lesson you presented. This implies thinking critically about how you could improve its effectiveness and develop your teaching skills. You should then write down some reflective comments on how you perceived the teaching–learning process. Ask yourself:

- What worked well?
- Where could I improve?
- Why did a particular aspect *not* work?
- How did the learners relate to … ?
- Did I misjudge the prior knowledge I thought the learners had?
- Would I teach like that again?
- What if I do this instead?

Note what aspects of the lesson the learners had difficulties with, so you can avoid these next time. These comments could be written in a journal or in the margin of your lesson planning. These comments ought to guide you in becoming a more effective teacher. You should reflect not only on your lesson presentation but on your daily interaction with the learners, your colleagues and parents. Effective reflection requires practice. Keep daily notes in a journal about your own learning and personal growth. Write down descriptions of events and interactions that occur in the classroom, reflections on what you see happening or questions that pop up. Keep track of teaching ideas you read about or hear from other teachers. Describe what happens when you try things out. Do not just write a record of the day's events. You should analyse what worked and what did not work in your lesson and think of ways to do it better next time. You need to interpret everything that happens against the background of how you reacted to the events and how they contributed to your own learning and development as a professional teacher. Keeping a journal of your positive feelings, frustrations and daily experiences will help you chart your progress. All the best teachers are continually adapting their approaches and are only the wiser for rectifying their mistakes.

> **How to reflect effectively after teaching a lesson (DACA model)**
> - Sit where it is quiet and you are not distracted.
> - **Describe** what happened in the 35 minutes.
> - **Ask** yourself leading questions, for example: What changes could I make to improve? What went well and why? Jot down the answers. Spend time **analysing** your responses.
> - **Confront/challenge**: What new action is needed?
> - **Adapt**: Review. Implement. Review.
> - Talk through your ideas with someone who listens carefully. This is a powerful way to clarify confusion, find appropriate answers to questions you may have or identify solutions.
> - Consult practising educators and your peers for a shared experience.
> - Monitor your feelings, keep a journal, and learn from your reflective experience.

Asking for feedback from learners and parents using a simple questionnaire is another useful way of getting feedback on your teaching. Perhaps you may even like to invite another teacher to critique your lessons. Your professional bond and maturity should allow you to accept criticism and suggestions for adaptation readily. Use this opportunity to identify teething problems and to brainstorm solutions. Bouncing your problems off other colleagues and networking outside your school may also prove effective in assisting your professional development. You may even want to analyse official documentation and test results, or observe patterns of behaviour. Collecting such information and thinking carefully about what to do with it is the beginning of doing classroom research.

Practitioner reflection is very often neglected, but it plays a major role in your professional development. It helps you to remain accountable by providing evidence of your own growth and your ability to make adjustments in the interests of learning outcomes. It empowers you to address any problematic aspect of your teaching, with the sole aim of ensuring that effective teaching and learning can take place.

36

The teacher as researcher

Candice Livingston

Good teachers are inquisitive by nature. They are also lifelong learners, for if you wish to impart knowledge you need to have it! If you are curious about finding answers to things that puzzle or intrigue you, you have the makings of a good researcher. So what is a teacher-researcher? Why it is important to conduct research in your classroom? How can it be done? You are probably also asking 'Why must I do it?'

Teacher-researchers are lifelong learners who are able to continuously improve their knowledge and skills. The teacher as a researcher implies being an active participant in conducting research in your classroom or learning environment in order to:

- identify and solve problems regarding teaching practice or learner behaviour
- find a solution to learning problems
- enhance your working conditions
- revise the curriculum
- develop as a professional
- create a culture of inquiry within your classroom and school
- interpret classroom activities critically, and to make thoughtful or reflective instructional and classroom management decisions that are conducive to learning.

The most common and useful form of research for a teacher is classroom-based and is called action research. Action research is an organised and formal way of conducting research. Action research is cyclical. This means it takes place in various stages, but also comes back to its starting point, from where the next cycle starts again until a practical solution has been found.

Action research places the teacher at the centre of the research. You will frame the question that interests you, and then collect and analyse the data in order to find an answer. (Remember that all research will require the approval of your school and education department.) In order to conduct research in a systematic fashion, you need to follow a structured process.

Figure 36.1 shows the four stages related to action research: planning, acting, observing and reflecting.

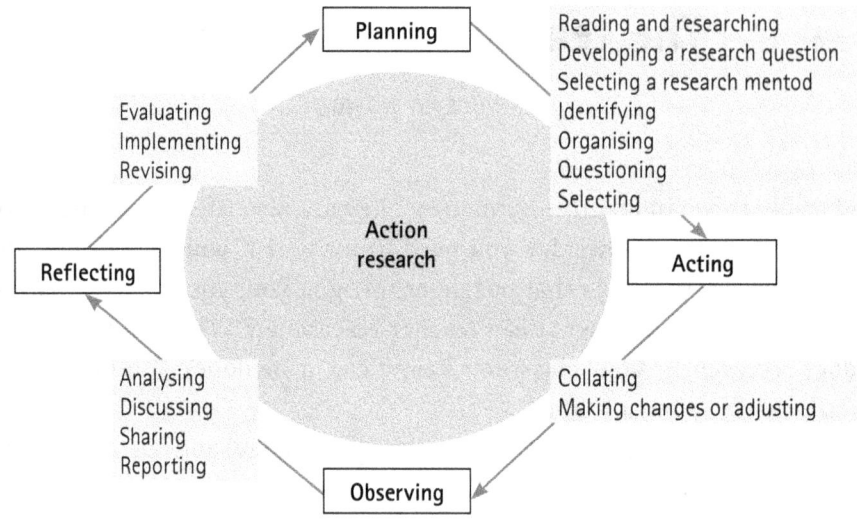

Figure 36.1   The action research cycle

Planning

Planning involves identifying a persistent problem or question that needs to be addressed, for example how to improve the reading speed of young learners or increasing learner participation in a large class. You will start by reading some literature or by making a study of similar projects developed by other teachers. Find as much information about the topic as you can in order to gain insight into the problem. The next step in planning is developing questions that must be answered and selecting the appropriate research methods.

Acting

After you have reflected on your situation/issue/problem, it is time to act. Before you choose an appropriate research strategy, it is always a good idea to pilot your project. This is to ensure that all the kinks have been ironed out and that you do not have to stop in the middle of your research project because of unforeseen problems. Now it is time to collect and collate your evidence. You may need to make changes as you go along.

Observing

Once you have collected the evidence, you need to analyse it and come up with findings. These may be the answers to the problem or the issue being investigated. It is a good idea to discuss the findings with colleagues. You may even want to share the outcome with colleagues at a cluster meeting or a workshop. You could even write an article for a teachers' magazine or newsletter, so that other teachers can benefit from your research.

Reflecting

Reflection entails evaluating the first cycle, deciding on how you will implement your findings or new strategy and revisiting your practice in order to decide on improvements or changes that may be necessary to the process. A wide variety of methods for collecting data can be used.

Advantages of using action research

Action research:
- allows you to focus on your own unique teaching problems
- helps you to examine and improve your classroom practices
- could strenghten relationships among colleagues
- provides you with alternative ways of viewing and approaching educational questions
- assists in developing a deeper understanding of programmes, processes and contexts.

You can improve your teaching and contribute to the improvement of your school by integrating research into your everyday practice. This means recognising the research skills that you already have, expanding those skills and using them in everyday practice. Consider collaborating with other teachers on focused mini-research projects. The collaborative research findings are then used to effect change within schools or society. By developing their research competencies, teachers are able to investigate their own pedagogy and specifically work to meet the needs of the learners in their classroom. They are empowered to find a voice and solve their own problems.

Researching your own practice should thus not be seen as an additional burden but, rather, an extension of your role as teacher. By conducting research, you as the teacher-researcher not only develop professionally, but get to understand your class and context better. This, in turn, benefits your learners and helps sustain improvements in your teaching and their learning. By developing specific research-related activities, you are able to find context-specific solutions to the problems you have identified in your classroom. Developing the habit of inquiry ought to make you a more thoughtful and observant teacher. The key question to keep asking is: How can I improve my practice?

37

Spending, saving and investing

Rinelle Evans

Holding that first payslip or receiving notification from the bank that says your account has been credited with your salary is a very special moment! But it could also be overwhelming if not handled with care and sensible decisions. Starting from the first month, you need to use and manage your money wisely.

Some novice teachers may have relied on bursaries, and others on parents or relatives to sustain them while they were trying to finish their studies. Earning your first pay cheque is an exhilarating feeling, not only because you probably have more money in your bank account than ever before, but also because it is a tangible sign of being independent.

> Don't forget to thank the people who directly or indirectly helped you graduate. These persons may have sacrificed much so that you could reap the benefits. All it takes is a bit of time to write a 'thank you' note in which you express your gratitude for their support, be it financial or emotional.

Being a working adult carries many new responsibilities. These include having to be conscientious about how you spend your monthly salary. Just because you have this new-found freedom to buy more things doesn't mean you should be spending more freely. Becoming financially literate is a skill and you need to be disciplined about what you do with your money each month, from the very start.

Before you even receive your salary, 'the taxman' – the South African Revenue Service (SARS) – will have deducted the mandatory portion due to them from your earnings. The amount will depend on how much you earn. You will also have had pension and medical scheme deductions. Many students will be obliged to pay so-called 'black tax', which also eats away at the amount you have to spend. So what are some of the first steps to financial security?

Open a savings account

Set aside a certain amount of money every month and pay yourself first. Treat this account like you would any other debtor. See where you can cut back on your spending by changing your habits or lifestyle a little. For example, pack your own lunch, or stop smoking or buying take-away coffee. Paint your own nails or reconsider that weave. Cut down on your drinks. Must you share an up-market house on an estate? Is a holiday more important than glitzy clothing? What about furthering your qualifications? Saving is a matter of prioritising your wants and needs and setting goals.

Set up your banking system so that your salary is paid into a current account, with debit orders going off directly towards your savings, paying off a loan, insurance policies, family commitments or retirement annuities before you spend money on anything else. Whatever is left is what you have to live on: rent, food, airtime, electricity, toiletries and transport. Only after you have made the essential payments can you consider luxuries such as entertainment, magazines and clothing.

Saving lays a solid financial foundation. Starting to save early is the best decision you'll ever make if you wish to eventually maintain an adequate standard of living.

Start an emergency fund

You have possibly heard the expression 'saving for a rainy day'. Well, it sometimes starts pouring with little advance warning. An emergency fund is used when an unexpected expense occurs, such as a medical emergency, a car breaking down or the death of a loved one. Such expenses can have a huge impact on your finances, and if you do not plan for them you might end up having to take on debt to cover the costs. Therefore it is advisable to create an emergency fund, which you should try to increase until it is at least three to six months' worth of income. If you have savings to tide you through such crises, it saves you from needless stress, having to borrow money and going into debt to pay for these unexpected costs. Taking out a funeral policy may also serve you well.

Budget

You can only manage your money if you know how much you are spending and what you are spending your money on. Most banks and financial institutions will be able to give you a simple chart on which you fill in the various expenses you have. Download one from the internet or, better still, look for a user-friendly application to access on your phone. Keep a weekly record of what you are spending and on which items. This will help you draft a simple budget to track your monthly spending patterns. Start by listing the expenses that you have to pay, such as accommodation, travel costs, food, electricity, your phone account or your student loan repayment.

Adjust your spending according to your available income

Most monthly expenses are fixed, but some are seasonal. Having a financial goal makes decisions easier. Only spend money on essential items. Not everything is a priority. *Never* spend more than you earn. If you plan carefully, you should not run out of money before the end of the month. Although acceptable to some people, borrowing money to survive until month-end is the start of financial uncertainty. You may be tempted to splurge on an item you have always desired. This could be the start of a downward spiral into debt and a very stressful life.

Clear or reduce your debt

A student loan is a common debt that you may have incurred and it may take several years to clear. Clear your debt diligently every month. If you do buy some big items, such as a fridge or television, try to get a six-month interest-free deal. Do not skip payments; rather renegotiate the amount you pay back. If you default on payments, there are often penalties and additional interest charges. Investing in stokvels or lay-byes are safer ways of eventually owning what you'd like.

Get insurance

Apart from short-term insurance for something like a car or your laptop, you should consider purchasing appropriate disability cover so that you will still have a monthly income should an unexpected illness or an unfortunate accident leave you unable to work. If you have dependants, it would be wise to take out life insurance to provide for them after your death. Your premium depends on your age and your health at the time of buying the policy.

Start investing

You may probably only be able to start investing once you have saved up some money. Educate yourself on investments first so that you can make informed choices. You will probably need the help of an unbiased expert to make sound investments. Every cent you can put away helps your money tree grow over the long term. The sooner you start investing, the better. Have short-, medium- and long-term financial goals and be disciplined.

Start as early as possible and leave your money for as long as you can. It is the power of compound interest that really makes the value of your money grow. This means interest is added to your initial investment and you earn more interest on that too. This money can be put towards buying a home or used as security.

Saving for your retirement

Even though a part of your salary is allocated to the government pension fund for the day when you retire, it is important that you start a retirement fund of your own. You may not stay in teaching or you may be retrenched, and having retirement annuities will enable you to have some funds until you earn again. This is another form of saving and helps reduce the amount of tax you pay. You will only be able to use these savings when you are 55, unless you become disabled.

Find a trustworthy financial advisor

Unless you know how to do this yourself, you will need an expert to design an investment plan for you. Shop around, and speak to senior colleagues and more mature adults about whose services they use. Be wary of financial advisors who might not have your best interests at heart. These persons usually earn their money via commission and the amount depends on the products they sell. Never sign any document until you have had time to read through it and speak to someone who can guide you, should you need clarity. Ask for the best rates and lowest fee. Make sure what the penalties are for cancelling or changing any recommended products. Meet with your advisor at least once a year so that you can revise your financial portfolio.

> **Mistakes to avoid**
> Accept that you won't be able to buy everything your heart desires right now. There are certain things that you should avoid doing if you want to save yourself much stress and financial difficulties:
>
> - **Buying big items all at once**
> Think twice before you buy that car, washing machine, fancy furniture and the mobile phone you have always wanted. Ask yourself each time you want to make a purchase: Do I just want it or do I really need it? List the essential items and look for ways to get along for a while without some of them. Instead of buying a car, can you use public transport or join a lift club? Rather than buying a washing machine, could you wash your own clothes or go to a laundromat? Must you have

state-of-the-art furniture? Will you still like the style in five years' time? What about all those brand-name shoes and sunglasses? Is your image and self-worth really tied up in what you wear and possess? It is not worth getting into debt just because you are not financially disciplined.

■ Buying on impulse
Buying something without planning for it has a direct impact on the money you have available each month. If you have not saved or budgeted for it, don't buy it. The best way to avoid buying is to not spend time just strolling through malls. Plan your purchases and shop around on websites for the best prices. Save up for the items that are really luxuries. Using the lay-bye system is a sensible way of eventually owning something you have long desired.

■ Buying on credit
It is just too easy to buy on credit, and many shops and even banks encourage you to open accounts with tempting promises of six-months' interest-free rates or buy-one-take-two options. Use cash or debit cards rather than credit cards. The interest rates are very high on credit cards and you can soon find yourself having to pay more on the interest than the item was worth. You might also damage your credit rating by defaulting on monthly payments. Being blacklisted is very troublesome and haunts you for many years. Also make sure you read and understand the fine print of any agreement you sign.

■ Giving in to peer pressure
Never buy something just because someone else has bought it. Be honest with yourself about what you can and cannot afford. Everyone's financial circumstances differ, so trying to keep up with your friends can be costly, and ultimately leads to financial strain.

■ Visiting loan sharks
Do not ever turn to a loan shark or *mashonisa* if you urgently need money. They are generally unscrupulous and deserve their bad reputation. They charge incredibly high interest rates, which just escalate the longer you take to pay back the money. They take your ID book, bank cards or other property and keep it until you have settled your debt. Some do not ever return what is yours. They are unregulated and you do not have recourse to a professional body for help.

> If you are forced to find money urgently, for example for a funeral, rather go to a registered micro-lender for a short-term loan. The rates are far more affordable and can be paid off over a longer period. There is also a limit to what creditors and their debt collection agents can charge you if you miss a payment. You are protected from abuse by the National Credit Act.

By understanding what you should be doing to strengthen your financial wellbeing, you can live life more confidently and enjoy greater peace of mind. You do not want to find yourself spending all the money you earn each month, living from pay cheque to pay cheque. Sliding into debt happens slowly, but it is a very deep and slippery pit from which to climb out.

You may find our advice on being financially disciplined restrictive, but in South Africa we live in uncertain economic times. We are not suggesting that you cannot enjoy your hard-earned money, but careful budgeting and disciplined saving will lessen your financial challenges. Heed the wise words of a bumper sticker: Money talks! It says goodbye!

Your elders were right: money does not grow on trees. Financial freedom requires planning and discipline.

38

Tips from top teachers

Franklin Lewis and Rinelle Evans

You are about to qualify as a teacher. For four years, you have been groomed in the history of education, professional studies and practices, leading pedagogical theories, as well as ICT skills. In addition, your knowledge of subject content and corresponding methodologies will enable you to interpret the national curriculum statement designed for the South African schooling system. If you have engaged with your studies these past years, most of the subject and pedagogical knowledge and skills that you have acquired could easily be transferred to an inner city school abroad. Well done! But are you truly ready for the post-modern South African classroom?

You might be appointed to a former Model C or private school located in an affluent suburb. In that case, you will have all the resources and opportunities that enable a quality education, and a space that accommodates the teaching and learning theories that your professors have taught you. You will be fortunate to engage with smaller classes, state-of-the-art technology and elaborate learning and teaching support material. However, you may also find yourself practising your teaching skills in a former Coloured township school on the Cape Flats, where you and your learners will have to duck under your desks when gangsters have a gun battle just before first break at 10 in the morning. You might even teach in a classroom in a township or informal settlement where the unpainted walls, thatched roofs, pit toilets and lack of electricity are glaring evidence of the legacy of the inferior system of Bantu Education imposed on the majority of South Africans during apartheid.

Professionally resilient teachers have various reasons why they remain employed under such onditions. For most dedicated teachers, the intrinsic reasons are their love for children or the passion for sharing the love for a particular subject. For others, extrinsic reasons such as the benefit of a permanent job or regular holidays become the primary reason to remain in teaching.

Your primary school teacher might have taught under more difficult conditions. She taught in an era where there were no data projectors, internet and smartphones. She only had the textbook. She had a large class and earned a small salary, and had little hope of being promoted to a senior position due to gender discrimination. Her primary goal was to teach you how to read and work with numbers, because she knew that literacy and numeracy skills would open the doors to tertiary education or the world of work. She wanted to make a difference to you and the other children around you. She was undaunted.

No doubt, from a young age you acquired the love for the subject that you intend teaching from one of your own dedicated teachers. The question is: How did they succeed even when faced by many challenges?

We asked teachers who currently work in inner city schools, rural schools, independent schools, faith-based schools and former Model C schools for their advice on how to cope with the demands of starting your career. Interestingly enough, much of their wisdom centred on behaviours to avoid.

Do's

- Some days the learners are simply not able to be proactive or focused. Have some simple or fun activities that they can do in such situations. Anything that gets them active will help them to be engaged in learning. When learners' attention or your own enthusiasm is flagging, change the pace or direction of the lesson. This can be done by playing a quick game, clapping or singing, changing seats, rearranging desks, reading a short story or dramatising a poem. Perhaps five minutes of 'tidy-up time' may help or, if possible, take a walk or do an activity on the field. Other in-class activities that could get learners focused again include 'discuss with neighbour' or 'quiz time'. You could also get the class to focus by doing or observing an experiment or activity (please remember: safety first). Showing a short relevant video also motivates learners.
- *There are no naughty learners, there are only learners who are not yet learning-ready.* Over time, you will find the activities that work for you and each particular class. You will get to know this by trying out various activities with them. If a class does not respond to a particular activity, it may just be circumstances or the way in which you approached it, but it is often a signal to try something different next time. It may even be that you have just chosen a particularly difficult worksheet and that you may need to make the introduction clearer and the questions easier in future.
- Even though you may be only a few years older than the learners you teach, and many years younger than some of your colleagues, you need to accept that your role has changed. You are no longer a student, but someone in authority and of whom your employer expects exemplary, adult behaviour. You will have to create what is called pedagogical distance

between yourself and the learners. You will have to think carefully about the places you frequent, and the way you dress and act in public. You can no longer hang out in clubs or afford to behave badly in public.
- Dress professionally and practically. Browse through the many marked-down railings or end-of-season sales. You will find several bargains. Invest in good shoes and a classic-cut coat/jacket. Wear clothing that has pockets.
- Pay attention to building the self-esteem of each and every learner, while transferring your knowledge and experience.
- Have some games or fun worksheets available. Sometimes, half the class will be at a special meeting or a quick athletics practice and you will be left with the other half to 'do something with'. It's much easier to keep them constructively busy than to just let them 'chat'.
- Keep a water bottle at your desk, and drink water every time the period ends. The days can be so busy that it will be 14:00 and you will not have had anything to drink. Your brain needs water!
- Write down in your planning every time you lose teaching time (evacuation drill, school nurse and so on). You might need to explain why you haven't completed the curriculum for the term.
- Use your 'admin' periods (if you are lucky enough to get any) for marking and making copies. Do not spend the whole period in the staff room chatting or on your phone. It will just mean you will have to do school work at home.
- Go out of your way to be good to the secretaries and other support staff.
- Learn how to say, 'I don't know, but I will find out.' Ask for help when needed. Learn how to say sorry if you were wrong.
- Let learners finish their sentences before deciding what you think they are going to say. As teachers, we are always in a hurry and we often cut learners off before they have finished telling us something.
- Keep your class tidy – it shows that you mean business. Spend five minutes tidying it up at the end of the day. You'll feel more positive the next morning when you walk into a tidy class. Give learners responsibilities so that they feel part of looking after their own class and school.
- Develop a reading culture in your class. Have educational magazines or books for learners who finish their work quickly to read quietly.
- Move around during your lessons. It can stop many problems before they start.

- Spend time at the beginning of the year training your learners not to shout out in class. The time spent doing this will be repaid for the rest of the year when you are not interrupted by learners who shout out. By all means, encourage them to ask questions, but in a manner that is orderly (such as raising their hands).
- Be prepared and be on time. Know what's going on in your grade, subject and teaching plan. Get clued up on the topics and computer skills.
- Remember that teaching is how you earn your salary. Try to leave school issues and problems at work, if you can.
- Use colleagues or social media groups as mentors to help you find different approaches to class development.
- Be strict but fair as well. Do not favour; be consistent.
- Be organised and believe in yourself.
- Trust your own judgement.
- Be willing to grow.
- Ask questions.
- Treat every learner as if he or she was your own sibling or child.
- Listen to both sides of the story when dealing with two learners.
- Be thorough when planning and delivering your lessons.
- Cater for all ability levels.
- Ensure you give positive feedback, especially after tasks and tests.
- Empower learners with good skills to build their confidence. Focus on all learners who struggle. If necessary, get them professional help as soon as possible.
- Rely on parental help and involvement to help you.
- Be kind, compassionate and caring. In order to teach, you need to reach out to colleagues, parents and learners.
- Ensure everyone has a common understanding regarding discipline, school uniforms and the school's code of conduct. Negotiate rules with the class and implement them consistently, even after the smallest transgression.
- Listen to learners' stories and gain their confidence. Get to know your learners' background. You should report matters of abuse to the relevant parties.
- Plan thoroughly! Keep up with any changes in your subject. Read widely and make sure you know your subject well. Be confident and positive in class.

> My surname happens to rhyme with a terribly vulgar word in my home language. I started my career at a predominantly boys' school – all speakers of the same language. One boy was particularly set on making life difficult for me by chanting the rude version of my surname at the most inappropriate times or in the most inappropriate places, which resulted in sniggering chaos. Athletics meetings, award ceremonies, school assemblies and many other group activities were made a living hell for me by this learner. It took me a long time to find the culprit and, upon confrontation, he denied all allegations. I felt there was really nothing I could do. I felt violated, exposed and helpless. It was only years later, with much more experience, that I learnt to use humour in class to deal with all the derivatives of my surname. Now when I meet new learners, I make a teaching point of introducing myself in a very specific fashion and explain upfront that I am aware of all the crude possibilities of my name. I let them know that I am aware of how they could 'mispronounce' my name and what it feels like when they do. I request that they should stick to addressing me appropriately, as one's name is an important part of one's identity.

Don'ts

- Be very careful of what you say to whom! Do not spread the word that you intend to resign, have received a better offer or are planning on emigrating. Speak to your line managers directly, as they ought to hear about these decisions first-hand.
- Do not tell everybody that the principal or HoD has made an appointment with you. Colleagues might be curious about the outcome and it could be something you do not wish to discuss.
- Do not fall for every sales person who arrives at school to sell you linen, crockery, life insurance, funeral plans or time share.
- Do not touch a learner, whether in anger or affection. When dealing with a learner in moments of anger or confrontation, put your hands behind your back, no matter how frustrated you may be, and lock your fingers! Count to 10 before responding.
- Do not plan any 'unofficial' activities with your direct peers. There is a reason why schools have schedules, year plans and management teams. Although you might view it as a brilliant initiative (which it probably is), SMTs prefer not to be surprised by novice teachers.
- Be mindful when wearing school-branded clothing and using equipment or vehicles that display your school's unique logo or branding. Do *not* go into

the nearest pub after school on a Friday afternoon dressed in the sportswear for staff. Do not give away school-branded clothing to anyone. Rather donate these to the school – it may be a good idea to start a community project or give it to someone who still has ties with the school. No one in any way related to your school wants to see a stranger dressed in the school's branded sportswear in a Saturday night brawl, nor do they want to find the school's emblem on the back page of the Sunday newspaper.
- Do not try to be 'friends' with the learners. Get them to respect you, not like you. If you prepare interesting lessons and treat everyone fairly and consistently, they will respect you and really like you. Do not socialise with learners. In fact, if you don't draw the boundary line, you will confuse the learners.
- Never:
  - take planning lightly
  - be late
  - panic
  - leave things for the last minute
  - doubt yourself
  - let the stress get to you
  - talk too much
  - take bad behaviour personally
  - be afraid to be different
  - get stuck in a rut
  - take the silent learners for granted
  - hold back your grievances – get it out and move on
  - stop listening
  - engage in drama, gossip or staff politics
  - look down on any learner, insult or humiliate learners, or show favouritism
  - say you know something when you don't – do proper research
  - send learners out of class to pass on messages or handouts, as they lose out on class time and learning.
- Avoid negativity.
- Do not discuss a learner's weakness, misbehaviour or confidences with another learner or other parents.
- Do not socialise with learners.
- Do not waste time.
- Do not teach above the learners' capabilities. Assess them before you stretch them.

- Time is of the essence, so plan ahead. Never wing it, as this will result in a wasted lesson. Avoid simply reading from a textbook, as it shows you have not prepared.

Once children venture beyond the domestic environment in which they are loved and cared for, traditionally called home, the next social context in which they spend a large portion of their life is a formal educational context, traditionally called school. This ought to be a safe, enjoyable space, as often children spend more time in the presence of their teachers than they do with their caregivers. Applying some of the wisdom shared in this section will make your daily life much easier and enjoyable. It could also change the lives of your learners. As a teacher you will seldom know how you have influenced a learner, but you can be certain that you do influence them each day they are in your class. Take your responsibility seriously and try to make a positive difference in the lives of young South Africans.

Concluding comments

You have chosen to become a teacher. Perhaps you had a teacher who inspired you. Perhaps you have parents who believe that this is a good career choice, especially if you should have a family of your own one day. Perhaps you are studying to be a teacher because you have a deep inner conviction to guide and empower other people to reach their potential. Whatever your personal reason is for working towards your education degree, not everyone considers teaching a noble profession. Many will say you have made the right choice; others will think you are not quite sane. Some may even ridicule you and think that you are not capable of doing more than 'looking after children'. Do not heed them. Teaching is an extremely dynamic and rewarding profession. You will soon have the opportunity to work towards exploiting the potential of our country's youth by offering them a quality education, despite the varied contextual and challenging conditions. Only education offers hope for a better future.

We hope that we have provided you with some valuable information for your teaching career, not only for the first year, but well beyond that. Read this book regularly, and you will find that some information is relevant at different times of your career.

Do your best and take pride in yourself as a professional teacher. May your best efforts be appreciated by learners, parents, colleagues and your community!

Our very best wishes for a shining career in education!

Sources consulted

Allen, DW. 1971. *The Teacher's Handbook*. USA: Scott.

An, D & Carr, M. 2017. 'Learning styles theory fails to explain learning and achievement: Recommendations for alternative approaches.' *Personality and Individual Differences* 116: 410–416. DOI: 10.1016/j.paid.2017.04.050.

Archer, S. 2006. *100 Ideas for Teaching Science*. London: Continuum.

Arista Training. 2017. Teachers' Legal Rights. Unpublished training manual. Johannesburg: Arista Global.

Ayres, AJ. 1979. Sensory Integration and the Child. Los Angeles: Western Psychological Services.

Avila, APC, Ran, A, Hui, C, Chen, JQ, Lin, JH, Sansanwal, S & Chia, SYS. 2013. *Teacher Education for the 21st Century: Developing Teachers who Are Thoughtful, Reflecting and Inquiring*. Singapore: National Institute of Education.

Bailey, R, Armour, K, Kirk, D, Jess, M, Pickup, I, Sanford, R & BERA Physical Education and Sport Pedagogy Interest Group. 2009. 'The educational benefits claimed for physical education and school sport: An academic review.' *Research Papers in Education* 24(1): 1–27. DOI: 10.1080/02671520701809817.

Beck, C & Kosnik, C. 2014. *Growing as a Teacher: Goals and Pathways of Ongoing Teacher Learning*. Netherlands: Sense Publishers.

Boaler, J. 2016. *Mathematical Mindsets*. San Francisco: Jossey-Bass.

Bowkett, W & Bowkett, S. 2008. *100 Ideas for Developing Good Practice in the Early Years*. London: Continuum.

Bradshaw, M. 2006. 'Creating controversy in the classroom: Making progress with historical significance.' *Teaching History* 125: 18–25.

Breaux, A. 2015. *101 Answers for New Teachers and Their Mentors: Effective Teaching Tips for Daily Classroom Use* (3rd edition). New York: Routledge.

Bremmer, LP. 2013. 'A legal interpretation of the duty of care of teachers regarding learner truancy.' Unpublished PhD Dissertation. Pretoria: University of Pretoria.

British Historical Association. 2007. *T.E.A.C.H. Teaching Emotive and Controversial History 3–19*. London: Historical Association.

Brownhill, S. 2009. *100 Ideas for Teaching Physical Development*. London: Continuum.

Cale, L & Harris, JO. 2005. *Getting the Buggers Fit*. London: Continuum.

Canter, L & Canter, M. 2001. *Assertive Discipline: Positive Behavior Management for Today's Classroom* (3rd edition). Los Angeles: Canter & Associates.

Carr, NS. 2013. 'Increasing the effectiveness of homework for all learners in the inclusive classroom.' *School Community Journal* 23(1): 169–182.

Clark, R. 2003. *The Essential 55: An Award-Winning Educator's Rules for Discovering the Successful Student in Every Child*. New York: Hyperion.

Cleary, S (ed). 2014. *Communication: A Hands-on Approach* (2nd edition). Cape Town: Juta.

Clement, MC. 2005. *First Time in the High School Classroom: Essential Guide for the New Teacher.* Maryland: Scarecrow Education.

Coakley, J. 2011. 'Youth sports: What counts as "positive development".' *Journal of Sport and Social Issues* XX(X): 1–9. DOI: 101177/0193723511417311.

Cooper, H, Robinson, JC & Patall, EA. 2006. 'Does homework improve academic achievement? A synthesis of research, 1987–2003.' *Review of Educational Research* 76(1): 1–62.

Cooze, A. 2006. *100 Ideas for Teaching English.* London: Continuum.

Cowley, S. 2003. *Getting the Buggers to Behave 2.* London: Continuum.

Cowley, S. 2004. *Getting the Buggers to Think.* London: Continuum.

Cowley, S. 2005. *Letting the Buggers Be Creative.* London: Continuum.

Cowley, S. 2009. *How to Survive Your First Year in Teaching* (2nd edition). London: Continuum International.

Davies, I. 2005. *100 Ideas for Teaching Citizenship.* London: Continuum.

DBE (Department of Basic Education). 2011a. Curriculum and Assessment Policy Statement. Life skills: Intermediate phase Grades 4–6. Pretoria: DBE. Available from: http://www.education.gov.za.

DBE. 2011b. Curriculum and Assessment Policy Statement. Life Orientation: Senior phase Grades 7–9. Pretoria: DBE. Available from: http://www.education.gov.za.

DBE. 2011c. Curriculum and Assessment Policy Statement. Life Orientation: Further Education and Training phase Grades 10–12. Pretoria: DBE. Available from: http://www.education.gov.za.

DBE. 2014. Basic Education on the importance of school sport and physical education. (Online) Available from: http://www.gov.za/2014-south-african-schools-national-championships (Accessed: 20 February 2017).

De Jager, M. 2009. *Mind Moves. Moves That Mend the Mind.* Johannesburg: Mind Moves Institute.

Dreyer, JM. 2008. *The Educator as Assessor.* Pretoria: Van Schaik.

Du Plessis, P. 2014. 'Problems and complexities in rural schools.' *Mediterranean Journal of Social Sciences* 5(20) 1109–1117.

Elkin, S. 2007. *100 Ideas for Secondary School Assemblies.* London: Continuum.

Eloff, I & Swart, E. 2018. *Understanding Educational Psychology.* Cape Town: Juta.

Emami, A, Sharif, MR & Jafarigohar, M. 2014. 'Extension homework and classroom assignments.' *Journal of Novel Applied Sciences* 3(1): 29.

Engelbrecht, A & Swanepoel, H (eds). 2013. *Embracing Diversity through Multi-level Teaching for Foundation, Intermediate and Senior Phase.* Cape Town: Juta.

Evans, R. 1995. 'The demands of the multicultural classroom on the ESL teacher in secondary schools with specific reference to Pretoria, Gauteng.' Unpublished MA dissertation. Birmingham, UK: University of Birmingham.

Evans, R. 2006. 'The impact of presenter speech personality on learner participation during televised instruction.' *Journal of Language Teaching* 40(2): 21–34.

Evans, R. 2011. 'Preparing pre-service teachers for multilingual classrooms: Designing a multiple African language module.' *Journal for Language Teaching* 45(2): 69–82.

Evans, R (ed). 2015. *Communication, Culture and the Multilingual Classroom* (2nd edition). Pretoria: Van Schaik.

Evans, R & Cleghorn, A. 2010. '"Look at the balloon blow up!": Student teacher-talk in linguistically diverse South African foundation phase classrooms.' *Southern African Linguistics and Applied Language Studies* 28(2): 123–133.

Evans, R & Cleghorn, A. 2012. *Complex Classroom Encounters: A South African Perspective*. Amsterdam: Sense.

Evans, R, Joubert, I & Meier, C. 2017. *Introducing Children's Literature: A Guide to the South African Classroom*. Pretoria: Van Schaik.

Evans, R & Nthulana, I. 2018. 'Linguistic challenges faced by rural Tshivenda-speaking teachers when Grade 4 learners transition to English.' *The Journal for Transdisciplinary Research in Southern Africa* 14(2): a545.

Farmery, C. 2005. *Getting the Buggers into Science*. London: Continuum.

Ferrance, E. 2000. *Action Research*. Office of Educational Research and Improvement. Providence, RI: LAB at Brown University.

Fisher, K. 2005. Research into identifying effective learning environment. Evaluating Quality in Educational Facilities, 9, 159-167

Fisher, L. 2006. *100 Ideas for Surviving Your First Year in Teaching*. London: Continuum.

Flanagan, N & Finger, J. 1989. *Management in a Minute: An Essential Tool for South African Managers*. Cape Town: Struik.

Flinders University. 2007. Teaching controversial issues. (Online) Available from: www.flinders.edu.au/teach/t41/inclusive/controversial.php?printview=1 (Accessed 12 November 2016).

Gauteng Provincial Circular. 04/2014. Prohibition of Corporal Punishment in Public Schools.

Gay, G. 2002. 'Preparing for culturally responsive teaching.' *Journal of Teacher Education* 53: 106–116.

Gillespie, H. 2007. 'Teaching emotive and controversial history to 7–11-year-olds: A report for the Historical Association.' *International Journal of Historical Learning, Teaching and Research* 7(1): no page numbers.

Glasgow, NA, Cheyne, M & Yerrick, RK. 2010. *What Successful Science Teachers Do*. California: Corwin.

Gous, I & Roberts, J (eds). 2015. *Teaching Life Orientation: Senior and FET Phase*. South Africa: Oxford University Press.

Graham, G, Holt-Hale, SA & Parker, M. 2007. *Children Moving: A Reflective Approach to Teaching Physical Education*. New York: Mc Graw-Hill.

Gravette, S, De Beer, J & Du Plessis, E. 2015. *Becoming a Teacher*. Cape Town: Pearson.

Griffith, N. 2005. *100 Ideas for Teaching Language*. London: Continuum.

Gultig, J & Stielau, J (eds). 2012. *Getting Practical: A Guide to Teaching and Learning*. Cape Town: Oxford University Press.

Hahn, CL. 1994. 'Controversial issues in history instruction', in *Cognitive Instructional Processes in History and the Social Sciences*, edited by M Carretero and JF Voss. New Jersey: Lawrence Erlbaum.

Harnett, P. 2007. 'Teaching emotive and controversial history to 3–7-year-olds: A report for the Historical Association.' *International Journal of Historical Learning, Teaching and Research* 7(1): no page numbers.

Heitzmann, R. 2007. 'Target homework to maximize learning.' *Education Digest* 40–43.

Hill, JD & Flynn, KM. 2006. *Classroom Instruction That Works With English Language Learners*. USA: ASCD Publications.

Hobson, A, Malderez, A & Tracey, L. 2009. *Navigating Initial Teacher Training*. London: Routledge.

Howarth, R. 2008. *100 Ideas for Supporting Pupils with Emotional and Behavioural Difficulties*. London: Continuum.

Jacobs, M & Gawe, N. 1996. *Teaching-Learning Dynamics: A Participative Approach*. Johannesburg: Heinemann.

Joubert, I (ed). 2013. *Literacy in the Foundation Phase* (2nd edition). Pretoria: Van Schaik.

Joubert, R. 2008. *Learner Discipline in Schools*. Pretoria: Centre for Education Law and Education Policy (CELP).

Kewley, G & Latham, P. 2008. *100 Ideas for Supporting Pupils with ADHD*. London: Continuum.

Kilpatrick, J, Swafford, J & Findell, B (eds). 2001. *Adding It Up: Helping Children Learn Mathematics*. Washington, DC: National Academy Press.

Kraut, H. 1996. *Teaching and the Art of Successful Classroom Management*. USA: NEA Professional Library and Aysa Publishing.

Krog, S & Krüger, D. 2011. 'Movement programmes as a means to learning readiness.' *South African Journal for Research in Sport, Physical Education and Recreation* 33(3): 73–78.

Krog, S, Naidoo, R, Cleophas, F, Du Toit, D, Krüger, D, Lewis, A, Rossouw, JP, Roux, CJ, Van der Merwe, N & Willemse, F (eds). 2017. *Teaching Physical Education and Sports Coaching*. South Africa: Oxford University Press.

Krolak-Schwerdt, S, Glock, S & Böhmer, M (eds). 2014. *Teachers' Professional Development: Assessment, Training and Learning*. Netherlands: Sense Publishers.

Kruger, AG & Van Schalkwyk, OJ. 1997. *Classroom Management*. Pretoria: Van Schaik.

Larsson, H & Nyberg, G. 2017. '"It does not matter how they move really, as long as they move." Physical Education teachers on developing their student's movement capabilities.' *Physical Education and Sport Pedagogy* 22(2): 137–149.

Lemov, D. 2010. *Teach Like a Champion*. San Francisco: Jossey-Bass.

Letseka, M. 2000. 'African philosophy and educational discourse', in *African Voices in Education*, edited by P Higgs, NCG Vakalisa, TV Mda & NT Assie-Lumumba. Cape Town: Juta.

Lister, K. 2013. https://twitter.com/search?q=%23RAG123.

Lucas, T (ed). 2011. *Teacher Preparation for Linguistically Diverse Classrooms: A Resource for Teacher Educators*. New York: Routledge.

Lunenberg, M, Dengerink, J & Korthagen, F. 2014. *The Professional Teacher Educator: Roles, Behaviours, and Professional Development of Teacher Educators*. Netherlands: Sense Publishers.

LRPS (Lynnwood Ridge Primary School). 2018. Discipline: teacher's pack. Unpublished school policy.

Mahdjoubi, L & Akplotsyi, R. 2012. 'The impact of sensory learning modalities on children's sensitivity to sensory cues in the perception of their school environment'. *Journal of Environmental Psychology* 32(3), 208-215. (Online) Available from: http://doi.org/10.1016/j.jenvp.2012.02.002

Manyane, M. 1995. *Teaching Controversial Issues in History: A Practical Guide for the Classroom.* Menlo Park: ACE Publishers.

Maphalala, M (ed). 2016. *Teaching and Learning Strategies in South Africa.* Hampshire, UK: Cengage Learning EMEA.

Martinet, MA. 2001. *Teacher Training: Orientation Professional Competencies.* Canada: Quebec.

Marzano, RJ, Pickering, DJ & Pollock, JE. 2001. *Classroom Instruction That Works.* USA: McREL.

McCann, TM, Jones, AC & Aronoff, GA. 2012. *Teaching Matters Most: A School Leader's Guide to Improving Classroom instruction.* USA: Corwin.

McCaughy, K. 2010. 'Ten great low-cost teaching tools.' *English Teacher Forum* 4: 24–29.

McCroskey, JC, Richmond, VP & McCroskey, LL. 2006. *An Introduction to Communication in the Classroom: The Role of Communication in Teaching and Training.* Boston: Allyn & Bacon.

McCully, A. 2005. 'Teaching controversial issues in a divided society: Learning from Northern Ireland.' *Prospero* 11(4): 38–46.

Meighan, R & Harber, C. 1981. *A Sociology of Education.* London: Continuum.

Mottet, TP & Beebe, SA. 2011. 'Foundations of instructional communication', in *Planning Effective Instruction: Diversity Responsive Methods and Management* (4th edition), edited by KM Price and KL Nelson. Belmont: Wadsworth.

Murphy, J. 2005. *100 Ideas for Teaching History.* London: Continuum.

Nel, JAP. 1998. Die belangrikheid en noodsaaklikheid van motorise ontwikkeling vir 'n positiewe selfbeeld, suksesvolle sportdeelname, sporttalentidentifisering en voorkoming van leerprobleme. Unpublished work. Cape Town: Tygerberg College (Department sport management and coaching).

Ntseane, G. 2007. 'African indigenous knowledge: The case of Botswana', in *Non-Western Perspectives on Learning and Knowing*, edited by SB Merriam and Associates. Florida: Krieger.

Okeke, C, Van Wyk, M, Wolhuter, CC, Adu, OE & Anangisye, WAL. 2016. *Learning to Teach: A Handbook for Teaching Practice.* Cape Town: Oxford.

Ollerton, M. 2007. *100 Ideas for Teaching Mathematics.* London: Continuum.

Orr, R. 2017. *100 Ideas for Primary Teachers: Differentiation.* London: Bloomsbury.

Paterson, A & Arends, F. 2009. *Teachers Graduate Production. South Africa.* Cape Town: HSRC.

Pica, R. 2008. 'Learning by leaps and bounds: Why motor skills matter.' *Young Children* July 2008.

Potgieter, JR. 2013. *Sport Psychology: Theory and Practice.* Diep Rivier: Peak Performance Coaching.

Prinsloo, IJ & Van Schalkwyk, OJ. 2008. *Education Management 1.* Pretoria: University of Pretoria.

Radford, CP. 2013. *Strategies for Successful Student Teaching: A Guide to Student Teaching, the Job Search, and Your First Classroom.* USA: Pearson.

Ramokgopa, IM. 2001. 'Developmental stages of an African child and their psychological implications: A comparative study.' Unpublished Phd dissertation. University of Johannesburg.

Reagan, T. 2005. *Non-Western Educational Traditions: Indigenous Approaches to Educational Thought and Practice* (3rd edition). Mahwah: Lawrence Erlbaum.

Reyes, SA & Kleyn, T. 2010. *Teaching in Two Languages: A Guide for K–12 Bilingual Educators.* California: Corwin.

Robertson, J. 1996. *Effective Classroom Control: Understanding Teacher-Student Relationship.* Britain: Redwood Books.

SACE (South African Council for Educators). 2016. The CPTD management system. Pretoria: SACE.

Sayed, Y, Carrim, N, Badroodien, A, McDonald, Z & Singh, M. 2018. *Learning to Teach in Post-apartheid South Africa: Student Teachers' Encounters with Initial Teacher Education.* Stellenbosch: African Sun Media.

Sedgwick, F. 2006. *100 Ideas for Primary Assemblies.* London: Continuum.

Senior, J. 2014. *100 Ideas for Secondary Teachers: Gifted and Talented.* London: Bloomsbury.

Senior, C. 2005. *Getting the Buggers to Read.* London: Continuum.

Siedentop, D 2007. *Introduction to Physical Education, Fitness, and Sport* (6th edition). New York: McGraw-Hill.

Siedentop, D & Tannehill, D. 2000. *Developing Teaching Skills in Physical Education* (4th edition). California: Mayfield.

Siegel, DJ & Bryson, TP. 2012. *The Whole-Brain Child: 12 Revolutionary Strategies to Nurture Your Child's Developing Mind.* New York: Bantam.

Smit, S. 2018. 'A psycho-educational model to facilitate adolescent boys' constructive management of proactive aggression.' University of Johannesburg.

Starratt, RJ. 2012. *Cultivating an Ethical School.* UK: Routledge.

Statistics South Africa. 2011. *Census in Brief (No 03-02-03).* Pretoria: Statistics South Africa. Available from: http://www.statssa.gov.sa (Accessed on 23 August 2105).

Stradling, R, Noctor, M & Baines, B. 1984. *Teaching Controversial Issues.* London: Edward Arnold.

Taole, MJ (ed). 2015. *Teaching Practice Perspective and Frameworks.* Pretoria: Van Schaik.

Thwaites, A. 2008. *100 Ideas for Teaching: Problem Solving, Reasoning and Numeracy.* London: Continuum.

University of Queensland. 2007. 'Inclusive practices for managing controversial issues.' Theory into practice strategies – teaching and learning. (Online) Available from: www.tedi.uq.edu.au/cdip (Accessed 10 December 2017).

Van der Walt, C & Evans, R. 2019. *Learn 2 Teach: English Language Teaching in a Multilingual Context* (5th edition). Pretoria: Van Schaik.

Van Deventer, KJ. 2015. 'The voice of Margaret Talbot on physical education and school sport: A tribute.' *South African Journal for Research in Sport, Physical Education and Recreation* 37(2): 143-157.

Vatterott, C. 2010. 'Five hallmarks of good homework.' *Educational Leadership* 68(1): 10-15.

Veriava, F, & Power, T. 2017. 'Corporal punishment', in *Basic Education Rights Handbook – Education Rights in South Africa*, edited by F Veriava, A Thom & TF Hodgson. Johannesburg: Section27.

Viola, S & Noddings, A. 2006. 'Making sense of every child: Meeting the needs of diverse students through Sensory Integration.' *Montessori Life: A Publication of the American Montessori Society* 18(4), 40-47.

Visano, L & Jakubowski, L. 2002. *Teaching Controversy*. Halifax: Fernwood Publishing.

Wagner, T. 2008. 'Rigor redefined.' *Educational Leadership* 66(2): 20-24.

Ward, B. 2003. *Getting the Buggers to Draw*. London: Continuum.

Wassermann, JM. 2018. 'Teaching Controversial Issues in History', in *Teaching and Learning History and Geography in the South African Classroom*, edited by P Warnich & ES van Eeden. Pretoria: Van Schaik.

Wassermann, JM, Francis, D & Ndou, L. 2008. 'The teaching of controversial issues in Social Science Education.' *Journal of Educational Studies* 6(4): 37-57.

Wessels, M. 1999. *Practical Guide to Facilitating Language Learning*. New York: Oxford.

Wheatley, M. 2005. *Finding Our Way: Leadership for an Uncertain Time*. San Francisco: Berrett-Koehle.

Wikipedia. 2018. What does the infinity symbol mean? Origins of an infinity sign. (Online) Available from: https://en.wikipedia.org/wiki/Infinity (Accessed 5 June 2018).

Willis, J. 1985. *Teaching English Through English: A Course in Classroom Language and Techniques*. London: Longman ELT.

Wong, HK & Wong, RT. 2009. *The First Days of School: How to be an Effective Teacher*. UK: Wong Publishers.

Wuest, DA & Bucher, CA. 2009. *Foundations of Physical Education, Exercise Science, and Sport* (16th edition). New York: McGraw-Hill.

Uys, AHC. 2006. A proposed model for training English medium of instruction teachers in South Africa. Doctoral dissertation. Potchefstroom: North-West University.

URLs

South African Schools' Act: https://www.education.gov.za/LinkClick.aspx?fileticket=aIolZ6UsZ5U%3D&tabid=185&

South African Children's Act: http://www.justice.gov.za/legislation/acts/2005-038%20childrensact.pdf

South African Council of Educators Code of Conduct for Teachers: https://www.sace.org.za/pages/the-code-of-professional-ethics

StatsSA: 2015 http://www.statssa.gov.za

Appendix A:
Outline of a CV for a graduate

1. The covering letter to the SGB:
- state why you are sending the CV
- explain your career objectives (focus on your main skills and strengths)
- state why you think the SGB should consider you
- indicate your willingness to relocate/undergo further training
- conclude with the anticipation of their positive response.

2. The cover page of your CV:
- the advertised post or position for which you are suited
- your name and full contact details; also add this as a footer to each page
- your nationality, with ID/passport number
- optional: indicate your state of health, gender and religious affiliation
- certified documents/testimonials available on request
- information valid as on (date).

3. The actual CV:
Present a positive yet accurate picture and show your potential. Try to tabulate as much information as possible, as such a format enables you to provide more detail in a limited space. Provide the information in descending chronological order. Do not report on matters earlier than Grade 12. Include the following:
- academic qualifications
- other qualifications or training, for example computer skills, first aid, coaching, driver's licence. Indicate the type of course, which institution awarded the certificate and when it was obtained
- experience to date: your teaching practice periods as well as any other extramural coaching, au pair work, religious teaching responsibilities or holiday clubs
- awards/achievements/financial grants
- leadership/managerial skills or experience
- extramural activities you could be involved in
- capabilities (short paragraph), for example:

My XXX demanded that I take on many organisational and managerial responsibilities. This experience has equipped me admirably to deal with a range of tasks. I consider myself multi-skilled with a strong bias for XXX. I am able to work with XXX. I am competent in the following: ...

- Language proficiency:

Language	Speak	Read	Write
Tswana	Excellent	Excellent	Excellent
English	Excellent	Excellent	Above average
Afrikaans	Average	Average	Average

- leisure interests
- list of referees (tabulate with full contact details and designation).

Do not forget to sign your document. (Add your contact number here again.) Attach any required documentation as appendices.

Appendix B:
Code of conduct: South African Council for Educators

Definitions

In this Code, unless the context indicates otherwise any word or phrase defined in the South African Council for Educators Act, 2000 has that meaning and:

1. **'Code'** means the Code of Professional Ethics of the South African Council for Educators
2. **'Council'** means the South African Council for Educators
3. **'Educator'** means any educator registered or provisionally registered with the Council
4. **'Learner'** means a pupil or a student at any early learning site, school, further education and training institution or adult learning centre
5. **'Parent'** means:
   1. any natural parent or guardian of a learner
   2. any person legally entitled to custody of a learner
   3. any person who undertakes to fulfil the obligations of a person referred to in paragraphs (a) or (b) towards the learner's education at school.

General

The educators who are registered or provisionally registered with the South African Council for Educators:

1. acknowledge the noble calling of their profession to educate and train the learners of our country
2. acknowledge that the attitude, dedication, self-discipline, ideals, training and conduct of the teaching profession determine the quality of education in this country
3. acknowledge, uphold and promote basic human rights, as embodied in the Constitution of South Africa
4. commit themselves therefore to do all within their power, in the exercising of their professional duties, to act in accordance with the ideals of their profession, as expressed in this Code

5. act in a proper and becoming way such that their behaviour does not bring the teaching profession into disrepute.

Conduct: The educator and the learner

An educator:
1. respects the dignity, beliefs and constitutional rights of learners and in particular children, which includes the right to privacy and confidentiality
2. acknowledges the uniqueness, individuality, and specific needs of each learner, guiding and encouraging each to realise his or her potentialities
3. strives to enable learners to develop a set of values consistent with the fundamental rights contained in the Constitution of South Africa
4. exercises authority with compassion
5. avoids any form of humiliation, and refrains from any form of abuse, physical or psychological
6. refrains from improper physical contact with learners
7. promotes gender equality
8. refrains from courting learners from any school
9. refrains from any form of sexual harassment (physical or otherwise) of learners
10. refrains from any form of sexual relationship with learners from any school
11. refrains from exposing and/or displaying pornography material to learners and/or keeping same in his/her possession
12. uses appropriate language and behaviour in his or her interaction with learners, and acts in such a way as to elicit respect from the learners;
13. takes reasonable steps to ensure the safety of the learner
14. does not abuse the position he or she holds for financial, political or personal gain
15. is not negligent or indolent in the performance of his or her professional duties
16. recognises, where appropriate, learners as partners in education.

Conduct: The educator and the parent

An educator, where appropriate:
1. recognises the parents as partners in education, and promotes a harmonious relationship with them
2. refrains from offering a bribe in any form to parents

3. does what is practically possible to keep parents adequately and timeously informed about the wellbeing and progress of the learner.

Conduct: The educator and the community

An educator:

1. recognises that an educational institution serves the community, and therefore acknowledges that there will be differing customs, codes and beliefs in the community
2. conducts him/herself in a manner that does not show disrespect to the values, customs and norms of the community.

Conduct: The educator and his or her colleagues

An educator:

1. refrains from undermining the status and authority of his or her colleagues
2. respects the various responsibilities assigned to colleagues and the authority that arises therefrom, to ensure the smooth running of the educational institution
3. uses proper procedures to address issues of professional incompetence or misbehaviour
4. promotes gender equality and refrains from sexual harassment (physical or otherwise) of his or her colleagues
5. uses appropriate language and behaviour in his or her interactions with colleagues
6. avoids any form of humiliation, and refrains from any form of abuse (physical or otherwise) towards colleagues.

Conduct: The educator and the profession

An educator:

1. acknowledges that the exercising of his or her professional duties occurs within a context requiring co-operation with and support of colleagues
2. behaves in a way that enhances the dignity and status of the teaching profession and that does not bring the profession into disrepute
3. keeps abreast of educational trends and developments
4. promotes the ongoing development of teaching as a profession
5. accepts that he or she has a professional obligation towards the education and induction into the profession of new members of the teaching profession.

6. refrains from any contravention of the statutes and regulations of the Republic of South Africa, relevant to the Code
7. refrains from indulging and/or being in possession of intoxicating, illegal, and/or unauthorised substances including alcohol and drugs within the school premises and/or whilst on duty
8. refrains from carrying and/or keeping dangerous weapons in the school premises without any prior written authorisation by the employer
9. refrains from engaging in illegal activities.

Conduct: The educator and his or her employer

An educator:
1. recognises the employer as a partner in education;
2. acknowledges that certain responsibilities and authorities are vested in the employer through legislation, and serves his or her employer to the best of his or her ability
3. refrains from discussing confidential and official matters with unauthorised persons
4. must inform and declare his or her business interests to the employer prior executing them.

Conduct: The educator and the council

An educator:
1. makes every effort to familiarise him/herself and his/her colleagues with the provisions of the Code
2. complies with the provisions of this Code
3. discloses all relevant information to the Council
4. informs Council and/or relevant authorities of alleged or apparent breaches of the Code within his/her knowledge
5. co-operates with the Council to the best of his or her ability
6. accepts and complies with the procedures and requirements of the Council, including but not limited to the Registration Procedures, the Disciplinary Procedures of the Council and the payment of compulsory fees.

Appendix C: Determining your personality style

In each row, tick the block that most applies to your way of thinking/feeling/doing.

	A	B	C	D
1	I thrive on compliments.	I don't believe people when they give me a compliment.	I mostly deserve people's compliments.	I return compliments when receiving them.
2	I cannot talk without using my hands.	I don't always need to use gestures when I speak.	Gestures help others understand what I am saying.	I sometimes use my hands when talking.
3	I make friends quickly and easily – the more the merrier!	I have one or two best friends and that's all I need.	I have more acquaintances than friends.	I enjoy being a friend, rather than often making new ones.
4	People always know what I'm thinking and feeling.	People never know what I really think or feel.	People always know what I'm thinking, but not what I'm feeling.	I let people believe that they know what I think and feel.
5	I always give my opinion, although I sometimes regret it.	I only give my opinion when asked.	I always give my opinion regardless of what people might think.	I like to agree with other people's opinions.
6	I like to tell funny stories to create a social atmosphere.	I enjoy, dry, witty humour with close friends.	I make people laugh, because I have the funniest stories.	I like to make people laugh to relieve tension.
7	I manage conflict until it is resolved fairly by giving and taking advice.	In conflict situations I retreat to my comfort zone.	I thrive in conflict situations because I am usually right.	I hate conflict, but will try to resolve it as quickly as possible.

Add your scores for each column.
If you scored highest in A, then you are primarily a **sanguine**.
If you scored highest in B, then you are primarily a **melancholic**.
If you scored highest in C, then you are primarily a **choleric**.
If you scored highest in D, then you are primarily a **phlegmatic**.

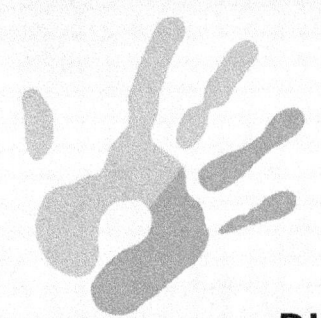

Appendix D:
Digital resources for teachers

We gratefully acknowledge this valuable contribution by Dr Ronel Callaghan and Jody Joubert from the Living Lab for Innovative Teaching Research unit at the University of Pretoria.

Resource websites

Open resources	www.creativecommons.org
Edutopia website	www.edutopia.org
Teacher videos	www.teachertube.com
Khan Academy	https://www.khanacademy.org
Phet simulations	https://phet.colorado.edu
Teacher toolkit blog	http://www.teachertoolkit.me/about/
Youtube	www.youtube.com
Mathematics resources	www.School-Maths.com
Mathematics resources	www.midhub.co.za
Commonwealth of learning resources	http://www.col.org/resources

Creating resources

Power Director	Creating videos
Photo Director	Editing photos
IMovie	Creating videos
Animaker	Creating animations
OnShape.com	Designing 3D models
Brainscape	Creating flashcards
GoQr.me	QR creating
QR Droid/QR scanner	QR reader

Assessment and feedback

Kahoot	Fun assessment
Plickers	Assessment – low on data
Socrative	Assessment
PollEverywhere	Visual feedback tool
ClassBadges.com	Create and manage badges

Learning Management

Class Dojo	(Children) Class management and assessment
Edmodo	Class and learner management
Schoology	Learning management system
TeacherKit	Learning management system

Interactive teaching apps

LiveBoard	Interactive digital whiteboard

Augmented reality (AR)

Chromville Science	AR colouring pages for science
Spacecraft 3D Nasa	AR resources
Aurasma	AR resources and creator
Quiver	Children's AR colouring pages

Virtual Reality (VR)

Discovery VR	VR resources
Cardboard Camera	Create your own VR
Cardboard	VR viewer

Other

Goosechase	Virtual scavenger hunt
ScratchJr / MIT App creator	Coding
Geogebra – Geogebra Geometry/Geogebra Graphing Calculator/Geogebra 3D Graphing Calculator	
OnProtractor	Mathematics
WordBubbles Free	Children's language
Interactive telling time	Children's language
Kids measurement science lite	Science

Appendix E:
Useful expressions to use during lessons

Greeting phrases	*Good morning/afternoon everybody/Grade 6 M ...* Use an ice breaker to make a connection with the class before you begin the lesson. *I'm excited about what we are going to do today ...* *Today we are going to learn about ...* *Have you ever thought about ... (name of topic)?* *Can anyone tell me what you know about ...?*
Setting the scene	Remember: the learners have come from a totally different situation and need to be eased into your lesson – you need to create the mood and atmosphere by what you say. *In our last lesson we discussed/learnt about .... Will you please remind us ...?* *Today we are going to discuss/talk about/debate ...* *Today we are going to conduct an experiment/research on ...* *We are going to divide our discussion into ... parts. First, we will ..., then ... and finally we will wrap up by exploring ...* *At the end of this lesson you will be able to ...* *This lesson will be useful for you to ...*
Instructional phrases	Instructions must be clear and brief – make sure the class is quiet and you are facing the learners so that your voice carries. Try to speak slowly. *Open your Maths/Science/novel/books at page ...* *You will need a pen/a new page/...* *For this lesson we will be working individually ...* *For this lesson we will be sharing our thoughts. Please turn to your neighbour on your right/left ...* For group work, make sure the movement into groups is easy and will not be disruptive. *Please get into the groups that you usually work in ...* *Turn around and get into groups of four ...* Ensure you give precise instructions. *You have five minutes to do this exercise ...* *Choose a group leader ...* *Choose a topic for your group to report on ...*

Appendix E – Useful expressions to use during lessons

	For report-back sessions, make sure there is attentive silence. *Leaders, give your group's answer/write it on the board.* *Right, we are now going to share our answers – listen carefully and please feel free to add your ideas.*
Asking questions	*Let's discuss topic two.* *Let's move on to the next part.* *We have been talking about ... Now, we turn our discussion to ...* Closed or display questions are used to establish factual understanding. These are 'what', 'where', 'who', 'when' questions. There is only one correct answer. *Where/when did the episode happen?* *Who was involved?* *What was the name of ...?* *What ingredients were used ...?* Open or exploratory questions allow learners to add their understanding and thoughts. These are 'why' and 'how' questions. They have no set answer and ask about possibilities/relationships/broader understanding of the topic. Learners also should provide the reasons as to why their answer is correct in their view. Remember to listen to the answers learners give. Avoid turning open questions into closed questions by imposing your ideas. *Why did the ...?* *Explain why you think that ...* *What do you think caused ...?* *Would you agree that ...?* *Describe the relationship/scene/event.* *What was the reason for the effect of ...?* *How did ... affect the situation?* While discussions are happening, check if everyone in the class understands or is listening. Avoid asking generally; rather ask an individual to explain to the class. *(Name), please will you summarise what we have been discussing.* *(Name), some of us may be feeling a bit lost, please explain what we have been discussing.*

Classroom management phrases	To get the learners' attention, change your tone and volume slightly. Try to use the 'we'/'us' pronouns to make the learners feel you are part of the process. *Okay, let's get started.* *Can you all see the board?* *Have we all found the place?* *Listen up everybody –* *Listen carefully as I explain what I want you to do.* *The purpose of this exercise is for us/you to …* Try to write instructions on the board and then ask an individual to read them out to the class. *(Name), please read the instructions for the class.* Establish key words that show you are moving on and keeping control of the discussions. *Right/Okay/Fine/Hmmm, now we will go onto the next question.* If learners are distracted, move towards them and address them by name. Avoid disrupting the class to discipline a learner. *(Name), I noticed while (name) was sharing her/his thoughts that you had some ideas – please share them with us.* *(Name), (name's) answer was very interesting. Please explain it to the class.* *(Name), you seem to be a bit lost. Are you okay?*
Interactive feedback phrases	Ensure your feedback is motivational or encouraging, otherwise learners will not try to answer a question again. *Thank you for your answer …* *I wonder if anyone else can add to (name)'s ideas.* *What are you thinking? Share your ideas with the person beside you.* Avoid telling a learner that his or her answer is wrong. Try to guide learners towards self-correction and even invite another learner to assist. *(Name), that is a very interesting answer/a different idea. Please explain it further to us all.* *(Name), thank you for your answer. Do you think it fully answers the question?* *Would anyone like to add to (name)'s ideas?* *Hmmm, that is a new way of looking at the question. Have you considered … or what about …?* *Please explain it in your own words.*

Appendix E – Useful expressions to use during lessons

	Use motivational encouragement and support. Asking questions or giving feedback is not intended to trick or test, but rather to enable learning. *Nearly there ... here is a clue.* *Have you considered ...?* *Remember .... Would that change your answer?* If you want to find out if learners have understood a concept, avoid stopping at a general question – add an individual element to it. *Has everybody understood ... put up your hand if you need me to explain further.* *(Name), would you please quickly explain what I have said to the class?*
Motivational phrases	Remember: the words you use can build or break a learner/person. Think before you speak. Never be sarcastic or belittle a learner/class – everybody must feel good and wanted. Address the learners by name. *Last lesson we spoke about .... (Name), please remind us all what we learnt. Who would like to read?* *(Name), could you try the next one?* *Let's all share our ideas/join in ... Everybody please ... Altogether now.* *(Grade ...), I love the way you are all listening to each other.* *You managed to work it out – how did you do that?* *Wow, that gave me an idea. Thank you.* *(Name), you haven't answered yet. Please help us answer the next question.* *(Name – individual or group), I was rather disappointed with your efforts. Did you feel you spent enough time on the work?* *You've improved a lot. Try to target your .... next time.*
Consolidation phrases: six minutes before lesson end	*So, to sum up, today we have learnt ...* *Quickly think of five things you have learnt today. Rate them.* *What was the most important thing you learnt today? Can you tell us why?*
Homework instructions	*Your homework is to do ... This will help you remember what we have learnt today.* *Hand it in tomorrow at the lesson/remember to put it on the shelf before 9.00 tomorrow.* *Tomorrow we will be doing ... so I want you to prepare by ...*

End of lesson	*Alright everybody, the bell will ring in two minutes. Please pack away and stand behind your chair.*
	Thank you all for sharing your ideas today. Please remember to add them to the homework task.
	I'm looking forward to seeing you all tomorrow/next lesson.
	You are a fantastic class. Please get to your next lesson quickly and quietly. Mr/Mrs ... is waiting for you.